a daily devotional for the rest of us

fLunking sainthoo̶d

→ Every Day

JANA RIESS

PARACLETE PRESS
BREWSTER, MASSACHUSETTS

2014   First Printing

Flunking Sainthood Every Day: A Daily Devotional for the Rest of Us

Copyright © 2014 Jana Riess

ISBN 978-1-61261-409-0

Scripture references are taken from the New Revised Standard Version Bible, copyright 1989, Division of Christian Education of the National Council of the Churches of Christ in the United States of America. Used by permission. All rights reserved.

The Paraclete Press name and logo (dove on cross) is a trademark of Paraclete Press, Inc.

Library of Congress Cataloging-in-Publication Data

Riess, Jana.
 Flunking sainthood every day: a daily devotional for the rest of us / Jana Riess.
    pages cm
 Includes bibliographical references and index.
 ISBN 978-1-61261-409-0 (hc jacket)w
 1. Devotional calendars. I. Title.
 BV4811.R54 2014
 242>.2--dc23   2014025943

10 9 8 7 6 5 4 3 2 1

Published by Paraclete Press
Brewster, Massachusetts
www.paracletepress.com

Printed in the United States of America

"Success is the ability to move from failure to failure without losing your enthusiasm."

Winston Churchill

Contents

Contents

*

vi

Introduction

The kind response to my memoir *Flunking Sainthood* floored me, to be honest. It's always uncomfortable to admit our disappointments and flaws in public, so to have that chronicle of repeated failure received with such grace has been a blessing. It seems there are a lot of us who are flunking sainthood—comrades-in-arms who have the courage to laugh at our shortcomings as we pick ourselves up to try, once again, to inch just a little closer to God.

Two recurring comments I've heard about *Flunking Sainthood* have prompted this companion devotional. The first is how much people loved the short quotations I sprinkled in the margins throughout the memoir. This delights me because I am a collector of quotations. I had been filling journals with them for years before I discovered that this is actually a long-standing devotional practice. (Who knew?) So the day-by-day compilation you're holding is a sort of commonplace book, a gathering of very short snippets by some of my favorite writers.

The second comment has been that people are enthusiastic to try many of the spiritual practices I undertook in *Flunking Sainthood*. To this end, each month in this book is organized in the same order that the practices occurred in the memoir. January is an opening month that addresses the spiritual journey—and, in particular, how we handle our failure to be perfect Christians. After that, there are twelve different spiritual practices, from fasting (February—hey, it's a short month) to generosity (December, just in time for the holidays). Note that June has two spiritual practices because I was so deficient with centering prayer that I wound up substituting the Jesus Prayer in the middle of that month.

Each day's devotion features a question for reflection, a prayer, or a short action item to help you integrate the monthly theme into your life. These action items are not intended to be guilt-inducing; please don't berate yourself if you only do some of them. This book is printed on flagellation-free paper. There may be entire months when you're not that interested in the assigned spiritual practice, and other months during which the practice feels totally natural and intuitive, like coming home. The hope behind this "daily devotional for the rest of us" is that you will discover some spiritual disciplines that speak to you, and find in the accompanying quotations additional resources where you can dive deeper into those practices.

God bless you on your journey.

JANUARY

The
Spiritual
Journey

———— **January 1** ————

I am about to do a new thing;
now it springs forth, do you not perceive it?
(Isaiah 43:19)

I am not so certain that we always enter into the new year with our focus on the whiteness, the freshness, the brand-new beginnings in our heart. I tend to believe that we let our glance rest a little too long on all those areas of our lives where we feel we have failed or not given our best. Why else would we still make resolutions based on what has gone before? . . .

Close your eyes and just imagine the clean, white, fluffy snow softly falling, covering all the drab spots of deadness on the earth. See that same soft, clean whiteness fall into your heart. Feel it heal the wounds, making clean your dreams and hopes. Hear the God of new beginnings speak to you about the fresh start being offered.

Joyce Rupp, *Fresh Bread and Other Gifts of Spiritual Nourishment*

ACTION

Commit this year to deepening your knowledge of God through spiritual practices. Also commit yourself to accepting that you are going to fail somewhere along the road. You are "on the way, though not necessarily very far along it," as Frederick Buechner puts it, and that is an acceptable place to be.

January 2

You were taught to put away your former way of life, your old self, corrupt and deluded. (Ephesians 4:22)

I constantly remind myself that real and total conversion is impossible. What *is* possible is the single act before me right now; that frame of mind, this word, another held back. I pray the breviary and read a page or two from an inspirational book each morning, kneel by my bedside at night, and utter prayers during the day. Realistically, this takes about twenty minutes all told. I find that I pray for alertness, insight, patience, courage—and, much of the time, help. I am not consciously aware of those prayers even moments later, but God knows that I have at least tried to put myself in his presence. . . .

Only I will know that I have or have not tried and, at times, tried valiantly. After all, if any of us were truly converted, we would become saints. Most of us do not.

Paul Wilkes, *Beyond the Walls: Monastic Wisdom for Everyday Life*

PRAYER
Focus my attention and energy on you, Lord, and help me find you in every moment. Amen.

January 3

"Be perfect, therefore, as your heavenly Father is perfect."
(Matthew 5:48)

Today we are caught in the tension between human nature and being children of God. To be perfect is not to add pressure to already overwhelmed lives; instead, it is to assure us that we are not alone in the world and that God continues to work in and through us. Perfection is less about getting things right and more about loving as God loves, and Jesus is God's concrete example of that love. . . .

In his Sermon on the Mount, Jesus lets us eavesdrop on his instructions to the disciples. We too are encouraged to live as sisters and brothers in God's realm. "Be perfect" is not an indictment; it is a promise that carries the possibility that we may love the world as God has loved us—fully, richly, abundantly, and completely.

———

Barbara Essex, *Feasting on the Word*

REFLECTION

What does the word *perfection* mean to you? Do Jesus's words conjure up hopefulness or performance anxiety?

——— **January 4** ———

. . . until all of us come to the unity of the faith and of the knowledge of the Son of God, to maturity, to the measure of the full stature of Christ. (Ephesians 4:13)

The Christian life is not a straight run on a track laid out by a vision statement formulated by a committee. Life meanders much of the time. Unspiritual interruptions, unanticipated people, uncongenial events cannot be pushed aside in our determination to reach the goal unimpeded, undistracted. "Goal-setting," in the context and on the terms intended by a leadership-obsessed and management-programmed business mentality that infiltrates the church far too frequently, is bad spirituality. Too much gets left out. Too many people get brushed aside.

Maturity cannot be hurried, programmed, or tinkered with. There are no steroids available for growing up in Christ more quickly. Impatient shortcuts land us in the dead ends of immaturity.

————

Eugene H. Peterson, *Practice Resurrection*

PRAYER

Teach me that I am on a journey, O God, and that you are with me even when I fail. Amen.

——————— **January 5** ———————

Not that I have already obtained this or have already reached the goal; but I press on to make it my own, because Christ Jesus has made me his own. (Philippians 3:12)

On the one hand, God's demand for perfection need not discourage you in the least in your present attempts to be good, or even in your present failures. Each time you fall He will pick you up again. And He knows perfectly well that your own efforts are never going to bring you anywhere near perfection. On the other hand, you must realise from the outset that the goal towards which He is beginning to guide you is absolute perfection; and no power in the whole universe, except you yourself, can prevent Him from taking you to that goal.

————

C. S. Lewis, *Mere Christianity*

REFLECTION

C. S. Lewis says that no power outside ourselves can prevent our realizing the perfection God has in mind for

The
Spiritual
Journey

*
6

us. Those words "except you yourself" are interesting. Have you ever gotten in the way of your own spiritual progress? (If not, you don't need this book and can likely return it for a full refund.)

———— **January 6** ————

For all of us make many mistakes. (James 3:2)

It seems that in the spiritual world, we do not really find something until we first lose it, ignore it, miss it, long for it, choose it, and personally find it again—but now on a new level. . . . Falling, losing, failing, transgression, and sin are the pattern, I am sorry to report. Yet they all lead toward home.

In the end, we do not so much reclaim what we have lost as discover a significantly new self in and through the process. Until we are led to the limits of our present game plan, and find it to be insufficient, we will not search out or find the real source, the deep well, or the constantly flowing stream.

Richard Rohr, OFM, *Falling Upward*

ACTION

Today, make a list of your failures—relationally, professionally, spiritually. Think about how God might use those failures and transgressions on your spiritual journey. Then throw the list away; you are a new creation.

January 7

"I am the way, and the truth, and the life. No one comes to the Father except through me." (John 14:6)

Jesus . . . didn't say that any particular ethic, doctrine, or religion was the way, the truth, and the life. He said that he was. He didn't say that it was by believing or doing anything in particular that you could "come to the Father." He said it was only by him—by living, participating in, being caught up by the way of life that he embodied, that was his way.

Thus it is possible to be on Christ's way and with his mark upon you without ever having heard of Christ, and for that reason to be on your way to God even though you don't even believe in God.

A Christian is one who is on the way, though not necessarily very far along it, and who has at least some dim and half-baked idea of whom to thank.

Frederick Buechner, *Beyond Words*

PRAYER

God, help me to remember that spiritual practices may help me grow closer to your Way, but that the most important thing is to be caught up in your Story.

January 8

But God, who is rich in mercy, out of the great love with which he loved us even when we were dead through our trespasses, made us alive together with Christ. (Ephesians 2:4–5)

Most of us are trying to live an authentic life. Deep down, we want to take off our game face and be real and imperfect. There is a line from Leonard Cohen's song "Anthem" that serves as a reminder to me when I get into that place where I'm trying to control everything and make it perfect. The line is, "There is a crack in everything. That's how the light gets in." So many of us run around spackling all the cracks, trying to make everything look just right. This line helps me remember the beauty of the cracks (and the messy house and the imperfect manuscript and the too-tight jeans). It reminds me that our imperfections are not inadequacies; they are reminders that we're all in this together. Imperfectly, but together.

Brené Brown, *The Gifts of Imperfection*

REFLECTION

Where and how are you "spackling" over your mistakes so that other people won't see them? What would it feel like to stop caring what other people think and recognize that your failures are essential instruments for new growth?

———— January 9 ————

Come to him, a living stone, though rejected by mortals yet chosen and precious in God's sight, and like living stones, let yourselves be built into a spiritual house, to be a holy priesthood, to offer spiritual sacrifices acceptable to God through Jesus Christ. (1 Peter 2:4–5)

W hen I have a sore throat, I gargle, and nobody gives me a medal. When I drive under the speed limit, the Department of Motor Vehicles doesn't send me a fruitcake. When I follow the practices that the community has found, through trial and error over long centuries, are helpful in drawing closer to God, I get the only reward I want: I get closer to God.

——

Frederica Mathewes-Green, *At the Corner of East and Now*

REFLECTION
Do you see spiritual practices as ways to grow closer to God, or as self-improvement projects? Or is it a combination of both? Be honest.

———— **January 10** ————

But God proves his love for us in that while we still were sinners Christ died for us. (Romans 5:8)

I used to think that I needed to get all my motives straightened out before I could pray, really pray. . . .

The truth of the matter is, we all come to prayer with a tangled mass of motives—altruistic *and* selfish, merciful *and* hateful, loving *and* bitter. Frankly, this side of eternity we will *never* unravel the good from the bad, the pure from the impure. But what I have come to see is that God is big enough to receive us with all our mixture. We do not have to be bright, or pure, or filled with faith, or anything. That is what grace means, and not only are we saved by grace, we live by it as well.

——

Richard J. Foster, *Prayer*

ACTION

Pray, today, in your worst moment. Pray when you're angry or anxious or bitter. You don't have to put on your "best self" for God. You can wear sweatpants and just be real.

———— January 11 ————

Immediately the father of the child cried out, "I believe; help my unbelief!" (Mark 9:24)

Often, when people speak about their faith, they describe it as a settled thing. A thing acquired, sometimes on a certain date, and utterly static. Not merely "once saved, always saved" . . . but "once saved, always the same," having the same exact faith as what they started out with their entire lives. . . .

Other faithful men and women of scripture, though, seem just the opposite. . . . Most heroes of faith, it seems to me, spend as much time wandering away from God as they do returning to him. And many great believers balk at the crucial moment, often late in their lives, when one would think their faith as mature and large as it will ever be. Theirs is a jagged faith trajectory at best. Like Jacob—like me—they must wrestle with God and with themselves for a long time before they can receive the blessing.

Patty Kirk, *Confessions of an Amateur Believer*

PRAYER

Help me understand that salvation is not stagnation, Lord. Show me ways to grow, even when growth is painful. Amen.

January 12

Your word is a lamp to my feet and a light to my path.
(Psalm 119:105)

Lead, kindly Light, amid the encircling gloom,
Lead Thou me on!
The night is dark, and I am far from home,
Lead Thou me on!
Keep Thou my feet! I do not ask to see
The distant scene; one step enough for me.

John Henry Cardinal Newman, "Lead, Kindly Light"

REFLECTION

I am a planner who would prefer my spiritual journey to come with not only a map but also a full-blown GPS system with longitudinal coordinates. What about you? Is "one step enough" for you, or are you clamoring for God to map out your journey in a predictable way?

January 13

You shall put these words of mine in your heart and soul,
and you shall bind them as a sign on your hand, and fix
them as an emblem on your forehead.
(Deuteronomy 11:18)

There is nothing winsome or goofy about God—or about the results for ourselves, and each other, of our failure to change our lives—and if there's a way of talking about God I find abhorrent, it's the way that says God is like a chocolate bar, God is a big teddy bear, God is the clouds in the sky. God is God of a world where drunks die in the gutter, and children get beaten to death by their mothers. . . . I can't combat those things by pretending they don't exist or that I don't have a part in them. . . . I combat them by the long slow crucifixion of trying to love God with my whole heart, mind, soul, and strength, and my neighbor as myself: the hardest, most complex, paradoxical, maddening, stimulating, challenging, inexhaustibly enriching, perpetually unfinished, bound-to-fail, sublime task in the world.

Heather King, *Redeemed*

PRAYER

God, I want to give you my whole heart, but I am often afraid. Help me to surrender everything to you. Amen.

———— **January 14** ————

Little children, let us love, not in word or speech, but in truth and action. And by this we will know that we are from the truth and will reassure our hearts before him whenever our hearts condemn us; for God is greater than our hearts, and he knows everything. (1 John 3:18–20)

In your life there may be unfulfilled yearnings. Your peace will depend on the acceptance of those unfulfillments.

Reconsider your expectations. Examine the demands you make on yourself. Are they realistic? What do you base them on? Does the pressure to meet these demands take away the centeredness you need to live in peace? Are these demands your own or do they come from others in spoken and unspoken messages? . . .

God helps you to let go of unfulfilled dreams and expectations. God helps you dream new dreams and hope new hopes. Let go of control. Surrender it to the love and mercy of God.

Adolfo Quezada, *Loving Yourself for God's Sake*

ACTION

Call to mind any unfulfilled yearnings that you have. What are they? What disappointments or unmet expectations have you experienced? Be candid with yourself about what those things are, then try to let them go.

——— **January 15** ———

Here is a call for the endurance of the saints, those who keep the commandments of God and hold fast to the faith of Jesus. (Revelation 14:12)

Don't adopt a practice that you have to force into an already crowded day. Somehow we always find the time for that which we like doing. Each of us has the ability to find a spiritual practice (perhaps, if we are fortunate, more than one) that fits our nature so well that we will perform it because we want to. When we discover that, we won't carry it out because it leads to something else or because it makes us a better person; we will do it because it is an end in itself.

John McQuiston II, *Finding Time for the Timeless*

REFLECTION

As we get ready to experiment with various spiritual practices, which are you most drawn to? Which are you dreading?

January 16

"Again, the kingdom of heaven is like a net that was thrown into the sea and caught fish of every kind." (Matthew 13:47)

Though we are taught to make plans and to keep to them, and though we work our way through predesigned courses of study to receive credentials and degrees, our attempts at real living don't happen this way.

For me, finding where I fit in the world feels a lot like spiritual fishing. The vast, mysterious ocean of experience keeps calling, and whether it is by buckets of question or nets of honesty, I keep hauling up food from the days. I keep hauling in shells and pearls and seaweed from a common depth that no one can see, and then I spend time cleaning what I've found and hearing what it has to say.

In this way, everyone alive must fish, and this requires stillness and patience and a willingness to drift. For we never know where deep things live.

Mark Nepo, *The Book of Awakening*

PRAYER

Guide me into stillness and patience, so that I may discover "where deep things live." Amen.

January 17

Rejoice with those who rejoice, weep with those who weep. (Romans 12:15)

A compassionate heart is the goal of our spiritual practice and will be the well from which we give cool water to ourselves and the other thirsty souls we encounter on the journey. But as the former presiding bishop of the Episcopal Church Frank Griswold points out, the first step on our journey comes when we ask the difficult question, "Do I want to have a compassionate heart?" Unless we can answer that question in the affirmative, then we will not enter into the hard work involved, because to have a compassionate heart calls us to a lifetime of spiritual homework.

———

Greg Garrett, *The Other Jesus*

REFLECTION

Do you *want* to have a compassionate heart, with its "lifetime of spiritual homework"? Are you ready for that?

——— **January 18** ———

Do not be conformed to this world, but be transformed by the renewing of your minds, so that you may discern what is the will of God—what is good and acceptable and perfect. (Romans 12:2)

We are in Christ, and Christ is in us. Spiritual practices can make this reality clear and evident. So many spiritual practices involve abiding or resting in God, and slowing down long enough to pay attention to the reality of our life in Christ and Christ's life in us. Contemplative prayer, contemplative approaches to Scripture, Sabbath keeping, and fasting all have strong components of waiting on God, resting in God, and allowing God to be God in our lives. When spiritual practices become a way to prove that we are spiritually profound or to earn God's approval, we are violating the essence of New Testament faith, which emphasizes this presence of God in us and beside us, at God's initiative and through the power of the Holy Spirit.

———

Lynne Baab, *Joy Together*

ACTION

Choose *one* of the spiritual practices that Baab mentions (contemplative prayer, contemplative Scripture reading/ *lectio divina*, Sabbath keeping, and fasting) and commit to trying it this week. You are not doing this to earn brownie points with God or make yourself over into a better person; you are doing it to cultivate sensitivity to God's presence.

———— January 19 ————

If we live by the Spirit, let us also be guided by the Spirit. (Galatians 5:25)

There is no condemnation for any inward sin still remaining in those who "walk by the Spirit." Even though sin may seem to cling tenaciously to everything we do, we are not guilty as long as we do not give way to it. So do not be disturbed because some ungodly imaginations remain in your heart. Do not feel dejection because you still come short of the glorious image of God, or because pride, self-will, or unbelief cling to all your words and works. Do not be afraid to face candidly all these distortions of your heart. Know yourself as you are known. Desire fervently of God that you may not think more highly of yourself than you ought to think.

———

John Wesley, *The New Birth*

The
Spiritual
Journey

——— **January 20** ———

But by the grace of God I am what I am, and his grace toward me has not been in vain. On the contrary, I worked harder than any of them—though it was not I, but the grace of God that is with me. (1 Corinthians 15:10)

*

17

Most people are willing to admit that no one in this life will attain moral perfection. Although we are often judgmental of others' shortcomings and too eager to rationalize our own, we recognize that the Christian life does not automatically engender perfection in virtue. When Jesus calls us to be perfect as he is perfect, we properly understand this as a goal to be attained through a lifetime of moral struggle. So the Christian life is goal-directed—we are to become children of God, heirs of eternal life. But we are now, it seems, infinitely far from that goal. In our moral shortcomings, we trust and hope that God will grant us mercy and not justice.

———

Kelly James Clark, *When Faith Is Not Enough*

PRAYER
Be merciful to me, O Lord, each time I fail. Amen.

The
Spiritual
Journey

*

18

——— **January 21** ———

"Why do you see the speck in your neighbor's eye, but do not notice the log in your own eye?" (Matthew 7:3)

Christ—as always, the model—never sat back, crossed his arms, and dismissed the annoying, the troublesome, or the unpromising. He never name-called, never judged, never treated a single person with contempt. Christ talked to everybody, he mingled with everybody, he shared his message with everybody, and he also loved everybody. . . .

Part of the overall plan seems to be that no matter how sad, wounded, neurotic, or needy we are, that may be exactly what some other person needs us to be at that time. We don't know the ways we comfort and save each other, not only in spite of our wounds, but also in some cases, *because* of them. No one is likely to be more sympathetic to an alcoholic than another alcoholic. No one is likely to have more compassion than the person, guided by love, who needs compassion him or herself. That is why we must never judge. That is why we must always look for the good in the other.

Heather King, *Shirt of Flame*

ACTION
Do not judge today. That's it. Do not judge. Look for the good in every person you meet. Yeah, even that person.

——— **January 22** ———

Think of us in this way, as servants of Christ and stewards of God's mysteries. Moreover, it is required of stewards that they be found trustworthy.
(1 Corinthians 4:1–2)

Avariety of small practices can reshape you from the outside in as you begin to let your eating and shopping and texting be informed, and transformed, by the person of Jesus and by your relationships with the ones he loves. Practicing sabbath—resting from your work or cell phone or Facebook—makes you available, in fresh ways, to God and to others. Fasting or forgoing meat or modifying your diet in some other way to honor the poor will make you more alert to their suffering. Joining your community for prayer, either daily or weekly, will begin to shape your heart and actions. . . . A consistent faithfulness to these small practices sets you free to be *for* others.

Margot Starbuck, *Small Things with Great Love*

REFLECTION

What spiritual practice has made you feel closest to God? This might be prayer, being in nature, fasting (or eating cake!), resting on the Sabbath . . . there are many ways to know God. What has felt right to you?

——— **January 23** ———

Blessed is anyone who endures temptation. Such a one has stood the test and will receive the crown of life that the Lord has promised to those who love him.
(James 1:12)

Mrs. March broke the silence that followed Jo's words, by saying in her cheery voice, "Do you remember how you used to play Pilgrim's Progress when you were little things? Nothing delighted you more than to have me tie my piece bags on your backs for burdens. . . .

"We never are too old for this . . . it is a play we are playing all the time in one way or another. Our burdens are here, our road is before us, and the longing for goodness and happiness is the guide that leads us through many troubles and mistakes to the peace which is a true Celestial City. Now, my little pilgrims, suppose you begin again, not in play, but in earnest, and see how far on you can get before Father comes home."

——

Marmee in Louisa May Alcott's *Little Women*

PRAYER

I am just a pilgrim on a journey, Lord, and sometimes the journey seems long and difficult. Please guide me along the road. Amen.

———— **January 24** ————

Charm is deceitful, and beauty is vain,
*but a woman who fears the L*ORD *is to be praised.*
(Proverbs 31:30)

I had to hand it to her. In less than fourteen days, the Proverbs 31 woman had made me feel guilty, inadequate, and poor. . . .

I knew from my research that Proverbs 31 was never meant to be turned into a to-do list, but there was something about the spectacularity with which I was blowing this that beleaguered my confidence. Most women walk around with the sense that they are disappointing someone. This year, I imagined that Someone to be God. Though Proverbs 31 represented a poetic ideal, I couldn't shake the feeling that if these were indeed the accomplishments of a competent, capable, virtuous, valiant, and worthy wife, then I must be none of those things.

———

Rachel Held Evans, *The Year of Biblical Womanhood*

ACTION

Read Proverbs 31 today. Remember that the woman represented here is a "poetic ideal," and that you—whether you are a woman or a man—don't need to feel inadequate next to her. You really don't need to plant a vineyard or make your own linen garments today. I'm just saying.

———— **January 25** ————

He called a child, whom he put among them, and said, "Truly I tell you, unless you change and become like children, you will never enter the kingdom of heaven." (Matthew 18:2–3)

We do not progress in the Christian life by becoming more competent, more knowledgeable, more virtuous, or more energetic. We do not advance in the Christian life by acquiring expertise. Each day, and many times a day, we return to Square One: God Said. . . . We adore and we listen.

———

Eugene H. Peterson, *Subversive Spirituality*

REFLECTION

What is God trying to tell you today? Are you listening?

———— **January 26** ————

*So we have known and believe the love that God has for us.
God is love, and those who abide in love abide in God, and
God abides in them. (1 John 4:16)*

A couple of years ago I went on a retreat. The director, a
very experienced guide, began with this simple instruction: "For this whole week, all I'm going to do is to try to
teach you to pray so that you can open yourselves up in
such a way that sometime—maybe not today, but sometime—you will hear God say to you, 'I love you!' Because
before that happens, nothing is ever completely right with
you—and after it happens, everything is really all right."

The words are simple but not simplistic. . . . Until we hear,
somehow, at the core of our being, God pronounce, in love,
our individual names, we will be incurably restless, chasing
after every kind of experience in the hope that it can make
us whole.

Fr. Ronald Rolheiser, *The Restless Heart*

ACTION

Tell someone today that God loves them. (The person
who most needs to hear it may be you.)

———— **January 27** ————

*Therefore let us go on toward perfection, leaving
behind the basic teaching about Christ, and not laying
again the foundation: repentance from dead works and
faith toward God. (Hebrews 6:1)*

Some people may seem to us to go to God by an escalator, where they can assist matters a bit by their own efforts, but much gets done for them and progress does not cease. Some appear to be whisked past us in an elevator; whilst we find ourselves on a steep flight of stairs with a bend at the top, so that we cannot see how much farther we have to go. But none of this really matters; what matters is the conviction that all are moving towards God, and, in that journey, accompanied, supported, checked, and fed by God. Since our dependence on Him is absolute, and our desire is that His Will shall be done, this great desire can gradually swallow up, neutralize all our small self-centered desires. When that happens life, inner and outer, becomes one single, various act of adoration and self-giving, one undivided response of the creature to the demand and pressure of Creative Love.

Evelyn Underhill, *Radiance*

REFLECTION

Do you feel you are moving toward God? If you think you are, what are the signs?

——— **January 28** ———

I lift up my eyes to the hills—
from where will my help come?
My help comes from the Lord,
who made heaven and earth. (Psalm 121:1–2)

And like a pilgrim who is traveling on a road where he has never been before, who believes that every house which he sees from afar is the hostel, and finding that it is not directs his belief to another, and so from house to house until he comes to the hostel; even so our soul, as soon as it enters upon the new and never-yet-made journey of life, directs its eyes to the goal of its supreme good, and therefore whatever it sees that appears to have some good in it, it thinks to be it. And because its knowledge is at first imperfect, through having no experience or instruction, little goods appear great to it; and therefore it begins first from them in its longing.

Dante Alighieri, *Convivio*

PRAYER

Lord, help me discern that the stages along the way are not the final destination. The final destination is you. Amen.

——— **January 29** ———

For though they fall seven times, they will rise again.
(Proverbs 24:16)

We are all on a journey in life. Hopefully, a journey toward the heart of God. . . . At times all of us stumble and fall along the way. Still, we are able to rise again—scarred, perhaps, but wiser for the experience—and continue on. Most critical for this journey is knowing that we are headed in a Godward direction.

To see the spiritual life as journey is to recognize that every step we take in life requires reflection and discernment if we are to see God's role in it. As we think our way along this journey, it is like following a path up a steep mountain. Occasionally we feel winded and need to stop—or even lose our footing and need to recover—but then suddenly we discover a whole new level of understanding we never knew existed.

Richard J. Foster and Gayle D. Beebe, *Longing for God*

REFLECTION

Have you ever had the experience that is described here—that just when you think you've failed or lost your footing, you discover a whole new level of understanding? What did you learn?

───── **January 30** ─────

And the peace of God, which surpasses all understanding, will guard your hearts and your minds in Christ Jesus. (Philippians 4:7)

When we try to live in this spirit [of loving without reserve], we begin to learn to let go peacefully of our anxieties, fears, resentments, and blindness. We become attentive to the world around us in a new way, aware of other people and their needs in a new way, and vividly conscious not only of the beauty and goodness of everything around us, but of suffering and despair as well. And strangely, to the extent that our focus shifts away from ourselves and our many concerns, instead of disappointment, we receive a fullness that remains with us despite our emotional highs and lows. We become perennially enthusiastic.

─────

The Monks of New Skete, *In the Spirit of Happiness*

ACTION

Release an anxiety today. Determine that for today you will not worry about that thing; every time you are drawn to worry about it, remember instead that you've decided to love and trust without limits.

The
Spiritual
Journey

*

26

———— **January 31** ————

"Those who try to make their life secure will lose it, but those who lose their life will keep it." (Luke 17:33)

I really hate that Jesus' Gospel is so much about death. I hate it. I wish that Jesus' message was, *Follow me and all your dreams of cash and prizes will come true; follow me and you'll have free liposuction and winning lotto tickets for life.* But obviously he's not like that. Jesus says, "Deny yourself, take up your cross and follow me." . . . And every single time I die to something—my notions of my own specialness, my plans and desires for something to be a very particular way—every single time I fight it and yet every single time I discover more life and more freedom than if I had gotten what I wanted.

————

Nadia Bolz-Weber, *Pastrix*

REFLECTION

As we finish our introductory month and begin diving into various spiritual practices, are you afraid of failure? Try to remove the focus from yourself—your own failures and accomplishments—and turn your eyes to Jesus.

FEBRUARY

Fasting

Fasting

*

28

——— February 1 ———

Blow the trumpet in Zion;
sanctify a fast;
call a solemn assembly. (Joel 2:15)

If you desire to make more space in your life for God, if you would like to deepen your prayer life, fasting can be very helpful. Look at your life. What activities are crowding out prayer? What activities or foods are becoming more important to you than God? Is something in your life taking up more space than you want it to? What activities are siphoning off time, money or energy in a way that isn't necessarily sinful but isn't helpful either? Consider fasting from that activity or that food for a day or a few days. Ask God to help your fast create more space for him.

Lynne Baab, *Fasting*

REFLECTION

Today we begin our emphasis on fasting. Have you ever fasted from food for a prescribed period? What was that experience like? And if you haven't, is that because you panic at the very thought of giving up your three square meals a day?

——— February 2 ———

"And whenever you fast, do not look dismal, like the hypocrites, for they disfigure their faces so as to show others that they are fasting. Truly I tell you, they have received their reward." (Matthew 6:16)

There follows a precept concerning fasting, having reference to that same purification of heart which is at present under discussion. For in this work also we must be on our guard, lest there should creep in a certain ostentation and hankering after the praise of man, which would make the heart double, and not allow it to be pure and single for apprehending God. . . . It is manifest from these precepts that all our effort is to be directed towards inward joys, lest, seeking a reward from without, we should be conformed to this world, and should lose the promise of a blessedness so much the more solid and firm, as it is inward, in which God has chosen that we should become conformed to the image of His Son.

St. Augustine of Hippo, "The Sermon on the Mount"

——

ACTION

Fast from one meal today. Do not let other people know what you are doing. Do not post it on Facebook. Try to begin and end your fast with a prayer.

———— **February 3** ————

I had eaten no rich food, no meat or wine had entered my mouth, and I had not anointed myself at all, for the full three weeks. (Daniel 10:3)

Perhaps the very point of the fast is to confront us with these questions [of how to find strength beyond ourselves]. How far can my body go? Why am I doing this? Each day we had to be aware of what we would eat or not. We could not grab whatever was convenient. We carefully examined the lists of ingredients on packages of prepared foods. We paid attention to what we were eating. We were thankful for whatever food we had. It had brought us through another day. It was precious manna.

The daily sensation of hunger and dependence marked out days of self-examination and repentance. We were remembering Jesus' way to the cross. We were confessing that we could not make sense of our lives on our own. We were living each day only by God's gracious provision.

———

John P. Burgess, *Encounters with Orthodoxy*

REFLECTION
What would it feel like to live each day "only by God's gracious provision"?

——— **February 4** ———

Is not this the fast that I choose:
to loose the bonds of injustice,
to undo the thongs of the yoke,
to let the oppressed go free,
and to break every yoke? (Isaiah 58:6)

Though the Bible describes people trying to demonstrate their sorrow before God through rituals like fasting, wearing sackcloth, and pouring ashes on their heads, prophets like the ones we read aloud on Ash Wednesday insist these acts do not constitute repentance unless there's a real change in behavior. . . .

Repentance means turning toward other human beings, our own flesh and blood, whenever they're oppressed, hungry, or imprisoned; it means acting with compassion instead of indifference. It means turning away, "fasting," from any of the little and big things that can keep us from God—drugs, religion, busy-ness, video games, lies—and accepting the divine embrace with all our hearts. Repentance requires paying attention to others, and learning to love, even a little bit, what God loves so much: the whole screwed-up world, this holy city, the people God created to be his own.

Sara Miles, *City of God*

PRAYER

Lord, reveal to me whatever things, big and small, are keeping me from you. Amen.

——— **February 5** ———

When I heard these words I sat down and wept, and mourned for days, fasting and praying before the God of heaven. (Nehemiah 1:4)

Fasting along with our prayer requests is not some kind of magic bullet to ensure the answer we want. Fasting doesn't reinforce the crumbling walls of our prayers like a flying buttress, nor is it a manipulative device. We fast because a condition arises—what we are calling the sacred moment—that leads us to desire something deeply. We fast because our plea is so intense that in the midst of our sacred desire eating seems sacrilegious.

A body plea occurs when the unified person gives himself or herself wholly to God to plead for something or someone. . . . Fasting can be a way for the unified person to turn to God to plead with God completely.

Scot McKnight, *Fasting*

ACTION

Fast again from one meal. Try to avoid the magical thinking that McKnight refers to here, where you are fasting only in order to manipulate God into behaving a certain way.

———— **February 6** ————

So God created humankind in his image, in the image of God he created them; male and female he created them. (Genesis 1:27)

"Why are you crying?" says Ginger, who knows why I am crying.

"I'll never be thin again," I wail. "I used to be thin." I tell Ginger about the purple pedal-pushers I had just taken to Goodwill because they, too, were a tad tight. Ginger reminds me that I bought the pedal-pushers in tenth grade.

This shopping expedition was good proof that, though I believe God has something to say about human bodies, I generally tune God out and listen to *Cosmopolitan* instead. I'm pretty sure that God, if He called me to chat about my body, would say things like, "I like your body. I created your body, and if you have read the first chapter of Genesis lately, you might recall that I called Creation good." Still, when I'm staring in the dress-shop mirror, I generally wish my body—or at least a few pounds of it—would vanish.

This desire to diet is not just bad feminism. It is also bad faith, for the biblical story of the body is very different from the bodily stories that *Cosmo* and *Maxim* tell. The magazines (and movies, TV shows, and advertising campaigns) speak of bodies that are both too important and not important at all. Scripture speaks of bodies that God created in His image, bodies that are both doing redemptive work and being redeemed.

Lauren F. Winner, *Mudhouse Sabbath*

REFLECTION

What body issues or preoccupations do you have that might stand in the way of a godly fast? Do you fast with the secret hope that you will lose weight?

——— **February 7** ———

For this perishable body must put on imperishability, and this mortal body must put on immortality.
(1 Corinthians 15:53)

Our bodies are a part of the creation God pronounced "very good," and Jesus demonstrated God's blessing on the human body when he became incarnate. He made the blessing more emphatic when he was resurrected, not as a mere spirit, but in a scar-marked body capable of eating fish. He sealed the blessing in the Ascension, taking that body into the very courts of heaven.

No doubt about it: we're going to have these same bodies forever, though in some transfigured form we can't now imagine. Our bodies are blessed, but we don't know how to live harmoniously in them. We drive them like vehicles, use them like tools to dig pleasure, and in the process damage and distort our capacity to understand them. Fasting disciplines help us quiet these impulsive demands, so that we can better hear what they need and how they are meant to work. It is a turning toward health, a way of honoring creation and preparing for eternity.

———

Frederica Mathewes-Green, *The Illumined Heart*

PRAYER

Fasting

Thank you, Lord, for the gift of my body! Amen.

———————— **February 8** ————————

*

34

Then I turned to the Lord God, to seek an answer by prayer and supplication with fasting. (Daniel 9:3)

Is fasting ever a bribe to get God to pay more attention to the petitions? No, a thousand times no. It is simply a way to make clear that we sufficiently reverence the amazing opportunity to ask help from the everlasting God, the Creator of the universe, to choose to put everything else aside and concentrate on worshiping, asking forgiveness, and making our requests known—considering His help more important than anything we could do ourselves in our own strength and with our own ideas.

———

Edith Schaeffer, cofounder of L'Abri Fellowship[1]

PRAYER

Lord, help me to resist the temptation to treat fasting like a talisman, or a way to get you to pay more attention to my prayers. Teach me humility and love. Amen.

February 9

The fast of the fourth month, and the fast of the fifth, and the fast of the seventh, and the fast of the tenth, shall be seasons of joy and gladness, and cheerful festivals for the house of Judah: therefore love truth and peace. (Zechariah 8:19)

We fast, not because we despise the divine gift [of food and drink], but so as to make ourselves aware that it is indeed a gift—so as to purify our eating and drinking, and to make them, no longer a concession to greed, but a sacrament and means of communion with the Giver.

———

Timothy [Kallistos] Ware, *The Orthodox Church*

ACTION

Do you ever slip into thinking that fasting is a way to manipulate God into doing your will? If you find yourself doing this, say aloud, "not my will but yours be done" (Luke 22:42). If you don't, pat yourself on the back for being so great at fasting righteously! (No, wait, don't do that either. That's what the Pharisee does in Luke 18, and he's not exactly the good guy in that chapter.)

February 10

And all of us, with unveiled faces, seeing the glory of the Lord as though reflected in a mirror, are being transformed into the same image from one degree of glory to another; for this comes from the Lord, the Spirit. (2 Corinthians 3:18)

Fasting is not a tool to pry wisdom out of God's hands or to force needed insight about a decision. Fasting is not a tool for gaining discipline or developing piety (whatever that might be). Instead, fasting is the bulimic act of ridding ourselves of our fullness to attune our senses to the mysteries that swirl in and around us. Sometimes God shows up. And sometimes he feeds us. And every now and then he throws his wild glory before us like bursting constellations, and it's all we can do to wait for him to leave, lest we be destroyed in his presence.

————

Dan B. Allender, *To Be Told*

REFLECTION

Allender writes that fasting is a "bulimic act" that purges us from all that stands in the way of spiritual union with God. Do you agree? You now have ten days of experience: what do *you* think is the true purpose of fasting?

——— **February 11** ———

Their end is destruction; their god is the belly; and their glory is in their shame; their minds are set on earthly things. (Philippians 3:19)

All the things of the earth are good, because God has made them. Yet there's no doubt that our desire for many of them is out of whack. Given the opportunity, most of us will eat more than our bodies need, and that's not good for us. In fact, this may be worse for the soul than it is for the body. For we become attached to created things and to the pleasure they bring us. And in time, we prefer the pleasure to spiritual goods. . . .

For earthly or heavenly goals, our bodies need discipline. Our bodies must be subject to our reason—or the order will be reversed: our reason will soon be subject to our bodies. The early Christians knew this, and they fasted frequently.

Scott Hahn, *Signs of Life*

ACTION

Today, at two meals, do not eat enough to feel full. Choose small portions, and don't snack between meals. Get familiar with how your body feels with a little less food.

FEBRUARY

Fasting

*

37

—————— **February 12** ——————

The poor shall eat and be satisfied;
those who seek him shall praise the LORD.
May your hearts live forever! (Psalm 22:26) 27

At a lunch meeting on Day 11 [of my juice fast] I notice a family in the restaurant join hands and bow their heads to pray before eating. I did this at every meal for almost twenty years. I thought I knew what it meant. I thought I was thankful. But as I watch the child squirm and the father pray, my stomach churns with emptiness. *I've never truly been thankful for food, because I've never before known hunger.* It's a good thing my client is in the restroom, because my eyes fill with tears. *So many go hungry around the world, and I've eaten my whole life without giving thanks.* I toy with the fork at my left and know I will never pick up an eating utensil again without being deeply, incredibly, thankful. Perhaps this is another function of fasting; can physical lack reveal spiritual deficiency?

Reba Riley, *Post-Traumatic Church Syndrome*

PRAYER

Lord, I pray that my fast will open my eyes and heart to those who are not hungry by choice. Teach me compassion and gratitude. Amen.

Fasting

*

38

———— **February 13** ————

For he will command his angels concerning you
to guard you in all your ways.
On their hands they will bear you up,
so that you will not dash your foot against a stone.
(Psalm 91:11–12)

An Angel came to Daniel upon his fast; so too in our Lord's instance, Angels came and ministered unto Him; and so we too may well believe, and take comfort in the thought, that even now, Angels are especially sent to those who thus seek God. Not Daniel only, but Elijah too was, during his fast, strengthened by an Angel; an Angel appeared to Cornelius, while he was fasting, and in prayer; and I do really think, that there is enough in what religious persons may see around them, to serve to confirm this hope thus gathered from the word of God.

John Henry Cardinal Newman, "Parochial and Plain Sermons"

REFLECTION

Can you imagine an angel beside you as you undertake a fast or other discipline of self-denial?

February 14

"But I say to you that listen, Love your enemies, do good to those who hate you, bless those who curse you, pray for those who abuse you. If anyone strikes you on the cheek, offer the other also; and from anyone who takes away your coat do not withhold even your shirt." (Luke 6:27–29)

Jesus encourages us to pray for our enemies, and even to revel in our persecution because it augurs a reward in heaven. But the Didache takes the love of enemy one step further than Jesus does in the gospel accounts when it bids the believer to "fast for those who persecute you."

. . . This stance isn't merely ideological. It's pragmatic, for the Didache promises that if you love those who hate you, "you shall have no enemies."

Tony Jones, *The Teaching of the Twelve*

ACTION

Who has harmed you or persecuted you? Plan to fast for that person according to the suggestion of the *Didache*, a first-century book of Christian teachings. Open and close your fast with prayers for that person's well-being. Come on, I know you can do it.

February 15

*But he answered, "It is written,
'One does not live by bread alone,
but by every word that comes from the mouth of God.'"
(Matthew 4:4)*

In fasting we abstain from our ordinary food to some significant degree and for some significant length of time. Like solitude and silence, it is not done to impress God or merit favor, nor because there is anything wrong with food. Rather, it is done that we may consciously experience the direct sustenance of God to our body and our whole person. . . .

When we have learned well to fast, we will not suffer from it. It will bring strength and joy. We will not be miserable, and so Jesus tells us not to look miserable. . . . He knew that we would "have meat to eat" that others "know not of." I and many others can report that we have repeatedly verified this in experience.

Dallas Willard, *The Great Omission*

PRAYER

Lord, as I fast, help me to lean upon you as the Bread of Life. Amen.

———— February 16 ————

For the grace of God has appeared, bringing salvation to all, training us to renounce impiety and worldly passions, and in the present age to live lives that are self-controlled, upright, and godly. (Titus 2:11–12)

Many people panic when you ask them to give something up. A desire to hoard immediately washes over them. They fear that they will never have access to the item again or that if they give up food for a time, they will die. . . .

On the other hand, some people are so paranoid about gaining weight that they skip meals all the time. These people need to fast from their attitude toward food and eat regular, joyful meals with thanksgiving.

The discipline of fasting will expose the true priorities of your life. If you want to know what really motivates and drives you in your daily life, engage honestly in the discipline of fasting.

_____

Valerie E. Hess, *Spiritual Disciplines Devotional*

REFLECTION

Do you panic at the thought of fasting from food for a time? On the other hand, do you ever obsess with a fear of gaining weight, and secretly view fasting as a vehicle to get the body you desire? If either of those questions applies to you, ask God for forgiveness and help.

——— **February 17** ———

To watch over mouth and tongue
is to keep out of trouble. (Proverbs 21:23)

Father Antony said . . . "Whoever has not experienced temptation cannot enter into the kingdom of heaven." He even added, "Without temptation no one can be saved."

Father Pambo asked Father Antony, "What ought I to do?" Antony replied, "Do not trust in your own righteousness, do not worry about the past, but control your tongue and your stomach."

_____

St. Antony the Great, quoted in *Eternal Wisdom from the Desert*

REFLECTION

In this passage, the Desert Father Antony makes an unexpected connection between guarding our speech and controlling our stomachs. Which is harder for you to restrain: a sharp tongue, or hunger?

Fasting

——— **February 18** ———

Day to day pours forth speech,
and night to night declares knowledge. (Psalm 19:2)

*
42

Now, though I had great openings, yet great trouble and temptation came many times upon me; so that when it was day I wished for night, and when it was night I wished for day; and by reason of the openings I had in my troubles, I could say as David said, "Day unto day uttereth speech, and night unto night showeth knowledge." When I had openings they answered one another and answered the Scriptures; for I had great openings of the Scriptures: and when I was in troubles, one trouble also answered to another. . . .

I fasted much, walked abroad in solitary places many days, and often took my Bible, and sat in hollow trees and lonesome places till night came on; and frequently in the night walked mournfully about by myself; for I was a man of sorrows in the time of the first workings of the Lord in me.

George Fox, *Journal*

ACTION

Fast in a time of sorrow. Does the experience of the fast help you to more closely discern God's will in a difficult situation?

February 19

I do not understand my own actions. For I do not do what I want, but I do the very thing I hate. (Romans 7:15)

Awareness is one of the keys to spiritual eating and freedom from craving, obsession, and addiction. When we are unaware of our thoughts and our desires, we can be stretched like a rubber band between food control on one side and food lust on the other. I remember noticing, on a recent visit to a bookstore, that the diet books and cookbooks were positioned directly opposite each other in the same aisle. It actually makes a lot of sense. If we're obsessed with food at all, we will always be faced with an ongoing struggle and the question, Which way to turn?

Donald Altman, *Art of the Inner Meal*

PRAYER

Teach me to love my body as your creation, but not be preoccupied with it. Amen.

February 20

"So when you are offering your gift at the altar, if you remember that your brother or sister has something against you, leave your gift there before the altar and go; first be reconciled to your brother or sister, and then come and offer your gift." (Matthew 5:23–24)

Do not limit the benefit of fasting merely to abstinence from food, for a true fast means refraining from evil. Loose every unjust bond, put away your resentment against your neighbour, forgive him his offences. Do not let your fasting lead to wrangling and strife. You do not eat meat, but you devour your brother; you abstain from wine, but not from insults. So all the labour of your fast is useless.

St. Ambrose, quoted in *The Doubleday Christian Quotation Collection*

REFLECTION

Are you harboring any resentment or bitterness toward anyone?

*

———— **February 21** ————

Then Jesus was led up by the Spirit into the wilderness to be tempted by the devil. He fasted forty days and forty nights, and afterwards he was famished. (Matthew 4:1–2)

Jesus was in the wilderness for forty days, not eating for the duration. I tried to imagine it, then gave up and instead tried to imagine relinquishing just one thing: my precious cup of coffee in the morning. No, no—I couldn't fathom it. All my reading . . . about those admirable spiritual athletes, those ascetics who survived on a nightly meal of bread and salt and water, had not prepared me in the least to give up a simple cup of coffee.

This constituted my first lesson about ascesis: It can't be read about or thought about—it must be practiced to have any effect whatsoever. Like those endless diets in the women's magazines, ascesis works only when we do it.

Paula Huston, *The Holy Way*

ACTION

Today, give up one small pleasure that matters to you, just for the day. It could be your morning coffee, or a television show, or using cosmetics. What are you learning about yourself as you try to practice relinquishment?

——— **February 22** ———

Then after fasting and praying they laid their hands on them and sent them off.
(Acts 13:3)

Fasting

It's true, Jesus fasted alone. He withdrew into the mountains in a desert of Jericho for forty days. And there will certainly be times we desire solitude to read, pray, and rest. This will be a season of reflection. However, if we allow ourselves to become isolated, if we completely withdraw, the journey will be even more challenging, mainly because you and I are not Jesus. We tend to experience our greatest failures when we are alone. . . . Find a group of friends and embark on [a] fast together. Pray for one another, support one another. Be honest about the struggles and failures.

*
45

Chris Seay, *A Place at the Table*

ACTION
However you are fasting this month, enlist the help of at least one other person to fast with you for a time. Share with one another your struggles and prayers.

——— **February 23** ———

"But when you fast, put oil on your head and wash your face, so that your fasting may be seen not by others but by your Father who is in secret; and your Father who sees in secret will reward you." (Matthew 6:17–18)

It is sobering to realize that the very first statement Jesus made about fasting dealt with the question of motive (Matt. 6:16–18). To use good things for our own ends is always the sign of false religion. How easy it is to take something like fasting and try to use it to get God to do what we want. At times there is such stress upon the blessings and benefits of fasting that we would be tempted to believe that with a little fast we could have the world, including God, eating out of our hands.

Richard J. Foster, *Celebration of Discipline*

PRAYER

Remind me again, O God, to fast for the right reasons, and not to obtain something I want. Amen.

—————— **February 24** ——————

As a deer longs for flowing streams,
so my soul longs for you, O God. (Psalm 42:1)

Fasting represents an attitude of detachment from the things which gratify man temporally, whether it be from food, pleasure, marital cohabitation, or lawful ambition. It is a mental discipline which constructs a competent personality and character. The Christian fast is a voluntary disuse of anything innocent in itself, with a view to spiritual culture. It does not necessarily apply to food only. . . . Fasting is really putting God first when one acts. It is wanting God more than wanting food or sleep; more than wanting fellowship with others; and more than wanting to attend to business.

Alan P. Johnson, *Fasting*

REFLECTION

Do you want God more than food, sleep, sex, success, or friendship? Be honest.

——— **February 25** ———

"I am the living bread that came down from heaven. Whoever eats of this bread will live forever; and the bread that I will give for the life of the world is my flesh."
(John 6:51)

We accept our constant dependence on food as a natural and inevitable thing. Yet it is not necessarily so: there are creatures which are free from it for very long periods of time. But perhaps because of his border-line status, his embryonic capacity for God, man is kept in constant memory of his own fragility, unable to maintain his existence for long without food from beyond himself; his bodily life dependent on the humble plants and animals that surround him, his soul's life on the unfailing nourishment of the life of God.

Evelyn Underhill, "Food"

REFLECTION

How does the knowledge of your dependence on God for physical sustenance bring you closer to God spiritually?

——— **February 26** ———

Or look at ships: though they are so large that it takes strong winds to drive them, yet they are guided by a very small rudder wherever the will of the pilot directs.
(James 3:4)

When you have to fast, do not pretend illness. For those who do not fast often fall into real sicknesses. If you have begun to act well, do not turn back through constraint of the enemy, for through your endurance, the enemy is destroyed. Those who put out to sea at first sail with a favorable wind; then the sails spread, but later the winds become adverse. Then the ship is tossed by the waves and no longer controlled by the rudder. But when in a little while there is a calm, and the tempest dies down, then the ship sails on again. So it is with us, when we are driven by the spirits who are against us; we hold to the cross as our sail so we can set a safe course.

The Desert Mother Amma Syncletica

PRAYER

Be the rudder of my ship, Lord, and guide me through the rough seas. Amen.

 **February 27**

I appeal to you therefore, brothers and sisters, by the mercies of God, to present your bodies as a living sacrifice, holy and acceptable to God, which is your spiritual worship. (Romans 12:1)

Fasting reveals the things that control us. This is a wonderful benefit for those who long to be transformed into the image of Christ. . . . During our fast, we encounter the inadequacies of will-power and self-discipline. They work for a while, but then we succumb to our cravings. It is this unavoidable encounter with hopelessness that can become the vehicle for a breakthrough that can change us forever.

We finally admit that we do not have control of our lives and that we need help in a way and at a level we may never have experienced before. Now we are ready to pray.

———

Patricia D. Brown, *Paths to Prayer*

ACTION

Fast for two meals (up to twenty-four hours). Whenever you feel that you're at the end of your own power and can't continue with the fast, pray to God to take control and give you strength.

——— **February 28** ———

Like a city breached, without walls,
is one who lacks self-control. (Proverbs 25:28)

When we fast, we learn to recognize and control our many appetites by first controlling our most basic and vital appetite, hunger. We learn to exercise discipline in our relationships with others, with external reality, and with God, relationships in which the temptation of voracity is always present. Fasting is a way of disciplining our need and educating our desire. . . . Fasting is actually the way a Christian confesses faith in the Lord with his or her entire body.

———

Enzo Bianchi, *Echoes of the Word*

REFLECTION

Has fasting this month helped you to educate your desire and confess faith in God with your entire body, as this quote suggests? If not, what do you think might be standing in the way?

MARCH

Daily Work

——— **March 1** ———

Like good stewards of the manifold grace of God, serve one another with whatever gift each of you has received.
(1 Peter 4:10)

Daily
Work

*

52

Even though by nature he had a great aversion to doing kitchen work, [Brother Lawrence] became accustomed to doing everything there out of love for God, and asked Him in every situation for grace to do his work. So he found that kitchen work became easy for him during the fifteen years he was assigned there.

Now he found delight in cobbling shoes, but he was ready to leave this task like the others because no matter where he was assigned, the thing that brought him joy was to do little things for the love of God. . . .

He was much more united to God in his ordinary occupations than when he left them to do the spiritual exercises of a retreat, from which he usually emerged in spiritual dryness.

Reflections on Brother Lawrence, *Practicing the Presence of God*

REFLECTION

This month we will be thinking about the spiritual value of work, particularly household chores but also the work we do outside the home. Do you feel close to God when you are washing dishes, cooking, or gardening? (Note that feeling close to God does not necessarily imply, as it did for Brother Lawrence, that you find "delight" in the household task itself. That's a pretty tall order for changing diapers, for example.)

———— **March 2** ————

Jesus said to them, "Come and have breakfast." . . . Jesus came and took the bread and gave it to them, and did the same with the fish. (John 21:12–13)

Lord of the pots and pipkins,
   since I have no time to be
A saint by doing lovely things
   And vigiling with Thee,
By watching in the twilight dawn
   and storming Heaven's gates—
Make me a saint by getting meals
   and washing up the plates!

Lord of the pots and pipkins,
   please, I offer Thee my soul,
The tiresomeness of tea leaves,
   and the sticky porridge bowls!
Remind me of the things I need,
   not just to save the stairs,
But so that I may perfectly lay tables
   into prayers.

Cecily Hallack, "The Divine Office of the Kitchen"

ACTION

Spend an hour cleaning the kitchen where you live. Set the timer and get to scrubbing. While you are cleaning, thank God for this chore and the chance to prepare good food in a clean, nurturing place. And if your kitchen is already so clean that another hour spent scouring it would be an hour wasted, then come and clean mine.

—— **March 3** ——

Then he said, "Come no closer! Remove the sandals from your feet, for the place on which you are standing is holy ground." (Exodus 3:5)

Daily
Work

*

54

We are always in the presence of this God, even though we may not always be aware of it because of our frenetic busyness; and we have to pause, reassemble our scattered faculties, become recollected as we savor the sanctity of the present moment, to be still. . . . Every bit of ground we trample is actually holy ground. . . .

In these ways we would be like Brother Lawrence, who found the clatter of the pots and pans in the kitchen as good in inducing holy thoughts as the liturgical acts in the sanctuary at the celebration of the Eucharist. . . . The sacred could erupt anywhere at any time, every bush being potentially a burning bush. One of my confessors and spiritual counselors used to say, "Nothing is secular except sin."

Desmond Tutu, Preface to *Words for Silence*

PRAYER

Lord, help me recognize that each room where I live is holy ground, and that you are found everywhere in the daily round of life. Amen.

—— **March 4** ——

Once Jesus was asked by the Pharisees when the kingdom of God was coming, and he answered, "The kingdom of God is not coming with things that can be observed; nor will they say, 'Look, here it is!' or 'There it is!' For, in fact, the kingdom of God is among you." (Luke 17:20–21)

I understand and know from experience that: *"The kingdom of God is within you."* Jesus has no need of books or teachers to instruct souls; He teaches without the noise of words. Never have I heard him speak, but I feel that He is within me at each moment; He is guiding and inspiring me with what I must say and do. I find just when I need them certain lights that I had not seen until then, and it isn't most frequently during my hours of prayer that these are most abundant but rather in the midst of my daily occupations.

St. Thérèse of Lisieux, *Story of a Soul*

REFLECTION

Thérèse reported that she was more likely to find God in her regular daily occupations than in her hours of prayer. (Feel better—she said that and is still considered a saint!) When do you feel closest to God?

——— **March 5** ———

Whatever your task, put yourselves into it, as done for the Lord and not for your masters. (Colossians 3:23)

Hence these ordinary works are God's order. What more glorious commendation are you asking for, or what clearer testimony? Hence when a milk maid milks the cows or a hired man hoes the field—provided that they are believers; namely, that they conclude that this kind of life is pleasing to God and was instituted by God—they serve God more than all the monks and nuns, who cannot be sure about their kind of life.

Martin Luther, *Lectures on Genesis*

ACTION

Today, say thank you to all the "providers" you come across—people who are serving God by serving others. These could be cooks, waiters, teachers, bus drivers, veterinarians, or what have you. Just appreciate what they have done for you.

——— **March 6** ———

Let us come into his presence with thanksgiving;
let us make a joyful noise to him with songs of praise!
(Psalm 95:2)

Do not fret about your prayer life. For the moment, a spiritual yearning suffices. Besides, everything is prayer. If you can see for yourself that "the world is charged with the grandeur of God"; if in certain times and places you can exclaim, "Heaven is under our feet as well as over our heads," you are praying, grateful for the awe and wonder of the natural world. If before entering your favorite class, or when sitting down each evening to do homework, you were to say, "For what I am about to receive, Lord, make me truly thankful," that would be a most appropriate prayer, for, as they used to say in the good-old-Latin-speaking days, "*Laborare est orare*." Work of all kinds done joyfully, thankfully, unselfishly, conscientiously—all such labor is prayer.

William Sloane Coffin Jr., *Letters to a Young Doubter*

PRAYER

Help me remember that everything is prayer, Lord, including my work. Amen.

March 7

Where can I go from your spirit?
Or where can I flee from your presence? (Psalm 139:7)

The nonmaterial things you and I can't buy and sell are at the very core of our sense of freedom and joy. Shooting the waves at the beach after a storm, walking through the woods at sunrise, sitting quietly alone in a garden, having a siesta with your spouse, are not wastes of time. . . . We should feel free to spend more time in contemplation, prayer, and meditation, when we fill our own hearts with light and faith and hope. We don't have to go to a chapel or a synagogue or a mosque to do this. We can meditate standing over the dishes in the kitchen sink, or fall to our knees in appreciation of our blessings as we wipe up the bathroom floor after a bath.

Alexandra Stoddard, *Feeling at Home*

ACTION

Spend fifteen minutes today in work-as-prayer. See if you can practice the presence of God by choosing a chore that keeps your hands busy but frees your mind to think about counting your blessings.

March 8

"Give us this day our daily bread." (Matthew 6:11)

Things exercise a certain tyranny over us. Whenever I am checking bags at the airport, I recall St. Teresa of Avila's wonderful prayer of praise, "Thank God for the things I do not own." Things are truly baggage, our *impedimenta*, which must be maintained with work that is menial, steady and recurring. But, like liturgy, the work of cleaning draws much of its meaning and value from repetition, from the fact that it is never completed, but only set aside until the next day. Both liturgy and what is euphemistically termed "domestic" work also have an intense relation with the present moment, a kind of faith in the present that fosters hope and makes life seem possible in the day-to-day.

Kathleen Norris, *The Quotidian Mysteries*

REFLECTION

When have possessions become *impedimenta* for you, slowing you down and impeding your spiritual growth? On the other hand, when has caring for those possessions through an almost liturgical round of repetitive work helped you to become closer to God?

——— **March 9** ———

Paul had gathered a bundle of brushwood and was putting it on the fire. (Acts 28:3)

You will never arrive at the state in life where you're too important to help with menial tasks. God will never exempt you from the mundane. It's a vital part of your character curriculum. . . . It is in these small services that we grow like Christ.

Jesus specialized in menial tasks that everyone else tried to avoid: washing feet, helping children, fixing breakfast, and serving lepers. . . .

Small tasks often show a big heart. Your servant's heart is revealed in little acts that others won't think of doing, as when Paul gathered brushwood for a fire to warm everyone after a shipwreck. He was just as exhausted as everyone else, but he did what everyone needed. No task is beneath you when you have a servant's heart.

———

Rick Warren, *The Purpose Driven Life*

ACTION

Perform three small acts of service today in the form of menial tasks. Don't call attention to the fact you are doing them; just be grateful that you can.

——— **March 10** ———

"So if I, your Lord and Teacher, have washed your feet, you also ought to wash one another's feet. For I have set you an example, that you also should do as I have done to you."
(John 13:14–15)

Redemption is profoundly, essentially physical; the Jesus who shared, and shares, your humanity and mine lived and suffered and died on our behalf.

Housework, too, is essentially physical. Indeed, a complaint commonly lodged against housework is that it is "menial"—work for servants—in contrast to other, higher-status kinds of work that may not include getting one's hands dirty. But if in Jesus God himself could take up a towel and wash people's feet, surely we, as Jesus' adopted brothers and sisters, can find it in us to wash one another's dirty clothes and dirty dishes and dirty floors. Active engagement with fundamentally physical practices like housekeeping can be a way of remembering that a properly human life is a life of service in and through the body. It was so for Jesus, and it is so for us.

——

Margaret Kim Peterson, *Keeping House*

REFLECTION

When you were growing up, what was your parents' attitude toward menial work? What are your attitudes about it now?

——————— **March 11** ———————

He provides food for those who fear him. (Psalm 111:5)

Before you ate, you probably gave thanks to God for your food, as is fitting. He is caring for your physical needs, as with every other kind of need you have, preserving your life through His gifts. . . . And He does so by using other human beings. It is still God who is responsible for giving us our daily bread. Though He could give it to us directly, by a miraculous provision, as He once did for the children of Israel when He fed them daily manna, God has chosen to work through human beings, who, in their different capacities and according to their different talents, serve each other. This is the doctrine of vocation.

——

Gene Edward Veith Jr., *God at Work*

PRAYER

Holy God, thank you for all the hands that brought me my food today: those who grew it, shipped it, prepared it, and served it. Amen.

———— **March 12** ————

For if those who are nothing think they are something, they deceive themselves. (Galatians 6:3)

Sometimes a disaster such as an earthquake or a flood is required to remind us that we depend for survival on people performing some work that seems rather mundane in more normal times. We want our water to be drinkable, we want food to be available, we want our garbage to be picked up, we want our electricity to work, we want the telephone to operate properly, we want the roads to be passable if not free of potholes, and we want to feel the security of living in an ordered society.

These and similar needs call for some rather mundane work to be done by someone. We do ourselves and the workers who do such work a disservice if we fail to recognize its value and indeed its necessity. Furthermore, people of faith who do such work would do well to see meaning in it and indeed to see it as an act of ministry and an expression of their calling.

Ross West, *Go to Work and Take Your Faith Too!*

ACTION

Try to keep track today of all the mundane services you take for granted: the water that comes from the faucet, the light that spills forth at the flip of a switch. Thank God for those services and the people who provide them.

——— **March 13** ———

If the part of the dough offered as first fruits is holy, then the whole batch is holy; and if the root is holy, then the branches also are holy. (Romans 11:16)

Daily
Work

*

62

When you wake up in the morning, Pooh," said Piglet at last, "what's the first thing you say to yourself?"

"What's for breakfast?" said Pooh. "What do *you* say, Piglet?"

"I say, I wonder what's going to happen exciting *today*?" said Piglet.

Pooh nodded thoughtfully.

"It's the same thing," he said.

———

A. A. Milne, *Winnie-the-Pooh*

REFLECTION
"What's going to happen exciting *today*?"

——— **March 14** ———

Now as they went on their way, he entered a certain village, where a woman named Martha welcomed him into her home. She had a sister named Mary, who sat at the Lord's feet and listened to what he was saying. But Martha was distracted by her many tasks. (Luke 10:38–40)

There Martha was, running around the house, getting food on the table for all the disciples. The entertaining pressure was on. This food was for Jesus for crying out loud. And Martha's making it all happen, because somebody has to.

In order for some people to sit around being still and having deep thoughts, I guarantee you there's always another group of people running around behind the scenes making it all possible, making sure the space is ready, the food is cooking, the music is prepared, and the atmosphere is just right for the other folks to have this deep spiritual connection in the moment.

Lillian Daniel, *When "Spiritual But Not Religious" Is Not Enough*

PRAYER

Lord, teach me to find a balance between serving others and becoming closer to you. Amen.

———— **March 15** ————

O taste and see that the Lord is good;
happy are those who take refuge in him. (Psalm 34:8)

From my vantage point, the idea that faith and meaning and all the other important things happen in your mind or soul where no one can see them is one of the worst by-products of modern Christianity. We are, whether we choose to acknowledge it or not, physical beings. And *physical* isn't negative. If we didn't have bodies, we couldn't feel the sun on our faces or smell the earthy, mushroom-y rich smell of the ground right after the rain. . . . I'm so thankful to live in this physical, messy, blood-and-guts world. I don't want to live in a world that's all dry ideas and theorems. Food is one of the ways we acknowledge our humanity, our appetites, our need for nourishment. And so it may seem trivial or peripheral to some people, but to me, when I'm telling a story, the part about what we ate really does matter.

Shauna Niequist, *Bittersweet*

REFLECTION

How does food *matter*? What does it mean to you to have this daily reminder of our dependence on God?

——— **March 16** ———

Let the favor of the Lord our God be upon us,
and prosper for us the work of our hands—
O prosper the work of our hands! (Psalm 90:17)

One of the Shakers' chief maxims was "Put your hands to work and your hearts to God." Well, of course, this is normal for us. You work and your heart is lifted up to God while you are working and you are working for God. Now, to work for God means not this business of working and looking at God, but working in such a way that your work is your union with God. . . . There is no point in my rushing like mad through a work period and typing fifteen or twenty pages and getting it out by four o'clock and then going to pray. It is not a question of working in a sort of half daze, so you will sort of work and go off a little bit, and come back, and float a little bit, and so forth. It is more a question of when you work, you *think* about your work.

Thomas Merton, ocso, "Work and the Shakers"

ACTION

When you work today, be fully present in what you are doing. Sometimes it helps to set a timer and determine that for the next half hour or hour, you will pursue a single task without distractions. Put your hands to work and your heart to God.

—— March 17 ——

Blessed are those who wash their robes, so that they will have the right to the tree of life and may enter the city by the gates. (Revelation 22:14)

Today, for the first time this year, the weather was fine and mild enough to hang the laundry out. So I spent the morning washing and filling the line with sheets—there is nothing like air-dried bedding, one of life's greater minor pleasures. For once, instead of seeing all the yardwork which needs to be done and which I don't think I can possibly accomplish singlehandedly, I let myself fall into Martha-prayer, the contemplation possible when the hands are busy and the mind is free.

Molly Wolf, *Hiding in Plain Sight*

PRAYER

Keep my mind free as my hands are busy, so that I can find you in my daily life. Amen.

—— March 18 ——

When they had gone ashore, they saw a charcoal fire there, with fish on it, and bread. Jesus said to them, "Bring some of the fish that you have just caught." So Simon Peter went aboard and hauled the net ashore, full of large fish, a hundred fifty-three of them; and though there were so many, the net was not torn. Jesus said to them, "Come and have breakfast." (John 21:9–12)

Jesus had cooked breakfast for his disciples on the beach. I loved how mundane it was. Every example I had of

God's "miraculous" provision in my life was a lot like this one. No one could ever prove that Jesus had put those fish in the water. The miracle wasn't a display of power. It was a reminder of who He was—the one who cared for them with abundance. The one who served them. It was a reminder of who they were—the ones called to receive from Him. The ones called to follow Him.

_____

Amy Julia Becker, *A Good and Perfect Gift*

ACTION
Make breakfast for someone today with love.

March 19

Day by day, as they spent much time together in the temple, they broke bread at home and ate their food with glad and generous hearts. (Acts 2:46)

The family dinner table is no longer something to be taken for granted. In some families it doesn't even exist. . . . It is a great loss. Often during my marriage Hugh and I had to work hard to keep the tradition, eating at odd hours just so that we could get everybody together, but the effort is worth it, it is *worth* it. For me the shared evening meal is the time for gathering together, the time when meaning is made clear—the value and validity of our lives. There have been times of trouble when the dinner table has been the only affirmation available.

_____

Madeleine L'Engle, *Glimpses of Grace*

PRAYER
Be with us at our table, Lord. Amen.

——— March 20 ———

Commit your work to the LORD,
and your plans will be established. (Proverbs 16:3)

The ordinary arts we practice every day at home are of more importance to the soul than their simplicity might suggest. For example, I can't explain it, but I enjoy doing dishes. I've had an automatic dishwasher for over a year, and I have never used it. What appeals to me, as I think about it, is the reverie induced by going through the ritual of washing, rinsing, and drying. Marie-Louise von Franz, the Swiss Jungian author, observes that weaving and knitting, too, are particularly good for the soul because they encourage reflection and reverie.

Thomas Moore, *Care of the Soul*

REFLECTION

What is your favorite household occupation, and why?

——— March 21 ———

. . . but all things should be done decently and in order.
(1 Corinthians 14:40)

Prayer and housekeeping—they go together. They have always gone together. We simply know that our daily round *is* how we live. When we clean and order our homes, we are somehow also cleaning and ordering ourselves. We know this by virtue of being human creatures. How we hold the simplest of our tasks speaks loudly about how we hold life itself.

Gunilla Norris, *Being Home*

REFLECTION

Have you known someone who seemed to find peace and joy through housekeeping? Do you feel that tranquility is attainable for you in the reality of your own house or apartment? Why or why not?

———— **March 22** ————

So I sent messengers to them, saying, "I am doing a great work and I cannot come down. Why should the work stop while I leave it to come down to you?" They sent to me four times in this way, and I answered them in the same manner.
(Nehemiah 6:3–4)

There are times when working in the kitchen is unavoidably a hassle, but often this is because the cook has become focused on a mindset that fosters stress. Instead of simply being yourself, you try to live up to an image of what you imagine a cook should be. Cooking then becomes a limiting rather than a liberating experience.

Around the world, various spiritual traditions have developed techniques to facilitate . . . internal silence. Many of these methods are based on a simple but very important fact: The mind can only accommodate one thought at a time.

Isaac Cronin, *The Mindful Cook*

ACTION

Be mindful in whatever cooking or food preparation you do today. Keep your aspirations simple—this is *not* the time to master Julia Child's techniques—and give yourself plenty of time, so you can enjoy the experience without stress.

March 23

Unless the LORD builds the house,
those who build it labor in vain. (Psalm 127:1)

Our rooms will only be as generous and nurturing as the spirit we invest in them. The Bible gives us the same warning, more sternly: Unless God builds the house, it will not stand. The one I live in has been standing for just over sixty years, a mere eyeblink, not long enough to prove there was divinity in the mortar. I do know, however, that mortar and nails alone would not have held the house together even for sixty years. It has also needed the work of many hands, the wishes of many hearts, vision upon vision, through a succession of families.

Scott Russell Sanders, *Staying Put*

PRAYER

Build my house, Lord; fill it with your presence and love.
Amen.

March 24

How lovely is your dwelling place,
O LORD of hosts! (Psalm 84:1)

My poor housekeeping and limited income keep me from the trap of believing that contentment comes with perfection. My ceilings will never be free of cobwebs; I will never own a first-rate shelving system for my canned goods. I cannot make the assumption (which advertising preaches so loudly) that having everything *just so* will satisfy my needs. I'm forced to explore the alternatives. How can I put myself in a healthy relationship with this pantry? What changes can I make to bring more peace into meal making—move the microwave onto a pantry shelf? Learn not to feel shame at my shortcomings? Only a small part of being at home is the home itself. The rest is the being, the creature who dwells, and the very nature of our dwelling.

Elizabeth J. Andrew, *Home, Hardwood, and Holiness*

REFLECTION

When you look around the place where you live, are you satisfied with what you see? Is it possible for you to find God in the process of creating a welcoming place to live, rather than in some ideal finished product? (Yes, I read those home decorating magazines too. Darn you, Pinterest!)

——— March 25 ———

Your wife will be like a fruitful vine
within your house;
your children will be like olive shoots
around your table. (Psalm 128:3)

It is impossible not to be inspired by the sentimental portrait of the large family sitting down to the Thanksgiving table as the mother places a huge turkey in front of them. That's exactly the home we would all prefer to gather for the holidays. But that family doesn't exist, and the portrait is an unfortunate judgment on the family we have.

Rockwell wasn't painting our family tables, but our aspirations of them. If he had wanted to give us a glimpse of the true family table it would have been stained with painful memories, a chair would have been vacant to remind the family of a loved one who had recently died, and at least one person at the table wouldn't be able to smile. There isn't a family on earth that is spared any of these harsh realities.

Craig Barnes, *Searching for Home*

ACTION

If a family member is causing difficulty or pain in your life, make a special effort today to be grateful for that person. If gratitude is impossible right now—and sometimes it is, in the non-Rockwellian family realities we have—just pray for God's light to be felt in your family.

———— **March 26** ————

So I saw that there is nothing better than that all should enjoy their work. (Ecclesiastes 3:22)

Some people choose to do physical labor as a hobby in their free time because it satisfies them spiritually. One clergywoman I know shared with me that she would like to make her passion for knitting a true vocation, and she now is leading workshops about how the "click click" of knitting needles can be a prayer. . . . I have friends whose most authentic prayer happens as they knead and bake fresh loaves of bread, as a "fragrant offering" to God. Especially for those of us who work mostly in our heads, we feel more human, more connected in bodyspirit when we work with our hands.

Nancy Roth, *Spiritual Exercises*

PRAYER

Thank you for work, Lord! I offer my work up to you today. Amen.

——— **March 27** ———

All must test their own work; then that work, rather than their neighbor's work, will become a cause for pride.
(Galatians 6:4)

I once visited the shop of a woodworker in Ireland. He had selected only woods grown on plantations, so as not to use endangered trees. He used nontoxic oils for polishing. He kept the organic colors and shapes of the wood in his finished bowls rather than cutting them away. In all these ways he presented a philosophy of life as much as a practical bowl, and his satisfaction at work seemed all the more solid for his ideas. . . . This is concrete work with a spiritual dimension.

Spirituality without a ground in daily work tends to be abstract and ultimately irrelevant. Practical labor without a spiritual base is unconscious, narcissistic, and one-dimensional. . . . The spiritual and the practical need each other. Without the spiritual, work is a mere job.

Thomas Moore, *A Life at Work*

REFLECTION

Do you think of yourself as a pragmatic, down-to-earth person, or more of an idealist? How does work help you grow closer to God?

——— **March 28** ———

For all must carry their own loads. (Galatians 6:5)

As long as the washer and dryer spin, I tell myself, I am safe and those I love may choose to keep living alongside me. For there is laundry to be done and so many chores—chores of the living. There is so much to be remembered under the dust of our old contempt for cleaning up after ourselves, picking up our own socks. There is much to be swept away and shined bright and scrubbed down to its deepest, most illuminating level. Think of all the chores we have yet to do, quietly and on our knees—because home is holy.

————

Brenda Peterson, *Nature and Other Mothers*

REFLECTION

Brenda Peterson suggests we should be grateful for household chores, because they are a reminder that we are among the living: where there's life, there's work. Can you point to your household tasks and be grateful for the full life they represent?

——— **March 29** ———

For they will scarcely brood over the days of their lives,
because God keeps them occupied with the joy of their hearts.
(Ecclesiastes 5:20)

To stand stubbornly in Nowhere, rejecting the restlessness that urges us to move on, silencing the voices that entice us into tomorrow, and blowing off the demonic whisper, "Look busy—Jesus is coming," is an act of unflappable trust in the presence of God. . . .

Sue Monk Kidd quotes her mentor, Beatrice Bruteau: "Be what you are actually doing in the present moment. If you are plowing, plow fully in the moment with your whole mind and heart—in other words, 'become plowing.'" Kidd adds, "I once read an Hasidic story about a teacher who was said

MARCH

Daily
Work

*

74

to have lived an unusually abundant life. After his death, one of his pupils was asked, 'What was the most important to your teacher?' The pupil replied, 'Whatever he happened to be doing at the moment.'"

Brennan Manning, *Ruthless Trust*

PRAYER

Help me be present, Lord, no matter what I am doing. Amen.

─────── **March 30** ───────

So the wall was finished on the twenty-fifth day of the month Elul, in fifty-two days. (Nehemiah 6:15)

If what you and I are doing is God's will, it qualifies as a "great work," whether it is cooking dinner for the kids or designing a bridge to span the Amazon River. We need Nehemiah's resolute response to the many forms of opposition we face, including procrastination, distraction or discouragement. . . .

Among scriptural mentors who integrate faith and work, Nehemiah is without peer. He was submissive both to his God and his employer. He was spiritually mature, wise, focused, determined and effective.

John D. Beckett, *Mastering Monday*

REFLECTION

Nehemiah faced great opposition in his building of the wall. What opposition do you face in your work, whether in or out of the home? How can you overcome it?

"You are the salt of the earth; but if salt has lost its taste, how can its saltiness be restored? It is no longer good for anything, but is thrown out and trampled under foot."
(Matthew 5:13)

Flour and salt—the makings of bread—were frequently brought to our early altars. The sacrifices were made in recognition of the fact that we are fundamentally creatures of need. These offerings were petitions for sustenance. We have understood from the beginning how dependent and vulnerable we are. We have known that in order to live we will always have to receive and care for the gifts of life.

And we have also known that we must share these gifts. They are not for us alone. Hoarded, they molder just as uneaten bread molders. We must share life, share bread with one another.

Gunilla Norris, *Becoming Bread*

REFLECTION

As we come to the end of our spiritual practice for March, what have you learned about finding God in daily chores and occupations? Do you feel contented with your work, your home, and your family?

APRIL

*Lectio
Divina*

——— **April 1** ———

Open my eyes, so that I may behold
wondrous things out of your law.
(Psalm 119:18)

Reading the Bible, if we do not do it rightly, can get us into a lot of trouble. The Christian community is as concerned with *how* we read the Bible as *that* we read it. It is not sufficient to place a Bible in a person's hands with the command, "Read it." That is quite as foolish as putting a set of car keys in an adolescent's hand, giving him a Honda, and saying, "Drive it." And just as dangerous. The danger is that in having our hands on a piece of technology, we will use it ignorantly, endangering our lives and the lives of those around us; or that, intoxicated with the power that the technology gives us, we will use it ruthlessly and violently. . . .

And so, as we hand out Bibles and urge people to read them, it is imperative that we also say, *caveat lector*, let the reader beware.

———

Eugene H. Peterson, *Eat This Book*

PRAYER

Lord, help me have humility as I approach the Scriptures.
Amen.

——— **April 2** ———

This book of the law shall not depart out of your mouth;
you shall meditate on it day and night. (Joshua 1:8)

Lectio literally means reading, from which terms like lection and lectionary are derived. It signifies the kind of reading we have been portraying: reflective, gentle paced, one-bite-at-a-time. It means reading as if you had a love letter in hand. You allow the words that are pregnant and weighty with meaning to sink in and expand and nourish your heart. With scripture, it entails reading each sentence as if for the first time, expecting that God will address you with a direct and personal message. The message may not be comfortable. Sometimes letters from those who love us contain painful words, but they are offered out of love and may be just what we need to hear. The question behind our reading is, God, what are you saying to me just now?

Marjorie Thompson, *Soul Feast*

ACTION

During this month, as we focus week by week on the four stages of *lectio divina,* I'd like you to start slowly and build gradually. So in the first week, you will do only *lectio*. Take a small section of Scripture, ask God to open your heart, and then slowly read it.

——— **April 3** ———
LECTIO

Make me to know your ways, O Lord;
teach me your paths. (Psalm 25:4)

The practice of spiritual reading involves a series of movements of mind and heart: reading, meditating, and praying. These movements bring us into conversation with God and prompt us to action—doing what God tells us to do. We *read* a Scripture text, intent on understanding it. We read with listening ears to hear what God is saying. Then we *meditate* on the text, letting the Holy Spirit show us its message for our lives. Reading and meditating on a text draw us to *pray*. The words we speak in prayer respond to God, who has initiated the conversation in our reading and meditating.

———

Bert Ghezzi, *Everyday Encounters with God*

REFLECTION

What does it mean for you to read Scripture with "listening ears"?

——— **April 4** ———

LECTIO

"But as for what was sown on good soil, this is the one who hears the word and understands it." (Matthew 13:23)

Be realistic as you think about when and for how long you will try to practice this prayer, but also plan on being regular. It may be that daily will work for you. However, do not feel that you need to start with this. Many people try to take this time of prayer three or four times a week. Remember, pray as you can, not as you ought. Similarly, be realistic about how long a period a time you might set aside for *lectio divina*. . . . It could be as short as five minutes. Longer is better (ten to fifteen minutes is ideal), but not always possible.

———

David G. Benner, *Opening to God*

ACTION

Spiritual director David Benner wisely advises that we begin a practice of *lectio divina* slowly and with a healthy reality check. Today, take just five minutes to work through the parable of the sower (Matthew 13:18–23). Remember that we are only working with the first stage: slowly read the text at least once. Sometimes reading aloud is helpful because it is a natural way of slowing down.

——— April 5 ———
LECTIO

"But whenever you pray, go into your room and shut the door and pray to your Father who is in secret. . . ."
(Matthew 6:6)

> I weave a silence on to my lips
> I weave a silence into my mind
> I weave a silence within my heart
> I close my ears to distractions
> I close my eyes to attractions
> I close my heart to temptations

David Adam, "Before Prayer"

ACTION

When you next sit down to *lectio*, pray this prayer out loud twice to help you settle in to God's presence.

——— **April 6** ———

LECTIO

*Hear, O Israel: The L*ORD *is our God, the L*ORD *alone. You shall love the L*ORD *your God with all your heart, and with all your soul, and with all your might. Keep these words that I am commanding you today in your heart. (Deuteronomy 6:4–6)*

There's a lovely Hasidic story of a rabbi who always told his people that if they studied the Torah, it would put Scripture on their hearts. One of them asked, "Why *on* our hearts, but not *in* them?" The rabbi answered, "Only God can put Scripture inside. But reading sacred text can put it on your hearts, and then when your hearts break, the holy words will fall inside."

———

Anne Lamott, *Plan B*

PRAYER

Teach me your words, O God, so that I can remember them and be sustained by them when life falls apart. Amen.

——— **April 7** ———

LECTIO

Oh, how I love your law!
It is my meditation all day long. (Psalm 119:97)

Prayer is easily recognized as a spiritual practice and many of us imagine that we might profit from spending more time at prayer. Few of us give much thought to spending more time reading and studying as a discipline. It isn't necessarily that we think poorly of these activities; it is rather that we just don't think of them at all or not as part of our rule of life.

Reading, however, is a key way of encountering aspects of God that are unfamiliar to us. If we take the time to explore challenging reading—the Bible, the lives of the saints, books of spirituality or Bible study, poetry, fiction, etc.— we provide ourselves with the opportunity to expand our knowledge of God and God's activity here on earth.

Debra Farrington, *Living Faith Day by Day*

REFLECTION

What have you read that helped you feel God's presence? It does not have to be from the Bible, though it can be.

——— **April 8** ———

MEDITATIO

Let the words of my mouth and the meditation of my heart
be acceptable to you,
O Lord, my rock and my redeemer.
(Psalm 19:14)

One can choose any length of time that satisfies, but ten or fifteen minutes can be enough for the Lord to give us a word of life. We are busy people; it is difficult to make time—we don't find it, we have to make it, for all the things we want to do each day. But who cannot make ten minutes for something he or she really wants to? The point here is that we listen for a period of time. . . . What we want to avoid is setting a goal for ourselves to read a page, a chapter, or a section. We are so programmed to speed reading, to getting things done, that if we set ourselves to read a certain amount, we will be pushed to get it done. We do not want that. We want to be able to listen to the Word freely. . . . That is why in the second point we say "we listen," not "we read."

M. Basil Pennington, OCSO, *Praying the Holy Scriptures*

ACTION

In this second week of *lectio divina*, you will continue doing *lectio* but also add the second stage of *meditatio*, deep listening to the text. Aim for ten minutes each time you sit down to do these two stages this week. Read your chosen passage at least twice and then focus on *deep listening.* What particular words or phrases strike you?

——— **April 9** ———

MEDITATIO

Now the LORD came and stood there, calling as before, "Samuel! Samuel!" And Samuel said, "Speak, for your servant is listening." (1 Samuel 3:10)

When I pick up the sacred Book, the speaker is present before me as a divine "Thou." At that moment God speaks those words for me. God wishes to create a dialogue of love, to take hold of my life and insert it into God's life. What power there is in those words, if I receive them from God's lips in this way! . . . In the presence of a message so alive, relevant and personal, I pay full attention. The words of the young Samuel spring spontaneously to my lips: "Speak, Lord, for your servant is listening." My entire soul is present in that listening, which is then expressed in the adherence of faith and in total surrender.

Mariano Magrassi, *Praying the Bible*

PRAYER

Speak, Lord, for your servant is listening. Amen.

———— April 10 ————

MEDITATIO

With my whole heart I seek you;
do not let me stray from your commandments.
(Psalm 119:10)

To take the holy scriptures and read them is the first thing we have to do to open ourselves to God's call. Reading the scriptures is not as easy as it seems since in our academic world we tend to make anything and everything we read subject to analysis and discussion. But the word of God should lead us first of all to contemplation and meditation. Instead of taking the words apart, we should bring them together in our innermost being; instead of wondering if we agree or disagree, we should wonder which words are directly spoken to us and connect directly with our most personal story.

Henri J. M. Nouwen, *Seeds of Hope*

REFLECTION

Is it difficult for you to turn off the analytical part of your mind and just sink into the Scriptures, regarding them as God's word to you?

———— **April 11** ————

MEDITATIO

Create in me a clean heart, O God,
and put a new and right spirit within me.
Do not cast me away from your presence,
and do not take your holy spirit from me. (Psalm 51:10–11)

Another difficulty arises as *lectio divina* is practiced regularly and takes on a life of its own. When this happens, as with all spiritual practices, fidelity is tested. Resistance arises alongside the greater union with God. Remembrance of sin and longing for God produces compunction of heart, sometimes accompanied with the *gift of tears*. Memories stored in the body arise and the psychological effects of repressed emotion peel off either gradually or suddenly as the false self is purified.

Mary Margaret Funk, in *The Gethsemani Encounter*

ACTION

Spend ten minutes in the first two stages of *lectio divina* with Psalm 51. Pray this Psalm by calling to mind your own sin and desire for reconciliation with God.

———— **April 12** ————

MEDITATIO

"Let anyone with ears to hear listen!" (Mark 4:9)

At the beginning of his gospel, the apostle John wrote: "The word became flesh and lived among us." This is the process of sacred reading. We read the Bible slowly and reverently, listening for the Word made flesh in our own lives.

In sacred reading we aren't studying the Bible for historical, theological, or cultural contexts. We are looking to encounter the living God. *Lectio divina* invites the Holy Spirit to bring the Word to life in a way that grips us and speaks to us right in the midst of our daily lives. We let the word descend from our minds to our hearts where it can penetrate and transform us.

Sharon Garlough Brown, *Sensible Shoes*

REFLECTION

How might the Word dwell inside you today?

─────── **April 13** ───────

MEDITATIO

[Jesus] said to him, "What is written in the law?
What do you read there?"(Luke 10:26)

I resolved, therefore, to direct my mind to the Holy Scriptures, that I might see what they were. And behold, I saw something not comprehended by the proud, not disclosed to children, something lowly in the hearing, but sublime in the doing, and veiled in mysteries. Yet I was not of the number of those who could enter into it or bend my neck to follow its steps. For then it was quite different from what I now feel. When I then turned toward the Scriptures, they appeared to me to be quite unworthy to be compared with the dignity of Tully. For my inflated pride was repelled by their style, nor could the sharpness of my wit penetrate their inner meaning. Truly they were of a sort to aid the growth of little ones, but I scorned to be a little one and, swollen with pride, I looked upon myself as fully grown.

St. Augustine of Hippo, *Confessions*

REFLECTION

What does Augustine mean that he "scorned to be a little one"? Do you ever feel that way?

—— **April 14** ——
MEDITATIO

Indeed, the word of God is living and active, sharper than any two-edged sword, piercing until it divides soul from spirit, joints from marrow; it is able to judge the thoughts and intentions of the heart. (Hebrews 4:12)

Maybe we need to work on our metaphors for scripture a little. Try something other than *rock* or *sword.* . . . Maybe it's more like an octopus than a rock, something more wriggly, something you can hardly keep track of, but it draws you in. And messes with you a little. It's not a thing that is laid out flat on a page; it's more of a creature that interacts with you to help you undergo something, dismantle something, usher you into relationship.

———

Debbie Blue, *From Stone to Living Word*

PRAYER

Lord, help me wrestle with and love the Scriptures at the same time. Amen.

—— **April 15** ——
ORATIO

But Jacob said, "I will not let you go, unless you bless me."
(Genesis 32:26)

Many people these days feel an absence in their lives, expressed as an acute desire for "something more," a spiritual home, a community of faith. But when they try to read the Bible they end up throwing it across the room. To me, this seems encouraging, a place to start, a sign of real engagement with the God who is revealed in scripture. . . . In the context of real life, the Bible seems refreshingly whole, an honest reflection on humanity in relation to the sacred and the profane. I can't learn enough about it, but I also have to trust what little I know, and proceed, in faith, to seek God there.

Kathleen Norris, *Amazing Grace*

ACTION

Today we are adding the third stage of *lectio divina*, which is *oratio* ("prayer"). Take fifteen minutes today for the first three stages of *lectio divina* on Genesis 32:24–29. Put yourself in Jacob's place. What are you wrestling with right now?

April 16

ORATIO

For there is no distinction, since all have sinned and fall short of the glory of God. (Romans 3:22–23)

The Bible is not a witness to the best people making it up to God; it's a witness to God making it down to the worst people. Far from being a book full of moral heroes whom we are commanded to emulate, what we discover is that the so-called heroes in the Bible are not really heroes at all. They fall and fail; they make huge mistakes; they get afraid; they're selfish, deceptive, egotistical, and unreliable.

. . . The overwhelming focus of the Bible is not the work of the redeemed but the work of the Redeemer. Which means that the Bible is not first a recipe book for Christian living but a revelation book of Jesus who is the answer to our un-Christian living.

Lectio Divina

———

Tullian Tchividjian, *One Way Love*

REFLECTION

Do you find it comforting or a bit threatening that so many of the Bible's characters—Noah, David, Jacob, Solomon—were not moral heroes?

——— **April 17** ———

ORATIO

For I know my transgressions,
and my sin is ever before me.
Against you, you alone, have I sinned,
and done what is evil in your sight.
(Psalm 51:3–4)

A recovering fundamentalist said to me that she had been taught never to question anything that anyone in the Bible did or said, because they were all holy people of God and could do no wrong! There are many of them who were holy people of God, but they did much wrong. . . .

The people of God are not all good and moral people. They do terrible things. But they know that they are utterly dependent on God, and if they do anything that is good, it is because God pushes them into it and helps them every inch of the way.

———

Madeleine L'Engle, *The Rock That Is Higher*

PRAYER

Lord, as I dig deeper into the Bible, help me to see my own frailty and sinfulness in the stories I read. Amen.

——— **April 18** ———

ORATIO

I treasure your word in my heart,
so that I may not sin against you. (Psalm 119:11)

To meditate for the ancient monastics was to repeat the words of the Scriptures until they were inscribed in the memory. The very muscles used to mouth the words and those parts in the ears that respond to the spoken sound "remember" the Scriptures.

Raymond Studzinski, "Lectio Divina: Reading and Praying"

ACTION

Memorize Psalm 119:11 above. (You can do it!) Memorizing it will help you to treasure the words in your heart.

——— **April 19** ———

ORATIO

The fear of the LORD is the beginning of wisdom;
all those who practice it have a good understanding.
His praise endures forever. (Psalm 111:10)

A slightly different form of *lectio divina* comes to us from Martin Luther, who shared his understanding of prayer when his barber asked him for guidance. Martin Luther instructed him to read a short passage from the Bible five times. The first time was simply to hear the words. The second time was to reflect on what teaching was present in the passage that needed attention. The third reading was to discover the gratitude the passage evoked. The fourth reading was to listen for the sin the passage reminded the reader of and to let reflection lead toward confession. The final reading was for rest.

———

Jane E. Vennard, *Be Still*

REFLECTION

How might you incorporate Luther's third instruction—to read in order to discover your gratitude—in your practice of *lectio divina*?

——— **April 20** ———

All scripture is inspired by God and is useful for teaching, for reproof, for correction, and for training in righteousness. (2 Timothy 3:16)

I put the Bible next to me on the bench and the wind surged. The pages started flapping and I started smiling. "Up to your old tricks again," I said out loud. "Okay, you want to play biblical roulette, let's see what you got, old man!"

The wind blew the pages to the left and then to the right and then to the left again and it all sounded like a gambler shuffling cards. When the wind died down, I looked over and the Bible had come to rest on the story of the parable of the talents.

"Okay, you have my attention," I said. With that I started to read.

———

Gary Jansen, *Exercising Your Soul*

ACTION

Just this once, we're going to play Bible roulette. Allow your Bible to fall open to any page and just start reading. What, if anything, are you hearing from God? (I don't recommend making Bible roulette a regular spiritual practice, but a very occasional foray into "*lectio* divination" is probably fine.)

Lectio Divina

*

93

——— **April 21** ———

ORATIO

Three times I appealed to the Lord about this, that it would leave me, but he said to me, "My grace is sufficient for you, for power is made perfect in weakness." So, I will boast all the more gladly of my weaknesses, so that the power of Christ may dwell in me. (2 Corinthians 12:8–9)

We should always consider the possibility that our difficulties with *lectio divina* are not the results of deficient will power but of some physical disability. Here we have to learn to accept reality graciously. If our attention span is very short or we find it very difficult to concentrate, then we need to experiment with brief—and perhaps more frequent—blocks of time. If our sight is impaired we will need to get new spectacles, find a large-print Bible, try listening to tapes, or have someone read to us. Some radical simplification of the content of our reading may be indicated: it might be better, for example, to stay with the Gospels.

———

Michael Casey, ocso, *Sacred Reading*

REFLECTION

Lectio Divina

Did you take to *lectio divina* like a duck to water, or is it a struggle for you? If it's the latter, are there ways that you might make the practice easier or more appealing, such as listening to Scripture read aloud online?

*

——— **April 22** ———

CONTEMPLATIO

They said to each other, "Were not our hearts burning within us while he was talking to us on the road, while he was opening the scriptures to us?" (Luke 24:32)

*L*ectio divina is like the experience of the disciples on the road to Emmaus (Luke 24:13–26). They were walking away from Jerusalem in a mood of great distress and discouragement—not good dispositions for *lectio divina*. Jesus came along hiding his identity at first, and asked them, "What is on your minds?" (Luke 24:17). When they related their inner turmoil, he began to explain the passages of scripture that referred to his passion and death. This is the discursive part of *lectio divina*, the careful reflection on what is actually said in the text. It was during this time that their hearts began to burn. . . . It is the Holy Spirit, the Spirit of Christ, dwelling in our hearts, who explains the meaning of scripture when we try to understand it, not as a science, not in order to teach others, but simply as a means of communing with God.

———

Thomas Keating, ocso, *The Heart of the World*

ACTION

For our final week of *lectio* practice, we are adding the fourth stage: *contemplatio.* The word sounds like it should just be translated "contemplation," but it's actually much deeper than that: it's integrating the text with your life. For today, spend twenty minutes doing all four stages of *lectio divina* on Luke 24:13–35. Imagine as you read that Jesus himself is opening the Scriptures to you.

—————— **April 23** ——————

CONTEMPLATIO

How sweet are your words to my taste,
sweeter than honey to my mouth! (Psalm 119:103)

A good image of the scriptures is the Greek dessert pastry baklava. It is rich, about an inch thick and cut into inch squares. It is made of thin layers of phyllo dough, honey, nuts and butter pressed down and packed firmly together. A good pastry maker packs the dough into one hundred and twenty or more layers. And when we read the scriptures, we take one layer at a time and savor it. Each time we eat a layer and incorporate it into our flesh and blood, we can discover another layer and eat more. But not to swallow, digest, and incorporate it into our bodies and lives means that we may just keep eating the same layer over and over again. . . . It is a many-course meal if we know how to eat it.

———

Megan McKenna, *Not Counting Women and Children*

ACTION

Your spiritual task today is to eat some baklava or other layered, rich sweet and reflect on how that treat reminds you of the Scriptures. Yes. You're welcome.

—————— **April 24** ——————

CONTEMPLATIO

*. . . making your ear attentive to wisdom
and inclining your heart to understanding. (Proverbs 2:2)*

L ectio teaches us to listen. Benedictine spirituality is about listening to God and listening to life. Lectio eventually moves us beyond reading Scripture to reading our lives, to reading our world. The important, core idea here is to listen. Listen.

A little while after beginning lectio, you discover that movies speak God, music speaks God, your friends become prophetic oracles. God begins to speak so persistently in all of life that you awake every day amazed that you didn't hear all this God-noise before. Lectio opens the ears of your heart.

Lonni Collins Pratt and Father Daniel Holman, OSB, *Benedict's Way*

PRAYER

Father, help me learn to listen to your words wherever I may find them. Amen.

—————— **April 25** ——————

CONTEMPLATIO

*But Mary treasured all these words and pondered them in
her heart. (Luke 2:19)*

In the same way that the word of a person who is dear to me follows me throughout the day, so the Word of Scripture should resonate and work within me ceaselessly. Just as you would not dissect and analyze the word spoken by someone dear to you, but would accept it just as it was said, so you should accept the Word of Scripture and ponder it in your heart as Mary did. That is all. That is meditation.

Dietrich Bonhoeffer, *Meditating on the Word*

REFLECTION

What would it mean for you to treasure God's word and ponder it in your heart today?

——— **April 26** ———

CONTEMPLATIO

*Then the angel showed me the river of the water of life, bright as crystal, flowing from the throne of God and of the Lamb through the middle of the street of the city.
(Revelation 22:1–2)*

Centuries ago, Ignatius of Loyola urged readers of scripture to participate in the life of Christ through a disciplined use of all the senses. When reading a story from the gospels . . . Ignatius tells us to enter the scene fully and to become each character in turn:

With the eyes of the imagination we should look at . . . the persons. With our hearing we should perceive how they are speaking or could speak. With the sense of smell and taste we should smell and taste the infinite sweetness and loveliness of the Godhead. With our sense of place we should embrace and kiss the place where these persons have set their foot and where they come to rest.

Roger Ferlo, *Sensing God*

ACTION

Lectio Divina

Read Revelation 22:1–5 for your *lectio* passage, doing all four stages and employing your imagination and senses. Imagine yourself in the scene. What are you seeing, smelling, hearing, and touching?

*

——— **April 27** ———

CONTEMPLATIO

He put a new song in my mouth,
a song of praise to our God. (Psalm 40:3)

Music lovers are in for a treat with this prayer. Instead of listening for a word from the written page, you will be listening for what is evoked in you by the music. You are allowing God to speak to you through musical notes, phrases, and images.

The choice of music used in this prayer is entirely up to you. . . . If you have a music collection, start with a selection that has moved you in some way previously.

After doing this prayer intentionally for awhile, you may find yourself moved to prayer spontaneously when listening to music. That's the beauty of *lectio divina*—it becomes a part of life as you practice it regularly. It helps us "pray always."

Teresa A. Blythe, *50 Ways to Pray*

ACTION

In this excerpt, a seasoned spiritual director suggests practicing the steps of *lectio divina* with a piece of music. Listen to your chosen piece four times. How might God be speaking to you through this music?

April 28

CONTEMPLATIO

In the beginning was the Word, and the Word was with God, and the Word was God. (John 1:1)

Every time we open the Scriptures, we should expect a personal encounter with the God-breathed Spirit of the living Word. This is reading at its very best. When the mind and spirit of a biblical author interact in vibrant dialogue with the mind and spirit of a reader the highest purpose of the inspired Word is fulfilled. We should soar every time we read the Word of God.

David McKenna, *How to Read a Christian Book*

REFLECTION

This author says twice that "every time" we read the Scriptures we should have a transcendent encounter. Has that been your experience? It has not been mine. As people flunking sainthood, let's not feel guilty about spiritual dry spells, but be grateful when we *do* have a glimpse of the holy.

April 29

CONTEMPLATIO

So shall my word be that goes out from my mouth;
it shall not return to me empty,
but it shall accomplish that which I purpose,
and succeed in the thing for which I sent it. (Isaiah 55:11)

To get at the inner dynamism of the word/event/experience, you must "act" it. This is an essential moment of *lectio divina.* To hear the word we must remove the obstacles and relate to the word/event/experience, as God becomes our reality. . . .

APRIL

Lectio Divina

*

99

Because this dynamic moment of *lectio divina* pervades our whole life, there's no sequence that orders this prayer. But we cannot move to the goal of sacred reading if we are not *doing* the word. We must truly live into the text. All wisdom literature was lived first, then written. So too, with us. We will understand the Scriptures only when we live them.

Mary Margaret Funk, *Tools Matter for Practicing the Spiritual Life*

PRAYER

Help me to be a doer of the Word, and not a hearer only. Amen.

—————— **April 30** ——————

CONTEMPLATIO

"Whoever is from God hears the words of God." (John 8:47)

By approaching Scripture in the personal, responsive mode suggested by *lectio divina*, we are able to listen to God speaking to us personally. We affirm the resurrection truth that the Spirit is as alive and involved with humankind as God has ever been. God longs to communicate love, grace, and truth to us. This is not meant to be difficult. The art of spiritual listening can be as simple as quieting our hearts and minds in God's presence and stopping long enough to be attentive to the words of God in Scripture so that we may live our lives today in communion with Jesus, the Word of God.

Alice Fryling, *The Art of Spiritual Listening*

REFLECTION

As we conclude our month with *lectio divina,* what has God been trying to tell you through this practice? What have you learned?

MAY

Simplicity

———— **May 1** ————

"For where your treasure is, there your heart will be also."
(Matthew 6:21)

Simplicity

*

102

In the spirit of quality over quantity, let us consider replacing the culture of consumption with a culture of appreciation. The culture of consumption fosters discontent with the present. The culture of appreciation is at home in today. The culture of consumption wants more and more. The culture of appreciation is content with what we have. The culture of consumption looks outside for meaning. The culture of appreciation gains meaning from internal resources. The culture of consumption is always restless. The culture of appreciation is at peace.

Richard J. Foster, *Freedom of Simplicity*

REFLECTION

Today we're beginning our focus on the spiritual practice of simplicity. Can you already identify areas in your life that are characterized by excess? In what areas do you want more and more?

———— **May 2** ————

He said, "Take your son, your only son Isaac, whom you love, and go to the land of Moriah, and offer him there as a burnt offering on one of the mountains that I shall show you." (Genesis 22:2)

Father, I want to know thee, but my coward heart fears to give up its toys. I cannot part with them without inward bleeding, and I do not try to hide from Thee the terror of the parting. I come trembling, but I do come. Please root from my heart all those things which I have cherished so long and which have become a very part of my living self, so that Thou mayest enter and dwell there without a rival. Then shalt Thou make the place of Thy feet glorious. Then shall my heart have no need of the sun to shine in it, for Thyself wilt be the light of it, and there shall be no night there. In Jesus' name, Amen.

A. W. Tozer, *The Pursuit of God*

ACTION

Pray A. W. Tozer's prayer, printed above, out loud.

──────── **May 3** ────────

And he said to them, "Take care! Be on your guard against all kinds of greed; for one's life does not consist in the abundance of possessions." (Luke 12:15)

If I am truly poor, then I am dependent on others for everything, and I feel useless and worthless, and I realize deep within that everything is a gift from the Father. Then in this attitude of complete dependence, I become useful again, for then I am empty of selfishness and I am free to be God's instrument instead of my own. In poverty I begin to value everything rightly again. I see how little really matters, and I see that only that which glorifies God is of value.

Murray Bodo, OFM, *Celtic Daily Prayer*

PRAYER

Lord, help me to see my dependence on you and others, so that I am freed to do your will. Amen.

———— **May 4** ————

*But we urge you, beloved, to do so more and more, to
aspire to live quietly, to mind your own affairs, and to work
with your hands, as we directed you.
(1 Thessalonians 4:10–11)*

And finally, live a modest and humble life because such a life exhausts the power of sin over you. The tax-collector who in sight of all, brought forward his humility, and laid aside the burden of his transgressions left that place, unlike the Pharisee beside him, a truly righteous man. Don't be lazy; but walk these five paths everyday: condemnation of your sin, forgiveness of others, prayer, generosity, and humility. Let us constantly apply these medicines and heal our wounds, in order that we may return to health, and enjoy the sacred table with assurance; and with much glory, reach Christ the king of glory, and attain to everlasting good by the grace, and compassion, and loving kindness of our Lord Jesus Christ, by whom and with whom be glory, power, honor, to the Father, together with the all holy, and good and quickening Spirit, now and always and for ever and ever. Amen.

St. John Chrysostom, "Concerning the Power of Demons"

PRAYER

Heavenly Father, give me today all that I need and help me to share with others. Amen.

———— **May 5** ————

*Therefore, let us celebrate the festival, not with the old
yeast, the yeast of malice and evil, but with the unleavened
bread of sincerity and truth. (1 Corinthians 5:8)*

When Joanne and I lived in the Democratic Republic of the Congo, we learned from our poor neighbors how to celebrate with wholehearted communal joy at weddings, church holidays, and end-of-school-year feasts. We observed how people who normally eat a meager fare can get ecstatic over goat meat sauce and a double portion of greens with groundnuts on a doughy lump of *fufu*. After food, the feast was extended with soccer games till dusk, followed by drumming, singing, and dancing through the night. Our Congolese friends knew how to feast "with glad and joyful hearts" because their palates were not so jaded that to celebrate, they needed something more exotic than they had ever eaten before. They taught us the "more with less" lesson, that when our daily food is simple and basic, celebrations are less stressful to pull off and generosity can extend until all are included and satisfied.

David Janzen, *The Intentional Christian Community Handbook*

ACTION

It's Cinco de Mayo, people! Today, do something in spontaneous but simple celebration with others. It may not feel "spiritual," but it can be.

——— **May 6** ———

The rabble among them had a strong craving; and the Israelites also wept again, and said, "If only we had meat to eat! We remember the fish we used to eat in Egypt for nothing, the cucumbers, the melons, the leeks, the onions, and the garlic." (Numbers 11:4–5)

We live in a consumerist culture that encourages forgetfulness. Dissatisfaction is at the very root of our modern economy. . . . It is a culture driven by a perpetual dissatisfaction machine that inundates us with the message that our lives won't be complete until we have the shiniest toy, the latest gadget, the most exclusive memberships, a younger wife, smoother skin, bouncier hair, the right hands, a nicer car and a bigger house. We're surrounded by advertising and other media that tells us from an early age that it is possible to buy happiness . . . at least until the next must-have item comes around.

C. Christopher Smith and John Pattison, *Slow Church*

ACTION

Be aware of advertising today, including television commercials, magazine enticements, pop-up Internet ads, and the promoted results that appear in your Google searches. What is being marketed to you? Are you able to ignore it, or does it create in you a dissatisfaction that wants you to buy, buy, buy?

——— **May 7** ———

"And can any of you by worrying add a single hour to your span of life?" (Matthew 6:27)

If nothing grew in the field unless we were anxious about it, we would all have died in our cradles; and during the night, while we are lying asleep, nothing could grow. Indeed, even by worrying ourselves to death we could not make a single blade of grass grow in the field. We really ought to see and understand God gives everything without any anxiety on our part, and yet we are such godless people that we refuse to give up our anxiety and our greed. Though it is up to Him to be concerned, as a father is concerned for his children, we refuse to leave it to Him.

———

Martin Luther, "Do Not Be Anxious"

PRAYER

Calm my anxiety and fear, Lord, and teach me to trust in your care. Amen.

——— **May 8** ———

See, I have set before you today life and prosperity, death and adversity. (Deuteronomy 30:15)

We are a nation of choosers: paper or plastic? Small, medium, large, or super? Fries or chips? Organic or conventional? Having a choice has become a staple of the American dream. Political agendas of all flavors are sold on a platform of choice—everything from private school vouchers to health-care reform. More choice is always the preferred value. The choice offered in Deuteronomy does not sit well with a people inundated by choices. Actually "offered" is too generous—Deuteronomy does not *offer* a choice so much as *require* that a particular choice be made: "If you obey the commandments of the LORD your God . . . then you shall live. . . . But if your heart turns away . . . you shall perish" (30:16–18).

———

Andrew Foster Connors, *Feasting on the Word*

REFLECTION

Do the all-or-nothing choices God seems to offer in Deuteronomy 30 resonate with you, or do you feel that your own decisions inhabit more of a gray area? Does unlimited choice appeal to you, or is it sometimes overwhelming?

———— **May 9** ————

Set your minds on things that are above, not on things that are on earth. (Colossians 3:2)

Plan to take some time off, and give some thought as to what you'd do with that time; hopefully, you'll spend part of it reviewing God's favors to you in the past. What else? Lock up ye olde curiosity shop. Devote more time to reading your spiritual books than your survival manuals. Withdraw from casual conversations and leisurely pursuits. Don't contract for new ventures, and don't gossip about old ones. All these having been done, you'll find more than enough time to undertake a program of meditation. Most of the Saints did just that, avoided collaborative projects whenever they could, choosing instead to spend some private time with God.

—

Thomas à Kempis, *The Imitation of Christ*

ACTION

Your task today is a no-brainer: unsubscribe from five email lists. Digital detox probably isn't exactly what Thomas à Kempis had in mind back in the fifteenth century, but it's certainly one way to simplify.

———— May 10 ————

He who supplies seed to the sower and bread for food will supply and multiply your seed for sowing and increase the harvest of your righteousness. (2 Corinthians 9:10)

Simplicity is not a universal fit. What is extravagance to one is necessity to another. My interpretation of wants and needs will not be yours. . . . The life of simplicity does not mean owning a bare minimum of goods. It is a commitment to live a liberated life, freed from constant distraction, devoted to our spiritual and emotional growth and the betterment of others. . . . While our journey toward a simpler life might well take different roads, it begins with the same step—the discernment between *wants* and *needs.*

Philip Gulley, *Living the Quaker Way*

REFLECTION

How skilled are you at distinguishing wants from needs?

———— May 11 ————

Why do you spend your money for that which is not bread, and your labor for that which does not satisfy? (Isaiah 55:2)

There is a certain irony in the fact that the perception of too much work and too many activities exists side-by-side with spending four-and-a-half hours a day watching television, the average for U.S. adults. Perhaps partly because of what is feeding our hearts and minds, and partly because it is passive entertainment, watching television gives us remarkably little satisfaction. Psychologist David G. Myers cites a study that showed only 3 percent of those watching television were fully absorbed in that diversion, while 39 percent felt apathetic. For those engaged in activities such as gardening or talking to friends the figures flipped: 47 percent were fully absorbed and 4 percent apathetic.

Arthur Simon, *How Much Is Enough?*

ACTION

Kill your television. Well, fast from television for at least one day this week when you are going to be home. (No fair fasting from TV when you won't be around anyway!) Do you have a lot of extra time when you give up the TV habit?

 **May 12**

He said to them, "Why were you searching for me? Did you not know that I must be in my Father's house?" (Luke 2:49)

If we get busy with something that isn't God's business, we feel God turns away from us. When we are preoccupied with ourselves, we fall under the influence of Satan's angels. But whenever we regret our wrong steps and our too-busy ways, and pray, "Help us, God!" He sends angels to protect us. They fly to our aid. Satan can't bother us then. . . .

Don't forget that God is balanced in all things. He isn't one way too-much-this or the other way too-much-that. No. Although He has absolute authority in everything, He never loses His sense of balance.

St. Hildegard of Bingen, *The Book of Divine Works*

PRAYER

O God, continuously renew my spirit and help me break the cycle of doing too much and wanting too much. Send your angels to protect me from my own selfishness, and teach me to be about my Father's business. Amen.

———— **May 13** ————

*He makes me lie down in green pastures;
he leads me beside still waters; he restores my soul.
(Psalm 23:2–3)*

The world is fairly studded and strewn with pennies cast broadside by a generous hand. But—and this is the point—who gets excited by a mere penny? . . . It is dire poverty indeed when a man is so malnourished and fatigued that he won't stoop to pick up a penny. But if you cultivate a healthy poverty and simplicity, so that finding a penny will literally make your day, then, since the world is in fact planted in pennies, you have with your poverty bought a lifetime of days.

———

Annie Dillard, *Pilgrim at Tinker Creek*

REFLECTION

What are ways to cultivate some simple joys in your life?

———— **May 14** ————

But do not ignore this one fact, beloved, that with the Lord one day is like a thousand years, and a thousand years are like one day. (2 Peter 3:8)

When we intentionally slow down we open up the possibility for a different quality of time. The *kairos* of which St. Paul speaks is different from the *chronos* which drives most of our calendars and our lives. . . . Once in a while, try moving through a day in half-time. If you become anxious about the *chronos*, i.e., worried about accomplishing all you've set out for yourself, follow the practice of a Methodist pastor I read about long ago. Each morning at the end of his prayer time he writes a list of all he thinks he ought to do that day. After a prayer for guidance, he crosses out half the list. Over the years this small step has helped him to focus on the few things that really matter.

Dolores R. Leckey, *7 Essentials for the Spiritual Journey*

ACTION

Today, follow this pastor's excellent advice about your to-do list. Cross off half the items on your list, then focus on the remaining items that matter most.

 **May 15** ────────

For the love of money is a root of all kinds of evil, and in their eagerness to be rich some have wandered away from the faith and pierced themselves with many pains.
(1 Timothy 6:10)

As long ago as the 1830s, Alexis de Tocqueville blamed the shopping instinct for jacking up the pace of life: "He who has set his heart exclusively upon the pursuit of worldly welfare is always in a hurry, for he has but a limited time at his disposal to reach, to grasp, and to enjoy it." That analysis rings even more true today, when all the world is a store, and all the men and women merely shoppers. Tempted and titillated at every turn, we seek to cram in as much consumption and as many experiences as possible. . . . The result is a gnawing disconnect between what we want from life and what we can realistically have, which feeds the sense that there is never enough time.

———

Carl Honoré, *In Praise of Slowness*

PRAYER

Lord, protect me from the allure of wealth and keep my heart focused on you. Amen.

——— **May 16** ———

And this is my prayer, that your love may overflow more and more with knowledge and full insight to help you to determine what is best. (Philippians 1:9–10)

Another way in which greater choice can lead to greater regret is the very fact that it *does* increase the potential benefits of choosing well, even as it makes the process of choosing more difficult. When the options are few, we can be happy with what we choose since we are confident that it is the best possible choice for us. When the options are practically infinite, though, we believe that the perfect choice for us must be out there somewhere and that it's our responsibility to find it. . . .

We're aware of the positive effects of choice but not the negative ones, so we attribute any harm caused by too much choice to some other cause, perhaps even to too little choice. After all, at first glance it seems that the best solution to not being able to find the perfect option is to add more options—

but an excess of possibilities can keep us from being happy with our choices.

Sheena Iyengar, *The Art of Choosing*

REFLECTION

Simplicity

Studies have shown that the more choices we have, the more paralyzed we become by the prospect of choosing—and the more likely we are to be unhappy when we *do* finally make a choice. One way to simplify our lives is to reduce the number of choices available to us. What might that mean for you, today?

*

——— **May 17** ———

So we do not lose heart. Even though our outer nature is wasting away, our inner nature is being renewed day by day. (2 Corinthians 4:16)

Aging has always been about simplifying and letting go. Sooner or later we realize that we can't manage all the stuff and activity anymore. We have to let go. The practice of letting go and embracing simplicity is one way we prepare ourselves for what is to come. One day we all will have to let go of *everything*—even our own breath. It will be a day of utter simplicity—a day when the importance of stuff fades. Learning to live simply prepares us for our last breath while cultivating in us the freedom to truly live here and now.

Adele Ahlberg Calhoun, *The Spiritual Disciplines Handbook*

PRAYER

Help me understand that all of life is a process of letting go, Lord; teach me to prepare for that "day of utter simplicity." Amen.

———— **May 18** ————

For God is a God not of disorder but of peace.
(1 Corinthians 14:33)

*

115

While you're giving stuff away and learning to say no, keep this profound thought in mind: The reason our lives are so complicated is that we're too self-centered. Richard Foster writes that "simplicity means moving away from total absorption in ourselves . . . to being centered in . . . God."

God isn't the one who leads you to a more complicated life (and more stress). You get there quite well all by yourself. God wants you to give the small stuff and the stress of your life over to Him. When you trust God and let Him take the lead in your life, you will find that your life will be more peaceful and productive. You will naturally want to clear out the clutter to make more room for God.

————

Bruce and Stan, *God Is in the Small Stuff*

ACTION

Give away ten items to charity. If you can't take them out of the house today, put them in a bag that you'll bring the next time you're headed toward the Salvation Army or a thrift store.

———— **May 19** ————

"Father, if you are willing, remove this cup from me; yet, not my will but yours be done." (Luke 22:42)

Here is a summary of everything I am trying to teach you: completely surrender to God, place your personal desires in his hands, and detach yourself from material things. By now, you should recognize the importance of this. We are preparing to complete a journey and will soon be drinking from the fountain of living water. Unless we totally turn our personal wills over to God, allowing God to do what is best for us, he will not allow us to drink it.

St. Teresa of Avila, *The Way of Perfection*

PRAYER

Lord, I surrender my desires and will to you. Amen.

———— **May 20** ————

The Lord is not slow about his promise, as some think of slowness, but is patient with you. (2 Peter 3:9)

I learned about slow rise by reading Julia Child. . . . In bread-making it works like this: You take flour, water, salt, and yeast, mix them together in the proper proportions, and form the dough into a ball. You then put it out of the way and forget about it for an hour and a half. What you do not do is rush it by warming it up; just let it grow at its own slow pace. . . . You want nature to work, character to develop. You do not want to rush the process.

Slow rise has taught me and is still teaching me a way to live, a way to be, and a way to see.

Brother Peter Reinhart, *Brother Juniper's Bread Book*

ACTION

If you have access to a kitchen, try baking a simple bread recipe sometime this week when you don't have to rush. What can you learn from "slow rise"?

——— **May 21** ———

give me neither poverty nor riches;
feed me with the food that I need,
or I shall be full, and deny you,
and say, "Who is the LORD?"
or I shall be poor, and steal,
and profane the name of my God.
(Proverbs 30:8–9)

When I came into the Country, and being seated among silent Trees, had all my Time in mine own Hands, I resolved to Spend it all, whatever it cost me, in Search of Happiness and to Satiate that burning Thirst which Nature had Enkindled in me from my Youth. In which I was so resolute, that I chose rather to live upon ten pounds a year, and to go in Leather Clothes, and feed upon Bread and Water, so that I might have all my time clearly to myself, than to keep many thousands per Annums in an Estate of Life where my Time would be Devoured in Care and Labour. And God was so pleased to accept of that Desire, that from that time to this I have had all things plentifully provided for me, without any care at all, my very Study of Felicity making me more to Prosper than all the Care in the Whole World. So that through His blessing I live a free and a Kingly Life as if the World were turned again into Eden, or much more, as it is at this Day.

————

Thomas Traherne, *Centuries of Meditations*

Simplicity

REFLECTION

The proverb "give me neither poverty nor riches" suggests that the path to God lies in a simple middle way. How might you chart that middle course, as Thomas Traherne did in the seventeenth century? When do you know you have enough?

*

118

————— **May 22** —————

The dogs have a mighty appetite;
they never have enough.
The shepherds also have no understanding;
they have all turned to their own way,
to their own gain, one and all. (Isaiah 56:11)

This passage is directed to the elders of Israel who turned aside from how they were supposed to act—as protectors, leaders, and guides to their flock—and went off on their own way, seeking their own gain. This is a textbook example of how excessities get turned around into "never enoughs." Often the behavior of an excessity starts out as harmless, even beneficial. . . . At some point the behavior becomes an excessity. When it does, you no longer have control over it.

————

Gregory L. Jantz, *Gotta Have It!*

REFLECTION

Dr. Jantz coined the term *excessity* to describe our tendency to regard our excesses as necessities. What excesses exist in your relationships to food, comfort, hobbies, or material things? What would it feel like to curb those appetites?

——— **May 23** ———

Better is a little with the fear of the LORD
than great treasure and trouble with it. (Proverbs 15:16)

How free it is not to own things! I have come to know a portion of that truth in my life. I once owned a house, but no longer; I used to collect rare books, but no more; and I'm grateful. St. Francis of Assisi used to teach his brothers that if they owned things, they'd have to worry about them, perhaps defend them, and if they had to defend them, they'd end up using violence and behaving in ways that they'd rather not. To live poorer than is required by your resources is one injunction that Jesus gave his first disciples, and I've found that to do it is not a virtue; it is both practical and rewarding.

Jon M. Sweeney, *Cloister Talks*

ACTION

Give away ten more things to charity. Refill that bag.

MAY

*So then let us not fall asleep as others do,
but let us keep awake.
(1 Thessalonians 5:6)*

Simplicity

*

120

Our life is frittered away by detail. An honest man has hardly need to count more than his ten fingers, or in extreme cases he may add his ten toes, and lump the rest. Simplicity, simplicity, simplicity! I say, let your affairs be as two or three, and not a hundred or a thousand; instead of a million count half a dozen, and keep your accounts on your thumbnail. In the midst of this chopping sea of civilized life, such are the clouds and storms and quicksands and thousand-and-one items to be allowed for, that a man has to live, if he would not founder and go to the bottom and not make his port at all, by dead reckoning, and he must be a great calculator indeed who succeeds. Simplify, simplify. Instead of three meals a day, if it be necessary eat but one; instead of a hundred dishes, five; and reduce other things in proportion.

Henry David Thoreau, *Walden*

ACTION

Build yourself a cabin in a remote wood and live there, just like Thoreau. Nah, just kidding. Just keep today's to-do list to a single Post-it note, with no more than five things to do today. Simplify, simplify.

Let your "Yes" be yes and your "No" be no.
(James 5:12)

I know a few wholesome self-stoppers. They're conscious—aware of what they want to do with time. They know when to say, "Enough is enough." They shut off their computers so that they can read, listen to *A Prairie Home Companion*, or tinker with toy trains. They unclog a choked-up itinerary so that they can play with their child. They take naps. They sleep soundly at night (unlike the two-thirds of us who complain of sleep disorders). They enjoy vacations. They are the self-definers who *trust* what they need or value and feel challenged—not overwhelmed—by the prospect of *being more*. For some, the phrase "being more" means doing less.

Marsha Sinetar, *Sometimes, Enough Is Enough*

ACTION

Say no to at least two requests today. Practice being more by doing less.

"For it is the nations of the world that strive after all these things, and your Father knows that you need them."
(Luke 12:30)

How often do we say to ourselves that happiness will be found when we own this one more special thing? It seems so reasonable at the time. So we buy it, and the same impulse returns the following day or the next, just as it was before. . . . Is that really what you want? I'm not saying that money and beautiful things are wrong or evil. Yet the desire to have more stuff feels like an insatiable beast feeding on the soul, much like the dread of those monthly bills breathing down your neck. Who are we kidding? Debt or no debt, we must come to terms with the difference between "needing" and "wanting."

———

Jeff Golliher, *A Deeper Faith*

PRAYER

Lord, help me be content with what I have, and stop always striving for more. Amen.

——— **May 27** ———

You show me the path of life.
In your presence there is fullness of joy;
in your right hand are pleasures forevermore.
(Psalm 16:11)

I gratefully turn to my Haitian cab driver as powerful proof of the link between simple pleasure and happiness. After learning my destination, he asked me what brought me to New York. Quite briefly I explained my series of talks about the concepts at the core of good living. His animated questions and comments lifted my spirits for the duration of our all-too-short ride. . . . "It's the little things. It doesn't take much to be happy, like music and dancing. Knowing for sure that people love you and loving them back strong. Laughing and sitting around the dinner table telling stories. Helping people out and being welcome wherever you go. A few lazy days with your shoes off, perfect! Oh, yes, I love talking about all these pure pleasures." . . . As the cab rolled to a slow stop, he faced me merrily and shared his last simple pleasure: "There is no charge, please. Our conversation makes me very happy."

Marietta McCarty, *The Philosopher's Table*

———— **May 28** ————

The rich rule over the poor,
and the borrower is the slave of the lender. (Proverbs 22:7)

I have yet to find a positive Scripture about debt. Everything I've ever read in the Bible about debt warns of its ability to enslave or bring darkness into your life. . . .

Visa once had an advertising slogan that began, "Life takes Visa." But ask yourself, is your Visa debt taking over your life? If you are in debt, then according to Scripture, you are a slave. If you are a slave, then you have a master. In fact, isn't that what many people have in MasterCard?

Michelle Singletary, *The 21 Day Financial Fast*

ACTION
Add up how much you owe in debt: mortgage, credit cards, student loans, everything. Take a long, hard look at that number. Remind yourself that debt stands in the way of freedom and simplicity.

—————— **May 29** ——————

In returning and rest you shall be saved;
in quietness and in trust shall be your strength. (Isaiah 30:15)

Simplicity

*

124

Men seek retreats for themselves, houses in the country, sea-shores, and mountains; and thou, too, art wont to desire such things very much. But this is altogether a mark of the most common sort of men, for it is in thy power whenever thou shalt choose to retire into thyself. For nowhere either with more quiet or more freedom from trouble does a man retire than into his own soul, particularly when he has within him such thoughts that by looking into them he is immediately in perfect tranquility; and I affirm that tranquility is nothing else than the good ordering of the mind.

Marcus Aurelius, *Meditations*

REFLECTION

Do you find your own company restful? Do you enjoy being alone?

—————— **May 30** ——————

Give us each day our daily bread. (Luke 11:3)

Mahatma Gandhi once said, "Earth provides enough to satisfy every man's need, but not every man's greed." I'd like to pray for loads of exotic foods and extravagant desserts, but the [Lord's] Prayer reminds me that I have no business asking for surplus in a world marked by poverty. We may pray earnestly for a house, a car, money to cover our credit card bills, a musical instrument, and a thousand other desires of our heart. But Jesus teaches us to pray for bread.

———

David Timms, *Living the Lord's Prayer*

PRAYER

Our father, who art in heaven, hallowed be thy name. Thy kingdom come. Thy will be done on earth as it is in heaven. Give us this day our daily bread. And forgive us our trespasses, as we forgive those who trespass against us. And lead us not into temptation, but deliver us from evil. For thine is the kingdom, and the power, and the glory forever. Amen.

——— **May 31** ———

May he remember all your offerings,
and regard with favor your burnt sacrifices. (Psalm 20:3)

From deep in the tradition, from *The Cloud of Unknowing*, a fourteenth-century text from an unnamed English monk: "You only need a tiny scrap of time to move toward God."

The words slap. Busyness is not much of an excuse if it only takes a minute or two to move toward God.

But the monk's words console, too. For, of time and person, it seems that scraps are all I have to bring forward. That my ways of coming to God these days are all scraps.

———

Lauren F. Winner, *Still*

MAY

Simplicity

REFLECTION

This month, we have focused on simplicity and decluttering our lives. We do this in preparation for the deep prayer practices we'll encounter in June. If you worry you have not simplified enough, or you aren't ready for centering prayer or the Jesus Prayer, believe that what you have done is enough for now. As today's quote suggests, you only need a tiny scrap.

*

126

JUNE

Centering
Prayer
and the
Jesus
Prayer

JUNE

Centering
Prayer
and the
Jesus
Prayer

*

128

—— June 1 ——

. . . because we look not at what can be seen but at what cannot be seen; for what can be seen is temporary, but what cannot be seen is eternal. (2 Corinthians 4:18)

Contemplation is not difficult or complex. Enthusiastic desire will accomplish much. With God's gift of spiritual hunger, you will make steady progress. Continue until your prayer life becomes enjoyable.

When you begin, you will experience a darkness, a *cloud of unknowing.* You cannot interpret this darkness. You will only comprehend a basic reaching out toward God. None of your efforts will remove the cloud that obscures God from your understanding. Darkness will remain between you and the love of God. You will feel nothing.

Accept this dark cloud. Learn to live with it, but keep looking, praying, and crying out to the one you love.

The Cloud of Unknowing, fourteenth century

REFLECTION

For the first half of this month, we'll be experimenting with centering prayer, which is an inner, mystical prayer tradition. Practitioners advise that most people will feel a darkness or "cloud of unknowing" when they first begin, but that this is actually a sign that the practice is starting to be effective. Can you commit to trying this daily practice even when it is difficult?

—— June 2 ——

To them God chose to make known how great among the Gentiles are the riches of the glory of this mystery, which is Christ in you, the hope of glory. (Colossians 1:27)

In introductory Centering Prayer workshops [a] gentle, laissez-faire attitude toward [our unbidden] thoughts is reinforced through a simple formula called "The Four Rs":

> Resist no thought
> Retain no thought
> React to no thought
> Return to the sacred word.
> ___

Cynthia Bourgeault, *Centering Prayer and Inner Awakening*

PRAYER

Lead me toward the gift of centering prayer, O God. Amen.

JUNE

Centering
Prayer
and the
Jesus
Prayer

*

129

——— **June 3** ———

All things are wearisome;
more than one can express;
the eye is not satisfied with seeing,
or the ear filled with hearing. (Ecclesiastes 1:8)

Of course, everywhere we go we hear people complaining about our wired world—about how complicated it has made life and about how frustrating it is—all the while utilizing every technological gadget at their disposal. The truth of the matter is we enjoy our technological gluttony.

Actually, the Internet culture is only a surface issue. Our deeper problem is something far more fundamental. This deeper, more basic issue can be summed up in one word: distraction. Distraction is the primary spiritual problem of our day. The Internet, of course, did not cause this problem; people were distracted long before it came along. Blaise

JUNE

Centering
Prayer
and the
Jesus
Prayer

*

130

Pascal observed, "The sole cause of man's unhappiness is that he does not know how to stay quietly in his room." . . . The moment we seek to enter the creative silences of meditative prayer, every demand screams for our attention.

Richard J. Foster, *Sanctuary of the Soul*

ACTION

Quiet your "noise" before you even attempt centering prayer. Remove yourself from every device and choose a place where you can think. Practice this today so that tomorrow you will be ready to attempt the practice for the first time.

——— **June 4** ———

Hear the voice of my supplication,
as I cry to you for help,
as I lift up my hands
toward your most holy sanctuary. (Psalm 28:2)

Virtually all personal correspondence begins with an apology for not writing sooner. When you receive a letter or an e-mail, do you want to dwell on how long it's been since the person wrote and their reasons for not doing so, or are you just excited to hear from them and to read the letter? Which way do you think God feels when we reach out in prayer, even after a long absence?

The people who are best at prayer almost universally advise us to stop feeling bad about it. . . . Brother Lawrence says that when his attention was drawn away from God, that God simply recalled it not with punishment but with a delightful sensation, and Brother Lawrence was only too happy to comply, remembering how miserable he had felt without God.

———

Julia Roller, *Mom Seeks God*

JUNE

Centering
Prayer
and the
Jesus
Prayer

*

131

ACTION

Today, choose a sacred word that you can return to as you begin your practice of centering prayer. Examples could be *Jesus*, *peace*, *Savior*, *Spirit*, or *holiness*; there are infinite choices, but please stay with the same word each day for the next two weeks.

Sit in the quiet place you identified yesterday. Set a timer for five minutes and simply let go of your mind. When (not if!) you find that your mind becomes crowded with thoughts, just calmly return to your sacred word without berating yourself. Centering prayer is a lifelong practice and you are just a beginner. Go easy on yourself.

——— **June 5** ———

But I have calmed and quieted my soul,
like a weaned child with its mother;
my soul is like the weaned child that is with me.
(Psalm 131:2)

There was a lovely silence in the Brethren assembled on Sunday morning as we waited for the Spirit. . . . We sat listening to the rain on the roof, distant traffic, a radio playing from across the street, kids whizzing by on bikes, dogs barking, as we waited for the Spirit to inspire us. It was like sitting on the porch with your family, when nobody feels that they have to make talk. So quiet in church. Minutes drifted by in silence that was sweet to us.

Garrison Keillor, *Lake Wobegon Days*

Centering
Prayer
and the
Jesus
Prayer

PRAYER

I come before you in silence, Lord, as I practice centering prayer today. Help me be mindful of the loveliness all around me. Amen.

*

————— **June 6** —————

But the Lord *God called to the man, and said to him, "Where are you?" He said, "I heard the sound of you in the garden, and I was afraid, because I was naked; and I hid myself." (Genesis 3:9–10)*

Now the moment of prayer is for me—or involves for me as its condition—the awareness, the re-awakened awareness, that this "real world" and "real self" are very far from being rock-bottom realities. I cannot, in the flesh, leave the stage, either to go behind the scenes or to take my seat in the pit; but I can remember that these regions exist. And I also remember that my apparent self—this clown or hero or super—under his grease-paint is a real person with an off-stage life. . . .

The attempt is not to escape from space and time and from my creaturely situation as a subject facing objects. It is more modest: to re-awake the awareness of that situation.

C. S. Lewis, *Letters to Malcolm: Chiefly on Prayer*

REFLECTION

As you practice centering prayer for five minutes each day, have you had the experience Lewis describes of becoming aware of a deeper reality that undergirds your daily life?

Centering
Prayer
and the
Jesus
Prayer

*
133

——— **June 7** ———

"Peace I leave with you; my peace I give to you. I do not give to you as the world gives. Do not let your hearts be troubled, and do not let them be afraid." (John 14:27)

Merton said to "establish ourselves in the present." Let go of the past. Lose it forever; abandon concern about the future. Focus attention on *now*, on the moment. This was the English monk's thought [in *The Cloud of Unknowing*]: "You must fashion a cloud of forgetting beneath you, between you and every created thing."

. . . How hard I found this. I think, I live, I act, I hurt, all in the present tense, but it was difficult to maintain that tense during prayer. The past pushed in mercilessly. Worry about the future nagged at me. Waiting in silence was a period that allowed concern for what might happen in the future to creep in. But I tried; often I failed.

Doris Grumbach, *The Presence of Absence*

ACTION

Today, increase the time you spend in centering prayer to ten minutes. You may find, as Grumbach mentions here, that during prayer you become anxious about the future or regretful of the past. If that happens, gently return to your sacred word and refocus yourself without judgment.

Centering
Prayer
and the
Jesus
Prayer

*

134

———— **June 8** ————

"God is spirit, and those who worship him must worship in spirit and truth." (John 4:24)

It is false to identify contemplative prayer with a marked state of Christian perfection or to consider its practitioner as one who has arrived there. A contemplative type of prayer is a way of prayer open to anyone who truly seeks God. And it is the type of prayer experience that will ordinarily best help one to make progress in the Christian life, to be purified and illumined, and to abide more integrally in union with God in and through all. It is, therefore, not something to be worked toward, a goal, but simply a way to be entered into, an experience that can be enjoyed—and struggled with—by all who seek God.

————

M. Basil Pennington, ocso, *Centering Prayer*

PRAYER

Keep me from pride, Lord, especially about prayer. Amen.

———— **June 9** ————

*Have mercy on me, O God,
according to your steadfast love;
according to your abundant mercy
blot out my transgressions. (Psalm 51:1)*

Contemplative prayer always requires hospitality to your deep self, to the deep parts of your self. It demands the openness to receive whatever might arise in you and then gently release it into God's hands. But in prayer you are not alone as you open yourself to whatever might emerge.

You do so in a relationship that provides safety and support in holding whatever emerges. . . . Tears may be intermixed with joy and sadness as repressed memories and fragments of past experience burst into consciousness. But whatever emerges in silence and stillness before God emerges in the place within you in which you are held within God.

———

David G. Benner, *Spirituality and the Awakening Self*

REFLECTION

Sometimes, darker parts of ourselves begin to surface when we silence the noise and focus our attention on the holy. How can you create a safe and hospitable place for those very human emotions to emerge in centering prayer?

———— **June 10** ————

For God alone my soul waits in silence;
from him comes my salvation. (Psalm 62:1)

To liberate our true self is an enormous undertaking, and it takes time. Centering Prayer is completely at the service of this program of liberation. It would be a mistake to think of Centering Prayer as a mere rest period or a period of relaxation, although it sometimes provides these things. Neither is it a journey to bliss. You might find some bliss along the way, but you will also have to endure the wear and tear of the discipline of cultivating interior silence.

Thinking our usual thoughts is the chief way that human nature has devised for us to hide from the unconscious. When our minds begin to quiet down in Centering Prayer, up comes the emotional debris of a lifetime in the form of gradual (and sometimes dramatic) realizations of what the false self is.

Thomas Keating, ocso, "The Practice of Attention/Intention"

ACTION

Increase your centering prayer time to fifteen minutes for the next few days.

————— **June 11** —————

In him we live and move and have our being.
(Acts 17:28)

Why do we think of the gift of contemplation, infused contemplation, mystical prayer, as something essentially strange and esoteric reserved for a small class of almost unnatural beings and prohibited to everyone else? It is perhaps because we have forgotten that contemplation is the work of the Holy Ghost acting on our souls through His gifts of Wisdom and Understanding with special intensity to increase and perfect our love for Him. These gifts are part of the normal equipment of Christian sanctity. They are given to all in Baptism, and if they are given it is presumably because God wants them to be developed.

Thomas Merton, ocso, *What Is Contemplation?*

REFLECTION

Have you sometimes thought of contemplative, mystical prayer as something only for *other* people? While it's true that some people take to it readily and others (myself included) find it a struggle, it's also true—as Merton suggests here—that we often underestimate our own capacity to develop these skills. How do you feel about your experiments with centering prayer so far?

———— **June 12** ————

Centering
Prayer
and the
Jesus
Prayer

*

137

O God, you are my God, I seek you,
my soul thirsts for you;
my flesh faints for you,
as in a dry and weary land where there is no water.
(Psalm 63:1)

Take everything that happens during the periods of centering prayer peacefully and gratefully, without putting a judgment on anything, and just let the thoughts go by. It does not matter where they come from, as long as you let them go by. Don't worry about them. Don't fret about them. Don't judge the prayer on the basis of how many thoughts come. Simply follow the fundamental directive. When you are interested in a thought, either positively or negatively, return to the sacred word—and keep returning to it. This is fulfilling the Gospel precept to watch and pray.

Thomas Keating, ocso, "Cultivating the Centering Prayer"

PRAYER

I will watch and pray, O Lord, and receive whatever comes. Amen.

———— **June 13** ————

. . . so that they would search for God and perhaps grope
for him and find him—though indeed he is not far from
each one of us. (Acts 17:27)

JUNE

Centering
Prayer
and the
Jesus
Prayer

*

138

All prayer disciplines are somehow trying to get head and heart and body to work as one, and that changes thinking entirely. "The concentration of attention in the heart—this is the starting point of prayer," says St. Theophane the Recluse, the nineteenth-century Russian mystic. Any other "handler" of your experience, including the rational mind or even mere intellectual theology, eventually distorts and destroys the beauty and healing power of Big Truth. One of my favorite teachers of the church, Evagrius Ponticus (345–399), said you could not be a theologian unless you knew how to pray, and only people who prayed could be theologians. This is surely true.

———

Richard Rohr, OFM, *Immortal Diamond*

REFLECTION

This is our last day of experimenting with centering prayer (though you are of course free to continue). How has the practice resonated with you?

——— **June 14** ———

"But the tax collector, standing far off, would not even look up to heaven, but was beating his breast and saying, 'God, be merciful to me, a sinner.'" (Luke 18:13)

The Jesus Prayer is united with the breath in two motions: the in breath and the out breath. Breathing in we say, "Lord Jesus Christ, Son of God." Breathing out we say, "Have mercy on me, a sinner."

. . . This works well with the actual meaning of the words. The first words fill us with all that is beautiful: the personal lordship of Jesus, personal salvation, the anointing of the Spirit, the Trinity, the incarnation, the church and the sacraments. The second group of words causes us to let go of anything standing between us and full communion with God through Jesus and with all people.

JUNE

Centering
Prayer
and the
Jesus
Prayer

*

139

John Michael Talbot, *The Jesus Prayer*

ACTION

Today we begin this month's second prayer practice, the Jesus Prayer, which is a traditional prayer for Eastern Orthodox monastics. Practice saying these twelve words by breathing in while you recite the first six and out during the last six, as described above. Do this six times, imagining that you are breathing in God's mercy and then exhaling your sin.

——— June 15 ———

"Abide in me as I abide in you." (John 15:4)

I pray the Jesus Prayer as much as I can. I'd like to say that I do it constantly, but I haven't quite reached that level yet. I'm working on it. I start my morning, first thing upon waking, with "Thank you, God." Then I begin, "Lord Jesus Christ, Son of God, have mercy on me, a sinner." I say it out loud, but often in a whisper so as not to disturb my wife next to me in bed. Then I say it again. Every so often, about every ten times, I'll replace the phrase "have mercy on me" with "thank you, thank you, thank you." I say the prayer when I get up and take some steps. I say it while making coffee, and over breakfast. After a while, it becomes automatic; that's when I begin to feel a connection with God. Sometimes I catch myself subconsciously saying it—in other words,

JUNE

Centering
Prayer
and the
Jesus
Prayer

*

140

saying it without realizing that I am. That tells me that it's getting deep inside my soul. . . . This prayer has changed my life.

———

Norris Chumley, *Mysteries of the Jesus Prayer*

REFLECTION

What are some different ways you might incorporate the Jesus Prayer into your daily life?

———— **June 16** ————

The spirit of God has made me,
and the breath of the Almighty gives me life. (Job 33:4)

As you inhale, you visualize your heart and say, "Lord Jesus Christ." As you exhale, you say, "Have mercy on me!" Do this as much and as often as you can, and soon you will experience a delicate but pleasant soreness in your heart, which will be followed by warmth and a warming tenderness in your heart. If you do this, with God's help you will attain to the delightful self-acting interior prayer of the heart.

———

The Way of a Pilgrim, fourth narrative

PRAYER

Lord Jesus Christ, Son of God, have mercy on me, a sinner. Lord Jesus Christ, Son of God, have mercy on me, a sinner. Lord Jesus Christ . . .

Mercy triumphs over judgment. (James 2:13)

People newly introduced to the Jesus Prayer often think: Why should we continually beg God for mercy? Can't we be certain that he has already forgiven us? What, do we have to grovel?

The problem, I think, is that we are imagining a prisoner in court, begging the judge for mercy. It is up to the judge whether to kill this man or free him, and she is justifiably angry. His only hope is to squirm and plead, and beg her to be lenient.

Picture instead the man in Jesus' parable (Luke 10:30–37) who was robbed and beaten on the road to Jericho, then left for dead. His helplessness was so extreme that he was not even able to ask passersby for mercy, and the priest and scribe passed by on the other side of the road. Yet, the Samaritan saw him and had compassion, and rescued him from death.

That's the kind of "mercy" the Jesus Prayer asks for. We are not trying to get off the hook for a crime, but recognizing how the infection of sin has damaged us. Revealing all the extent of our illness to the heavenly physician, we seek his compassionate healing.

———

Frederica Mathewes-Green, *The Jesus Prayer*

JUNE

Centering Prayer and the Jesus Prayer

*

141

ACTION

As you repeat the Jesus Prayer several times, call to mind one of your sins. Name it out loud. Remind yourself that Christ is merciful and will forgive you.

Centering
Prayer
and the
Jesus
Prayer

*

—————— **June 18** ——————

Pray without ceasing. (1 Thessalonians 5:17)

The thought of this verse should be turning unceasingly in your heart. Never cease to recite it in whatever task or service or journey you find yourself. Think upon it as you sleep, as you eat, as you submit to the most basic demands of nature. . . .

You will write it upon the threshold and gateway of your mouth, you will place it on the walls of your house and in the inner sanctum of your heart. It will be a continuous prayer, an endless refrain when you bow down in prostration and when you rise up to do all the necessary things of life.

Blessed Isaac, quoted in *Prayer: A History*

ACTION

Pray the Jesus Prayer five times (either aloud or silently) every time you sit down to eat a meal today. Does this prayer make you more aware of God's presence at your table?

—————— **June 19** ——————

Simon Peter answered, "You are the Messiah, the Son of the Living God." (Matthew 16:16)

So if you are breathing, "Lord Jesus Christ," you take in, you breathe in with your breath the name of the Lord; you hold it and take God into yourself. When you confess your sins, when you confess as Peter confessed, "You are the Lord," then you confess your sins ("have mercy on me"); you breathe them out.

This is a marriage of body and soul. This is a purification of your body by your prayer. It is already an accelerated way of silence because you arrive at a point where your mind is still because it's surrendered to Jesus.

Father Ruwais, quoted in *Mysteries of the Jesus Prayer*

PRAYER

Lord Jesus Christ, Son of God, have mercy on me, a sinner. Lord Jesus Christ, Son of God, have mercy on me, a sinner. Lord Jesus Christ . . .

JUNE

Centering
Prayer
and the
Jesus
Prayer

*

143

——— June 20 ———

If we say that we have no sin, we deceive ourselves, and the truth is not in us. If we confess our sins, he who is faithful and just will forgive us our sins and cleanse us from all unrighteousness. (1 John 1:8–9)

While the final self-referential tag, "a sinner," seems like a harsh conclusion, it is, of course, the truth. Many modern recitations of the Prayer omit this ending, but I always use it in my own practice. It stings me and awakens me to my own weakness. It also makes the Prayer a loop, for as I conclude by considering my own sinfulness, I'm compelled to once again call upon God's mercy for my life. In this way, when practiced rhythmically, the Prayer has no beginning and no end.

Tony Jones, *The Sacred Way*

REFLECTION

How does the continuous loop of the Jesus Prayer bring you from mercy to sin and back to mercy?

Centering
Prayer
and the
Jesus
Prayer

*

144

————— **June 21** —————

*So that at the name of Jesus
every knee should bend,
in heaven and on earth and under the earth.
(Philippians 2:10)*

This prayer can expose the sin that is living in us, and this prayer can eradicate it. This prayer can stir up in the heart all the power of the enemy, and this prayer can conquer it and gradually root it out. The name of the Lord Jesus Christ, as it descends into the depths of the heart, will subdue the snake which controls its ranges, and will save and quicken the soul. Continue constantly in the name of the Lord Jesus that the heart may swallow the Lord and the Lord the heart, and that these two may be one. However, this is not accomplished in a single day, nor in two days, but requires many years and much time. Much time and labor are needed in order to expel the enemy and instate Christ.

————

St. John Chrysostom, *Letter to Monks*

PRAYER

Lord Jesus Christ, Son of God, have mercy on me, a sinner. Lord Jesus Christ, Son of God, have mercy on me, a sinner. Lord Jesus Christ . . .

————— **June 22** —————

The LORD is my shepherd, I shall not want. (Psalm 23:1)

My season of winter was when I was least inclined to pray and most in need of it. I often in that season practiced a simple and ancient discipline called breath prayer. I breathed in a phrase from the Bible—"The Lord is my shepherd" was my favorite—and breathed out the corresponding phrase— "I shall not want." I'd do this until the cadence of it slowed my mind and my breathing, stilled my anxiousness. I'd do it until all I wanted was God's shepherding presence. I'd do it until I experienced God's shepherding presence.

———

Mark Buchanan, *Spiritual Rhythm*

PRAYER

Lord Jesus Christ, Son of God, have mercy on me, a sinner. Lord Jesus Christ, Son of God, have mercy on me, a sinner. Lord Jesus Christ . . .

JUNE

Centering
Prayer
and the
Jesus
Prayer

*

145

——— June 23 ———

*Therefore God also highly exalted him
and gave him the name
that is above every name. (Philippians 2:9)*

About ten years ago my Catholic spiritual director told me I was long past time to begin centering prayer, so I should select a word and repeat it endlessly in my mind; later, when I went to the monk Father David for spiritual counsel, he emphasized that if we pray anything except the name of Jesus we open ourselves to unknown spirits. So I began repeating Jesus' name with every exhalation, for a half hour each night. In the last month I've started expanding that to the Jesus Prayer itself. The goal is to focus on those recurring words, not on other prayers or intercessions, not on Bible study or theological truths; you have all day long for that. For this half hour, just fall into the presence of God

JUNE

Centering
Prayer
and the
Jesus
Prayer

*

146

like warming your hands before a fire, without a conscious thought in your head.

———

Frederica Mathewes-Green, *Facing East*

REFLECTION

How does simply reciting the name of Jesus bring you closer to God?

——— **June 24** ———

"Go and learn what this means, 'I desire mercy, not sacrifice.' For I have come to call not the righteous but sinners." (Matthew 9:13)

To pray "have mercy" suggests that for the petitioner there are no names to drop, nor anything to bring, no hopes or dreams, no claim to stake, no honor to defend, no project or plan or intent to explain. Only nakedness and madness and queerness, things that typify the human predicament. Fatigue perhaps, perhaps regret, perhaps collapse, that is all. It is opening one's mouth wide and asking for nothing, waiting to receive whatever is given.

———

Wendy Murray Zoba, *On Broken Legs*

ACTION

Take your pleas for mercy out into the world today and pray the Jesus Prayer for other people, inserting their names ("Lord Jesus Christ, Son of God, have mercy on *x*, a sinner").

The one who calls you is faithful, and he will do this.
(1 Thessalonians 5:24)

Make the new habit a convenient part of your daily routine. "Pin it" to something else that you do every day. Do you read the news every morning? When you sit down with the paper or at the computer, close your eyes and say the Jesus Prayer first. If you read your e-mail every day, say the Prayer after you sit at your desk but before you open your e-mail account. Pick something that is already an established habit, and embed this new practice into what you're already doing.

Centering
Prayer
and the
Jesus
Prayer

*

147

Frederica Mathewes-Green, *Praying the Jesus Prayer*

ACTION

What is an established habit you already have that could accommodate a daily practice of the Jesus Prayer? This might be while waiting for the microwave to ding, or walking the dog. Make the Jesus Prayer a regular part of your routine.

Then Jesus told them a parable about their need to pray always and not to lose heart. (Luke 18:1)

Using a prayer rope is not essential in the practice of the Jesus Prayer, but it helps. Focusing on moving your thumb and forefinger from one knot to the next actually assists in focusing on the words of the prayer, mostly because this simple activity of the hand helps keep the mind from

JUNE

Centering
Prayer
and the
Jesus
Prayer

*

148

wandering elsewhere. This is but one example among many, I suppose, of the Eastern Church's insistence that the attitude and activity of the body are not unrelated to the actions of the soul.

_____

Scott Cairns, *Short Trip to the Edge*

PRAYER

Lord Jesus Christ, Son of God, have mercy on me, a sinner. Lord Jesus Christ, Son of God, have mercy on me, a sinner. Lord Jesus Christ . . .

———— **June 27** ————

And God, who searches the heart, knows what is the mind of the Spirit, because the Spirit intercedes for the saints according to the will of God. (Romans 8:27)

I received a prayer rope in the mail today from the Orthodox priest in Grand Rapids. I went on the Internet to discover meaningful ways to pray the Jesus Prayer. You are supposed to pray the prayer with your head bowed, and once you pray it through one time, you bow from the waist. When you get to the large beads, then you prostrate yourself on the ground. . . .

The Orthodox prayer rope is made of wool and contains a hundred knots. It is divided into ten sections of ten knots each. After each section there is a bead. At the bottom of the prayer rope is a cross, and beneath the cross, a tassel. The purpose of the tassel is to catch our tears and wipe them away.

_____

Ed Dobson, *The Year of Living Like Jesus*

REFLECTION

Are you open to the idea of using a prayer rope, beads, or a rosary to help refocus your mind on the Jesus Prayer?

——— **June 28** ———

Centering
Prayer
and the
Jesus
Prayer

*

149

And have mercy on some who are wavering; save others by snatching them out of the fire; and have mercy on still others with fear. (Jude 22–23)

I woke up in the night as I usually do with the words of the Jesus Prayer plashing up into my conscious mind like a little fountain, as they have been doing for years. And I thought bitterly, why on earth am I saying these meaningless and empty words? They mean nothing. . . .

And then I flung myself into the words of the prayer like a drowning person clutching at a rope thrown into the dark sea. I held onto it with all my strength and I was slowly pulled from the waters which had been sucking me under, pulled out of the dark and into the light and Lord Jesus Christ did indeed have mercy on me.

Madeleine L'Engle, *The Irrational Season*

ACTION

In this passage Madeleine L'Engle describes a dark night of the soul, a period when she was plagued by atheism. When you next have doubts about God, pray the Jesus Prayer.

Centering
Prayer
and the
Jesus
Prayer

*

——— **June 29** ———

Hannah was praying silently; only her lips moved, but her voice was not heard. (1 Samuel 1:13)

Some of the fathers taught . . . the saying of the prayer with the lips, others with and in the mind. In my opinion both are advisable. For at times the mind, left to itself, becomes wearied and too exhausted to say the prayer mentally; at other times the lips get tired of this work. Therefore both methods of prayer should be used—with the lips and with the mind.

———

St. Gregory of Sinai, "Instructions to Hesychasts"

ACTION

If you have been saying the Jesus Prayer out loud, today work on saying it silently. Go over the words in your mind at key points throughout the day.

——— **June 30** ———

*Let me hear of your steadfast love in the morning,
for in you I put my trust.
Teach me the way I should go,
for to you I lift up my soul. (Psalm 143:8)*

The Jesus Prayer . . . is to become through frequent repetition not just something that we do but something that we are—as much an instinctive part of ourselves as the drawing in of our breath and the beating of our heart. To use the terminology of St. Theophan the Recluse, it is to become "self-acting." The nineteenth-century Russian work *The Way of a Pilgrim* provides a striking illustration of this. After the anonymous Pilgrim had been reciting the Jesus Prayer for some time, he found that as he regained consciousness in the morning, the Prayer was already "saying itself" within him, before he had become fully awake. As he puts it, "Early one morning the Prayer woke me up."

———

Kallistos Ware, "The Beginnings of the Jesus Prayer"

REFLECTION

Today we conclude our practice of the Jesus Prayer. Has this "prayer of the heart" opened your eyes or illuminated your spirit? Do you plan to continue saying it?

JUNE

Centering
Prayer
and the
Jesus
Prayer

*

151

JULY

Sabbath

—— **July 1** ——

And on the seventh day God finished the work that he had done, and he rested on the seventh day from all the work that he had done. So God blessed the seventh day and hallowed it, because on it God rested from all the work that he had done in creation. (Genesis 2:2–3)

He who wants to enter the holiness of the day must first lay down the profanity of clattering commerce, of being yoked to toil. He must go away from the screech of dissonant days, from the nervousness and fury of acquisitiveness and the betrayal in embezzling his own life. He must say farewell to manual work and learn to understand that the world has already been created and will survive without the help of man. Six days a week we wrestle with the world, wringing profit from the earth; on the Sabbath we especially care for the seed of eternity planted in the soul. The world has our hands, but our soul belongs to Someone Else.

Abraham Joshua Heschel, *The Sabbath*

REFLECTION

This month we will be focusing on Sabbath rest. (Read: LEARN TO BE LAZY.) Can you make a commitment to having a full twenty-four-hour Sabbath at least once this month?

—— **July 2** ——

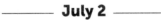

Six days shall work be done; but the seventh day is a sabbath of complete rest, a holy convocation; you shall do no work: it is a sabbath to the LORD throughout your settlements. (Leviticus 23:3)

For years of my life Sabbath didn't exist. I was unaware of it from week to week. . . . Saturday was all worldly purpose—errands and chores, laundry, haircuts, a jog in the park—topped off by an evening of special plans. . . .

There came a day, though, a Saturday morning years ago. I was already, or so I thought, confirmed in my views and ways. I handed my husband a To Do list. Forget it, he said, "It's *Shabbas*."

. . . Saturday rest was a reference point, something that never had left him. His father walked to the synagogue every Saturday, and his mother waited at home with a meal prepared the day before. He owned a separate time grid, the ancient lunar calendar, with its periodic soundings and pauses, and this he kept beneath and between his awareness of standard time.

———

Elizabeth Ehrlich, *Miriam's Kitchen*

PRAYER

O God of peace and delight, guide my restless heart toward your holy rest. Amen.

——— **July 3** ———

Remember the sabbath day, and keep it holy. (Exodus 20:8)

Busy, restless, sabbath-less people are idolaters. They have displaced the Creator God, who both worked and rested, with a god who is no true god, the god of relentless productivity who can never stop to enjoy, celebrate or—to use the commandment's resonant word—*remember*. Without remembering the sabbath, we cease to remember the Creator God who made the world and called it good; we cease to remember the one who brought us out of Egypt; we cease to remember the Eighth Day when God defeated death. We also cease to remember our future: that the end of the human story is a gift rather than an achievement. Sabbath requires us to "mark time," to stand still and pay attention to the unearned and infinite grace that is our origin and destiny.

———

Andy Crouch, *Playing God*

ACTION

Practice a mini-Sabbath today. The word *Shabbat* in Hebrew means to cease or to stop, so today you are going to stop all activity for half an hour. Don't work, don't check e-mail or social media, and don't attempt to "fill" the time. I am even heathen enough to suggest that for this half hour you don't read the Scriptures and don't pray. Just rest. Then reflect: how did half an hour of rest feel to you? Was it peaceful, or did the lack of constant motion make you feel anxious?

——— **July 4** ———

For in six days the LORD made heaven and earth, the sea, and all that is in them, but rested the seventh day; therefore the LORD blessed the sabbath day and consecrated it. (Exodus 20:11)

God rested on the seventh day. God did not show up to do more. God absented God's self from the office. God did not come and check on creation in anxiety to be sure it was all working. God has complete confidence in the fruit-bearing, blessing-generating processes of creation that have been instituted. God exhibits no anxiety about the life-giving capacity of creation. God knows the world will hold, the plants will perform, and the birds and the fish and the beasts of the field will prosper. Humankind will govern the earth in a generative way. All will be well, and all will be well, and all manner of thing will be well!

. . . God is not a workaholic. God is not a Pharaoh. God does not keep jacking up production schedules. To the contrary, God rests, confident, serene, at peace.

———

Walter Brueggemann, Sabbath as Resistance

REFLECTION

For the Hebrews, the prospect of a day of rest was thrilling, something they had never enjoyed during Egyptian slavery. Yet the Bible is filled with examples of Israel *not* keeping this commandment, just like most of us don't keep it today. If you have not observed the Sabbath, what is standing in your way?

——— July 5 ———

"Moreover I gave them my sabbaths, as a sign between me and them, so that they might know that I the Lord sanctify them." (Ezekiel 20:12)

One Sunday at noon, my twelve-year-old daughter received a very appealing invitation. A friend, and the friend's parents, wanted her to go along for an afternoon at the mall. . . . As my daughter knew, I don't shop on Sundays; stepping out of the rat race of consumerism is an important part of my sabbath practice. I said that she couldn't go.

"But Mom, I won't buy anything," she pleaded. "I'll just look." When I did not give in to her pleas, she stormed for a few minutes in her disappointment, first at me and then alone. But after a little while, we had one of our best conversations ever. What kinds of feelings are stirred up in us when we "just look" at the displays at the mall? We start to want things; but do we need them? Is this wanting good for us and for others? If we were poor, how would we experience the mall?

Dorothy Bass, *Receiving the Day*

ACTION

For a day, give up shopping. Don't make purchases or look at catalogs and commercial websites. Think about incorporating this freedom from consumption as a regular part of your Sabbath ritual.

———— **July 6** ————

Those of steadfast mind you keep in peace—
in peace because they trust in you. (Isaiah 26:3)

Drop thy still dews of quietness,
        Till all our strivings cease;
Take from our souls the strain and stress,
And let our ordered lives confess
        The beauty of thy peace.

Breathe through the hearts of our desire
        Thy coolness and thy balm;
Let sense be numb, let flesh retire;

Speak through the earthquake, wind, and fire,
O still, small voice of calm!

John Greenleaf Whittier, "The Brewing of Soma"

PRAYER

"O Lord, calm the waves of this heart. Calm its tempests. Calm thyself, O my soul, so that the divine can act in thee" (Søren Kierkegaard).

———— July 7 ————

In the beginning when God created the heavens and the earth, the earth was a formless void and darkness covered the face of the deep, while a wind from God swept over the face of the waters. (Genesis 1:1–2)

If we worry we are not good or whole inside, we will be reluctant to stop and rest, afraid we will find a lurking emptiness, a terrible, aching void with nothing to fill it, as if it will corrode and destroy us like some horrible, insatiable monster. If we are terrified of what we will find in rest, we will refuse to look up from our work, refuse to stop moving. We quickly fill all the blanks on our calendar with tasks, accomplishments, errands, things to be done—anything to fill the time, the empty space.

But . . . all life has emptiness at its core; it is the quiet hollow reed through which the wind of God blows and makes the music that is our life. Without that emptiness, we are clogged and unable to give birth to music, love, or kindness.

Wayne Muller, *Sabbath*

REFLECTION

Do you have emptiness at your core? If so, is that a frightful void, or an opportunity for creation?

Sabbath

*

160

——— **July 8** ———

In the morning, while it was still very dark, he got up and went out to a deserted place, and there he prayed.
(Mark 1:35)

When our absence from people means a special presence to God, then that absence becomes a sustaining absence. Jesus continuously left his apostles to enter into prayer with the Father. The more I read the Gospels, the more I am struck with Jesus' single-minded concern with the Father. . . . When he withdraws himself from the crowd and even from his closest friends, he withdraws to be with the Father.

Henri J. M. Nouwen, *The Living Reminder*

ACTION

Withdraw by yourself today for a time of solitude. Even fifteen minutes can be a restful, holy mini-Sabbath.

——— **July 9** ———

a time to throw away stones,
and a time to gather stones together;
a time to embrace, and a time to
refrain from embracing . . . (Ecclesiastes 3:5)

Lord of all creation, You have made us masters of Your world, to tend it, to serve it, and to enjoy it. For six days we measure and we build, we count and carry the real and the imagined burdens of our task, the success we earn and the price we pay.

On this, the Sabbath day, give us rest.

For six days, if we are weary or bruised by the world, if we think ourselves giants or cause others pain, there is never a moment to pause, and know what we should really be.

On this, the Sabbath day, give us time.

For six days we are torn between our private greed and the urgent needs of others, between the foolish noises in our ears and the silent prayer of the soul.

On this, the Sabbath day, give us understanding and peace.

Help us, Lord, to carry these lessons, of rest and time, of understanding and peace, into the six days that lie ahead, to bless us in the working days of our lives. Amen.

A Jewish blessing for the Sabbath

ACTION

Say this Jewish blessing out loud, inviting a spirit of Sabbath rest into your day.

———— **July 10** ————

He said to them, "Come away to a deserted place all by yourselves and rest a while." For many were coming and going, and they had no leisure even to eat. (Mark 6:31)

The number one enemy of Christian spiritual formation today is exhaustion. We are living beyond our means, both financially and physically. As a result, one of the primary activities (or anti-activities) of human life is being neglected: sleep. According to numerous studies, the average person needs approximately eight hours of sleep in order to maintain health. This tells me that God has designed humanity to spend nearly one-third of our lives sleeping. This is a stunning thought. We were made to spend a large portion of our existence essentially doing nothing.

James Bryan Smith, *The Good and Beautiful God*

REFLECTION

How many times a week do you get a full eight hours of sleep? How might chronic sleep deprivation damage a person's relationships with God and others?

———— **July 11** ————

"Come to me, all you that are weary and are carrying heavy burdens, and I will give you rest." (Matthew 11:28)

A major blessing of Sabbath keeping is that it forces us to rely on God for our future. On that day we do nothing to create our own way. We abstain from work, from our incessant need to produce and accomplish, from all the anxieties about how we can be successful in all that we have to do to get ahead. The result is that we can let God be God in our lives.

This was profoundly reinforced for me while I was writing my dissertation. Six days a week I felt enormous pressure to get the thing done and, later, to be successful in revising it. On Sundays, when I set that work aside, it invariably struck me that I was trying too hard to do everything on my own without trusting God to provide for my future. . . . My Sabbath keeping every week put things back into perspective and stirred in me a great repentance for my failure to let God be God in every aspect of my life, especially the academic.

Marva Dawn, *Keeping the Sabbath Wholly*

PRAYER

Heavenly Father, lead me into Sabbath rest and out of the path of perpetual anxiety. Amen.

July 12

When it began to be dark at the gates of Jerusalem before the sabbath, I commanded that the doors should be shut and gave orders that they should not be opened until after the sabbath. (Nehemiah 13:19)

For a large part of my life, I got stuck in the first few chapters of Nehemiah. I never stopped building the wall. Only in the last decade or so have I started to understand the greatest lesson of Nehemiah: once the people finished their work, they moved on. They took stock of who they were, confessed their sins, gave away money, and studied the Scriptures. . . .

Yes, work is good, but the purpose of work is not more work. The purpose of work is to live and to glorify God. One of the ways we do that best is by remembering the Sabbath and keeping it holy.

Matthew Sleeth, *24/6*

REFLECTION

When one major task is finished, do you take time to rest or do you immediately dive into tackling the next big challenge? (Guilty.) Can you make space in your life for a brief time of rest between responsibilities?

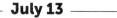

July 13

O come, let us sing to the Lord;
let us make a joyful noise to the rock of our salvation!
(Psalm 95:1)

Shoshe had done her washing for the week, and had given him a fresh shirt, underdrawers, a fringed garment, even a clean pair of stockings. She had already performed the benediction over the candles, and the spirit of the Sabbath emanated from every corner of the room. . . . The candlelight reflected in the window panes, and Shmul-Leibele fancied that there was a duplicate of this room outside and another Shoshe out there lighting Sabbath candles.

Isaac Bashevis Singer, "Short Friday"

ACTION

In Jewish life, advance planning goes into creating a peaceful Sabbath. Today, make a list of three things you can do to help you keep the Sabbath next weekend, whether you're planning for a full day or just a few hours. These tasks might include finishing (or tabling) a project, cleaning the house ahead of time, shopping for groceries, or telling your kids not to schedule any events.

────── **July 14** ──────

You who live in the shelter of the Most High,
who abide in the shadow of the Almighty,
will say to the LORD, "My refuge and my fortress;
my God, in whom I trust." (Psalm 91:1–2)

Sabbath: Uncluttered time and space to distance ourselves from the frenzy of our own activities so we can see what God has been and is doing. If we do not regularly quit work for one day a week we take ourselves far too seriously. The moral sweat pouring off our brows blinds us to the primal action of God in and around us.

Sabbath-keeping: Quitting the internal noise so we hear the still small voice of our Lord. Removing the distractions of pride so we discern the presence of Christ ". . . in ten thousand places, / Lovely in limbs, and lovely in eyes not his / To the Father through the features of men's faces."

Eugene H. Peterson, *Working the Angles*

REFLECTION

Peterson writes that when we don't keep the Sabbath, we take ourselves and our work too seriously. Do you feel this is true for you?

———— **July 15** ————

*For God alone my soul waits in silence,
for my hope is from him. (Psalm 62:5)*

The ancient monastic word used to describe the state of prayer was the Latin word *quies*, which contains the notion of being at rest, being in a state of silence, sometimes described as "staying quiet in the Lord." This state of being quiet suggested complete confidence and ease at being in the presence of God. In our society we are so used to striving for things, to owning things, to earning the approval of others, that it is very hard for us to think of ourselves as usefully employed if we are just "resting in the Lord" in this state of *quies*, of being quiet. But what those of us who try to tread this pilgrimage must always remember is that just being in His presence is all-sufficient.

———

John Main, *Being on the Way*

PRAYER

My hope comes from you, O Lord, and my soul waits for you in silence. Amen.

———— **July 16** ————

"For the Son of Man is lord of the sabbath." (Matthew 12:8)

As we settle into our yearlong experiment, I take comfort in how Jesus approaches the Sabbath in scripture. He doesn't always observe the sabbath day the way people want him to; he's constantly getting in trouble for healing on the Sabbath, for example. . . . He takes Sabbath seriously while still finding his own way. He doesn't postpone Sabbath until everyone else has been tended to. He doesn't cross everything off the messianic to-do list, nod, and say, "Now. Sabbath can begin." He just *goes*—to the mountain, to a deserted place. And people don't always understand it or make it easy on him. At one point, he comes back from one of these retreats to find the disciples saying, "Everyone is searching for you!" (Mk. 1:37). . . .

Jesus manages to carve out the time for Sabbath, despite the dire needs that confront him at every turn.

MaryAnn McKibben Dana, *Sabbath in the Suburbs*

REFLECTION

The rhythm of Sabbath creates a sense of peace and rest because the Sabbath comes right on schedule, week after week. We're called to organize our lives and priorities around that schedule, rather than trying to squeeze Sabbath in once all the work is finally done. (Which never happens.) What are the "dire needs" that threaten to keep you from enjoying regular weekly rest?

July 17

What do mortals get from all the toil and strain with which they toil under the sun? For all their days are full of pain, and their work is a vexation; even at night their minds do not rest. This also is vanity. (Ecclesiastes 2:22–23)

When you carry a mobile device, all things digital (and all people) are along for the ride. Home life is busier too. Much of what used to be called free time has been colonized by our myriad connective obligations, and so is no longer free.

It's easy to blame all this on the tools. Too easy. These tools are fantastically useful and enrich our lives in countless ways. Like all new technologies, they have flaws, but at bottom they can't make us busy until we make them busy first. We're the prime movers here. We're always connected because we're always connecting.

William Powers, *Hamlet's BlackBerry*

ACTION

For the next three nights, turn off all your digital devices by nine in the evening. How does it feel?

———— July 18 ————

"Be still, and know that I am God." (Psalm 46:10)

The psalmist's word here, *rapah,* though a fairly common word in the Old Testament, is translated as "still" in most translations only in this one passage. Elsewhere it means to go limp or slack, to let go or withdraw or give up, to sink, to relax, to be lazy. Pharaoh uses *rapah* pejoratively—twice, to emphasize its negative value in his eyes. . . .

"Lazy, that's what you are—lazy!" (Exodus 5:17), Pharaoh tells them and orders them back to work.

I read God's instruction to "Be still"—Be lazy!—"and know that I am God" as a simple presentation of cause and effect: that is, if we would just quit trying to *do* our faith and instead relax and enjoy the life we've been given, then we would become more intensely aware of God.

Patty Kirk, *The Easy Burden of Pleasing God*

———— **July 19** ————

*The LORD is near to the brokenhearted,
and saves the crushed in spirit. (Psalm 34:18)*

I f you decide to live on the fire that God has kindled inside
of you instead of rushing out to find some sticks to rub
together, then it does not take long for all sorts of feelings to
come out of hiding. You can find yourself crying buckets of
uncried tears over things you thought you had handled years
ago. People you have loved and lost can show up in their
ghostly lawn chairs, announcing they have nowhere else
they have to be all day. While you are talking with them,
you may gradually become aware of an aching leg and look
down to see a bruise on your thigh that you did not know you
had. How many other collisions did you ignore in your rush
from here to there?

*
169

————

Barbara Brown Taylor, *Leaving Church*

REFLECTION
Taylor notes that sometimes we are afraid to rest because
the moment we stop moving, buried emotions like grief
and pain can rise to the surface. Has this ever happened
to you?

———— **July 20** ————

*"The sabbath was made for humankind, and not humankind
for the sabbath." (Mark 2:27)*

Sabbath

I n my childhood, Sabbath observance was strictly enforced by my grandfather, but there was little joy in it. Like all good gifts of a good God, Sabbath too could be spoiled by those who, ironically, deeply treasured it. In Jesus' day too such Sabbath observers apparently existed. A day of rejoicing in the gifts of God could of course be transmuted into a day of punctilious religiosity. Jesus' warning, "The sabbath was made for humankind, and not humankind for the sabbath" (Mark 2:27), condemns such understandings.

Walter J. Jarrelson, *The Ten Commandments for Today*

*

170

PRAYER

I will rejoice in your Sabbath, Lord! Thank you for creating it and commanding me to rest. Amen.

—————— **July 21** ——————

But you are a chosen race, a royal priesthood, a holy nation, God's own people. (1 Peter 2:9)

T he seasons of life in which Sabbath-keeping seems impossible are the seasons you need it the most. Your children need to see you rest and to know that it's okay to stop achieving, running, and doing for a little while. One of the most important developmental skills you can give your children is the ability to daydream. You can't sign them up for a class on it. You can't direct them in how to do it. You have to give them, as small children, enough downtime simply to discover it on their own. . . .

You can facilitate this with very young children by continuing a daily nap time, even if they don't sleep. During that time, they must be quiet and on their own beds (no video games or music). They can read or just lay down and relax. Several families I've spoken to told me their Sabbath practice includes Sunday-afternoon naps for everyone in the family.

Keri Wyatt Kent, *Rest*

ACTION

If you have children, begin a routine of a weekly Sabbath time for them. Explain that parents need rest too. The season of life when your children are little is admittedly one of the most difficult in which to keep the Sabbath—but that is precisely why you may need to start the practice.

——— **July 22** ———

*. . . if you call the sabbath a delight
and the holy day of the Lord honourable. (Isaiah 58:13)*

Each person deserves a day in which no problems are con-fronted, no solutions searched for. Each of us needs to withdraw from the cares which will not withdraw from us. We need hours of aimless wandering or spates of time sitting on park benches, observing the mysterious world of ants and the canopy of treetops.

If we step away for a time, we are not, as many may think and some will accuse, being irresponsible, but rather we are preparing ourselves to more ably perform our duties and dis-charge our obligations.

Maya Angelou, *Wouldn't Take Nothing for My Journey Now*

JULY

Sabbath

REFLECTION

In your experience, does adequate, regularly scheduled rest make you more able to tend to your duties on the nonresting days?

172

───────── **July 23** ─────────

Six days you shall labor and do all your work. But the seventh day is a sabbath to the LORD your God; you shall not do any work—you, your son or your daughter, your male or female slave, your livestock, or the alien resident in your towns. (Exodus 20:9–10)

The Sabbath is a time of holiness—a day that inspires and ennobles one's soul. The best of everything comes out on the Sabbath: the finest food, dress, and dinnerware; the most joyous songs; the most sacred objects and treasured heirlooms. The many beautiful customs that families share on this day give the Sabbath an aura of holiness that is almost indescribable.

───

Barbara Rush, *The Jewish Year*

ACTION

For your Sabbath or mini-Sabbath, do something at the table that marks a Sabbath meal as special. This can be through food, table settings, heirlooms, flowers, music, or special guests. Warning: do not go over the top! This is not an HGTV show, and no one is judging your table centerpiece on a scale of one to ten. But find a simple, tangible way to remind yourself that the Sabbath is distinctive.

*"See! The L*ORD *has given you the sabbath, therefore on the sixth day he gives you food for two days; each of you stay where you are; do not leave your place on the seventh day." So the people rested on the seventh day. (Exodus 16:29–30)*

Our war is not with flesh and blood; our reluctance to [keep the] Sabbath is not a fight with busyness, drivenness, or time. We are caught in and fight battles against delight. Delight unnerves us; God's call to delight terrifies us. To surrender to delight is to hear God's passionate extravagance spoken in a manner that is uniquely crafted for our joy.

Do we really believe that Sabbath delight is God's heart for us? Are we willing to silence the rabble of idols and foul spirits to hear the intoxicating joy of God? We will never know Sabbath delight unless God delivers us from drowning in the noise and grime of our soiled days. Each day may involve countless wars, but every day can also contain the promise of an utterly different eon.

Dan B. Allender, *Sabbath*

PRAYER

Teach me to surrender to your delight, O God. Amen.

*Return, O my soul, to your rest, for the L*ORD *has dealt bountifully with you. (Psalm 116:7)*

I'm in the process of decorating a new house. On my shelf sits a thoughtful book on home design, by John Wheatman, voted one of America's top-ten designers by *House*

Beautiful. His very first reflection is both profound and terse: "Edit what you have." What does this mean? "When I work on a space, I like to begin by culling the objects in it down to a group of essential items, each of which has a role in meeting the needs of the inhabitants and has found a place in the overall scheme of the household." What a perfect description of the work of the Sabbath—to cull the things in our lives to what's essential and to determine how they fit into the overall scheme of our values and goals.

Greg Cootsona, *Say Yes to No*

REFLECTION

Sabbath observance is about editing—temporarily editing out those things in our lives that are not restful. What are the least restful and most stressful aspects of your weekends? What changes can you make so that rest is encouraged?

———— July 26 ————

I will both lie down and sleep in peace;
for you alone, O LORD, make me lie down in safety.
(Psalm 4:8)

Every single Sunday, along about mid-afternoon, my body goes into shut-down mode. It doesn't matter where I am or what I am doing at the time, as soon as two o'clock hits, I'm completely sapped of energy and start to wilt like a pansy in the summer sun. This has been true for as long as I remember, and I think I know why. As good Southern Baptists, my family went to church for most of the day on Sundays, with a few hours off in the afternoon. Each week we'd come home from church, eat a lavish meal and then be shooed off to bed by my mom and dad so they could get in some shuteye as well. ... Apparently my body adapted so well that to this day I can hardly get by without that Sunday afternoon siesta.

Tricia McCary Rhodes, *Sacred Chaos*

ACTION

This weekend, take a nice, long nap. That's your only assignment. Enjoy it. You can thank me when you wake up.

———— July 27 ————

Thus says the Lord God to these bones: "I will cause breath to enter you, and you shall live. I will lay sinews on you, and will cause flesh to come upon you, and cover you with skin, and put breath in you, and you shall live; and you shall know that I am the LORD." (Ezekiel 37:5–6)

From midway in chapter 36 of his book, Ezekiel has been communicating, through his apocalyptic visions, the good news of restoration. In this story, he uses the symbol of dry bones being restored to life. What better word picture could he have given us to communicate the mystery and wonder of redemption? What more appropriate picture would describe my overspent life in need to rest? . . . If anything ever described my burned-out condition and need for sabbath rest, it is old, dead, dry bones. Bones that once held flesh and muscle teeming with life have become useless even to the scavengers of the desert.

Kim Thomas, *Even God Rested*

PRAYER

Lord, take the dry bones of my spirit and breathe life in them through your Sabbath peace. Amen.

—————— **July 28** ——————

From the heavens you uttered judgment;
the earth feared and was still. (Psalm 76:8)

Sabbath

We lack time. Yet it frightens us. We complain about the hectic pressures of our busy schedules. Still, it often seems that what we really miss is the time to do even more things. The prospect of long stretches of uninterrupted time, solitude, or quiet can be dreadful. Cancel all appointments, clear our schedules, and what would we rather do? Turn on the television, reach for a newspaper, pick up the phone, or plan some excursion that will leave us more exhausted than we were before.

There is of course a true spirit of leisure, just as there is a true spirit of work. But something else is going on when what really drives us is the need to avoid sitting still.

*

176

Robert Ellsberg, *The Saints' Guide to Happiness*

REFLECTION
Are you ever afraid of silence and rest?

—————— **July 29** ——————

But this is the one to whom I will look,
to the humble and contrite in spirit,
who trembles at my word. (Isaiah 66:2)

This . . . commandment imposes a regular periodical holi-day—quietness of heart, tranquility of mind, the product of a good conscience. Here is sanctification, because here is the Spirit of God. Well, here is what a true holiday, that is to say, quietness and rest, means. "Upon whom," he says, "shall my spirit rest? Upon one who is humble and quiet and trembles at my words." So unquiet people are those who recoil from the Holy Spirit, loving quarrels, spreading slanders, keener on argument than on truth, and so in their restlessness they do not allow the quietness of the spiritual Sabbath to enter into themselves.

St. Augustine of Hippo, *Sermon* 8.6

PRAYER

Holy Spirit, fill me with peace and humility, so that I may enter into God's rest. Amen.

———— **July 30** ————

God saw everything that he had made, and indeed,
it was very good. (Genesis 1:31)

So why remember the Sabbath? Because the Sabbath comes to us out of the past—out of the bodies of our mothers and fathers, out of the churches on our streets, out of our own dreams—to train us to pay attention to it. . . . God stopped to show us that what we create becomes meaningful only once we stop creating it and start remembering why it was worth creating in the first place. . . . We could let the world wind us up and set us to working, like dolls that go until they fall over because they have no way of stopping. But that would make us less than human. We have to remember to stop because we have to stop to remember.

Judith Shulevitz, *The Sabbath World*

REFLECTION

What does it mean when Shulevitz says, "We have to remember to stop because we have to stop to remember"? When you stop your activities, what do you appreciate about what you've made or done?

Sabbath

———— **July 31** ————

a time to tear, and a time to sew;
a time to keep silence, and a time to speak . . .
(Ecclesiastes 3:7)

*
178

After the sun sets, when three medium-sized stars can be seen in the sky, Shabbat ends. It is escorted out with a special service called *havdalah* (separation). Just as we entered that sacred place through a portal of candlelight and accompanied by wine, so we leave it through a portal of candlelight and accompanied by wine. . . .

The candle is extinguished. The lights come on. Our rest is over. We return to where we left off. Our clothes need washing; food needs cooking; presents need to be bought; meetings need to be scheduled. We work for another six days with God at our side, until the next Shabbat, when we reenter God's palace in time.

Nina Beth Cardin, *The Tapestry of Jewish Time*

ACTION

Rabbi Cardin describes a traditional Jewish ritual marking the end of Sabbath. As we end this month of focusing on Sabbath, choose to do something that will create *havdalah* (separation) for you, whether it's a full-blown ritual with candles or a simple prayer at your desk on Monday morning.

AUGUST

Gratitude

AUGUST

Gratitude

*

180

Of course, there is great gain in godliness combined with contentment; for we brought nothing into the world, so that we can take nothing out of it; but if we have food and clothing, we will be content with these. (1 Timothy 6:6–8)

When you woke up this morning, chances are you slept on a comfortable bed. There was breakfast to eat and perhaps a glass of juice or a good cup of coffee or tea to sip. You put clean clothes on. Odds are that you are reasonably safe and that two more meals and a few snacks are still ahead of you today. For most of us, this is the way it has been nearly every day of our lives. We see evidence of the Creator's care and provision all around us. We hear the birds singing in the morning. The sun rises, rain falls to water the earth, and year after year plants grow that provide oxygen and food for our bodies—and not just calories but tasty morsels that excite the palate. . . . We embrace the abundance of life by learning to practice gratitude and trust.

Mark Scandrette, *Free*

REFLECTION

This month, we will be expressing gratitude as a spiritual practice. Have you considered gratitude to be a spiritual practice in line with prayer or fasting? Why or why not?

———— **August 2** ————

Pleasant words are like a honeycomb, sweetness to the soul and health to the body. (Proverbs 16:24)

I'm convinced of the virtue of giving praise because I have seen its effects so often. I don't gush or hand out empty compliments. But I have thanked janitors in public restrooms for keeping those places clean; I've complimented total strangers on their coats and hairdos. I've gone out of my way to tell some short-order cook that those were the best scrambled eggs I'd had in years. I'm not trying to earn points; I never expect to see these people again. But they've brought something good to my day, and they should be told about it.

Vinita Hampton Wright, *Simple Acts of Moving Forward*

ACTION

Compliment three strangers you encounter today.

——————— **August 3** ———————

"Whoever is faithful in a very little is faithful also in much." (Luke 16:10)

Only he who gives thanks for little things receives the big things. We prevent God from giving us the great spiritual gifts He has in store for us, because we do not give thanks for daily gifts. We think we dare not be satisfied with the small measure of spiritual knowledge, experience, and love that has been given to us, and that we must constantly be looking forward eagerly for the highest good. Then we deplore the fact that we lack the deep certainty, the strong faith, and the rich experience God has given to others, and we consider this lament to be pious. We pray for the big things and forget to give thanks for the ordinary, small (and yet really not small) gifts. How can God entrust great things to one who will not thankfully receive from Him the little things?

Dietrich Bonhoeffer, *Life Together*

Gratitude

PRAYER

Thank you, God, for all the little things and daily gifts I enjoy. Amen.

*

——— **August 4** ———

O give thanks to the Lord of lords,
for his steadfast love endures forever. (Psalm 136:3)

Inside the itchy hankering of every heart stirs an aching need to feel grateful. We are heavy until we feel the lightness of gratitude. We hear the sweet music of joy only when we feel some awe and wonder and delight, and surprise, too, at being our own best gift. But once we have felt it, we know that there is no pleasure on earth like it.

My mother had a heavier way with gratitude. Whenever I groused about my lot in life, she whacked my conscience with this solemn bromide: "Lewis, you *ought* to be grateful." She was right, I suppose, to press gratitude into the mode of duty: we ought to be grateful.

Lewis Smedes, *Days of Grace through the Year*

REFLECTION

How were you taught to express gratitude as a child? Was it a moral obligation, or an outpouring of joy?

August 5

"Blessed are the meek, for they will inherit the earth."
(Matthew 5:5)

Gratitude is a sign of maturity. It is an indication of sincere humility. It is a hallmark of civility. And most of all, it is a divine principle. I doubt there is anything in which we more offend the Almighty than in our tendency to forget His mercies and to be ungrateful for that which He has given us.

Where there is appreciation, there is also courtesy and concern for the rights and property of others. Without these, there is arrogance and evil. Where there is gratitude, there is humility instead of pride, generosity rather than selfishness.

Gordon B. Hinckley, *Standing for Something*

REFLECTION
How does gratitude cultivate humility?

August 6

Bless the LORD, O my soul,
 and all that is within me,
bless his holy name.
Bless the LORD, O my soul,
 and do not forget all his benefits.
(Psalm 103:1–2)

Wilkie said, "Sit right down at this table. Here is a yellow pad and a ballpoint pen. I want you to write down your blessings."

. . . The ship of my life might or might not be sailing on calm seas. The challenging days of my existence might or might not be bright and promising. From that encounter

AUGUST

Gratitude

on, whether my days are stormy or sunny and if my nights are glorious or lonely, I maintain an attitude of gratitude. If pessimism insists on occupying my thoughts, I remember there is always tomorrow. Today I am blessed.

Maya Angelou, *Mom & Me & Mom*

ACTION

For the next three days, list five things a day you are grateful for. If you feel comfortable doing so, share them with others publicly to spread the joy.

＊

184

———— **August 7** ————

May I never boast of anything except the cross of our Lord Jesus Christ, by which the world has been crucified to me, and I to the world. (Galatians 6:14)

Thankfulness points us away from what we have achieved or failed to achieve and makes us focus instead on God's love, which alone can warm our cold hearts and set them on fire with delight in God and in serving and obeying him. If we look only at our own efforts, we soon become overwhelmed by our failures and sink beneath the waves of discouragement. If we look only at any minor successes or at any experiences we may have had, we easily become proud and again there is a block in the way of loving God (1 Pet. 5:5).

As only the love of Christ can constrain us to change our sinful attitudes and habits, it is of fundamental importance that we understand what Christ has done for us and what our salvation cost him. Just as a person saved from drowning is thankful, so should we be when we understand our deliverance by Christ.

Ranald Macaulay and Jerram Barrs, *Being Human*

Thank you, Lord, for all you have done for me in Christ. Amen.

———— **August 8** ————

O LORD, how manifold are your works!
In wisdom you have made them all;
the earth is full of your creatures. (Psalm 104:24)

＊

185

I will be the gladdest thing
        Under the sun!
    I will touch a hundred flowers
        And not pick one.

    I will look at cliffs and clouds
        With quiet eyes,
    Watch the wind bow down the grass,
        And the grass rise.

    And when lights begin to show
        Up from the town,
    I will mark which must be mine,
        And then start down!

Edna St. Vincent Millay, "Afternoon on a Hill"

ACTION

Go outside today! Breathe the air and notice the flowers. Thank God for the beauty of this world. (But don't get your head so high in the clouds that you forget that this is the third day writing down your gratitude list.)

Gratitude

*

186

——— **August 9** ———

We welcome this in every way and everywhere with
utmost gratitude. (Acts 24:3)

What does it mean to pay back in life? To discharge our deepest debts of all? To fulfill our obligations for simply being human? How do we pay back our fathers and mothers? Were our parents just the "luck of the womb" for us, or more? How do we pay back the one teacher who made all the difference in our school years? Or the youth director or team coach whose noticing us in a special way drew out a part of us that was crucial in our becoming who we are today?

. . . All sorts of curious twists arise when we pursue such questions. Isn't it hypocritical, for example, that when we convict people for doing wrong to society, we say they "owe" something and must "repay the debt"—yet when society has so obviously showered so much good on the rest of us, we take it as our right and live as if we owe nothing in return?

Os Guinness, *The Call*

ACTION

Thank a parent or mentor today. Be specific about the ways this person influenced your life for good.

——— **August 10** ———

Then he ordered the crowds to sit down on the grass.
Taking the five loaves and the two fish, he looked up to
heaven, and blessed and broke the loaves, and gave them
to the disciples, and the disciples gave them to the crowds.
(Matthew 14:19)

I believe the old practice of pausing to thank God before meals is a wise and good one. It reminds me of my creatureliness; like the birds of the air and the flowers of the field, I am dependent on God for my daily sustenance. The simple act of table grace can certainly be practiced on mindless autopilot, but when it is done mindfully, with awareness, it can connect me at least three times a day with the Creator, who supplies soil and sunlight and rain to maintain the miraculous web of life, of which I am part. And true gratitude to God will also produce gratitude to my fellow creatures—wheat stalk, apple tree, and corn plant; chicken, salmon, and cattle; farmer, agricultural researcher, truck driver, grocer, and cashier too.

Brian D. McLaren, *Naked Spirituality*

PRAYER

Bless us, O Lord, and these thy gifts which we are about to receive from thy bounty, through Christ our Lord. Amen.

—————— **August 11** ——————

We know that all things work together for good for those who are called according to his purpose.
(Romans 8:28)

As I grew stronger and the crippling self-absorption of depression began to wane, I discovered a new sensation had taken root: gratitude. True, joyous gratitude. A blossoming within that flowered into a deep and abiding desire to tend to the well being of these most precious individuals [my friends]. Not because I owe them.

Because I love them with the kind of love they taught me. Experiencing the liberation of honest gratitude, I slowly began learning the inexplicable richness of servanthood. The unparalleled honor of serving others. . . .

I'm hard-pressed to say I'm glad I suffered clinical depression, but I am grateful even for the evils because of the incredible gifts that sprang from them.

Nevada Barr, *Seeking Enlightenment Hat by Hat*

REFLECTION

What terrible events can you look back on with gratitude? Are you glad now that those things happened to you, even though you were not happy about them at the time?

———— **August 12** ————

"But we had to celebrate and rejoice, because this brother of yours was dead and has come to life; he was lost and has been found." (Luke 15:32)

In the past I always thought of gratitude as a spontaneous response to the awareness of gifts received, but now I realize that gratitude can also be lived as a discipline. The discipline of gratitude is the explicit effort to acknowledge all that I am and have is given to me as a gift of love, a gift to be celebrated with joy. . . .

The choice of gratitude rarely comes without some real effort. But each time I make it, the next choice is a little easier, a little freer, a little less self-conscious. Because every gift I acknowledge reveals another and another, until finally even the most normal, obvious, and seemingly mundane event or encounter proves to be filled with grace.

———

Henri J. M. Nouwen, *The Return of the Prodigal Son*

ACTION

As you express gratitude today, become conscious of the way it gets a little easier each time, as gratitude becomes a habit.

——— **August 13** ———

For every wild animal of the forest is mine,
the cattle on a thousand hills.
I know all the birds of the air,
and all that moves in the field is mine. (Psalm 50:10–11)

Glory be to God for dappled things—
 For skies of couple-colour as a brinded cow;
  For rose-moles all in stipple upon trout that swim;
Fresh-firecoal chestnut-falls; finches' wings;
Landscape plotted and pieced—fold, fallow, and plough;
And áll trádes, their gear and tackle and trim.

All things counter, original, spare, strange;
  Whatever is fickle, freckled (who knows how?)
   With swift, slow; sweet, sour; adazzle, dim;
He fathers-forth whose beauty is past change:
   Praise him.

———

Gerard Manley Hopkins, "Pied Beauty"

PRAYER

Thank you, God, for the glorious beauty of nature. Amen.

———— **August 14** ————

I do not cease to give thanks for you as I remember you in my prayers. (Ephesians 1:16)

Gratitude

G ratitude begins in our hearts and then dovetails into behavior. It almost always makes you willing to be of service, which is where the joy resides. It means you are willing to stop being such a jerk. When you are aware of all that has been given to you, in your lifetime and in the past few days, it is hard not to be humbled, and pleased to give back.

*

190

Anne Lamott, *Help Thanks Wow*

REFLECTION
When has gratitude prompted you to serve others—like paying it forward?

———— **August 15** ————

Go, eat your bread with enjoyment, and drink your wine with a merry heart; for God has long ago approved what you do. (Ecclesiastes 9:7)

E very time we eat a meal, gratitude is our practice. We are grateful for being together as a community, we are grateful that we have food to eat, and we really enjoy the food and the presence of each other. We feel grateful throughout the meal and throughout the day, and we express this by being fully aware of the food and living every moment deeply. This is how I try to express my gratitude to all of life.

Thich Nhat Hanh, *Living Buddha, Living Christ*

PRAYER
Thank you for the gifts of food and fellowship. Amen.

So they took away the stone. And Jesus looked upward and said, "Father, I thank you for having heard me." (John 11:41)

The Gospels indicate . . . that at every moment of his life Jesus was aware that everything came from the love of God. He never took his life for granted but each moment received it as a free gift from his Abba.

The nameless gratitude that we feel after a narrow escape from injury or death, Jesus felt each morning as he rose from sleep. He lived without boredom, tranquilizers, or anesthesia, numb to neither the pain nor the joy of the human experience. He was a man with his arms open, his chest uncovered, and his heart exposed; and so the wild world, gift of his prodigal Father, leaped into his eyes, ravished his ears, and pierced his heart.

Brennan Manning, *Reflections for Ragamuffins*

REFLECTION

Have you ever gotten a "stay of execution" by an illness suddenly healing or a car accident being barely averted? How long were you able to sustain the immediate gratitude you felt after that narrow escape before you started taking your health or safety for granted again?

*The fig tree puts forth its figs,
and the vines are in blossom;
they give forth fragrance. (Song of Solomon 2:13)*

It is not necessary, as is very often supposed, to give up natural pleasures before we can gain spiritual ones. On the contrary, we enjoy them more exquisitely as we rise in the inner life. How wonderful is a bunch of grapes sent by a dear friend, with its rounded beauty and delicious fragrance—love, imagination, and poetry in substance! How rich and varied we find flowers in fragrant delights that quicken the brain and open our heart-blossoms! How endlessly the changes of sky and water and earth charm us and keep before us a lovely mirror of the higher world upon which our faith and our dreams are centered!

The world is so full of care and sorrow that it is a gracious debt we owe to one another to discover the bright crystals of delight hidden in somber circumstances and irksome tasks.

Helen Keller, *Light in My Darkness*

ACTION

Be grateful today for smell and touch, two of the senses Helen Keller got to enjoy. What fragrances are you enjoying? What sensations are at your fingertips?

 **August 18**

This is the day that the LORD has made;
let us rejoice and be glad in it. (Psalm 118:24)

"This is the day that the *Lord* has made." If God made this day, if he intended me to wake up this day, then there's purpose in it. It wasn't made because he was bored and had nothing better to do. He created it because that's his nature—he is creative. And he creates for his pleasure. And here I am right in the middle of a creation that was provided for his pleasure. . . .

"*I will rejoice* and be glad in it." I've got several choices ahead of me. I can worry. I can fear. I can hesitate. I can plan. I can be regretful. But these first words out of my mouth—*I will rejoice*—remind me that this, too, is an option. I have the option to choose rejoicing and to be glad.

Amy Grant, *Mosaic*

PRAYER

This is the day that you have made, Lord! I will rejoice and be glad in it. Amen.

——— **August 19** ———

Shout aloud and sing for joy, O royal Zion,
for great in your midst is the Holy One of Israel.
(Isaiah 12:6)

Another Saturday night, (January 1739) I had such a sense, how sweet and blessed a thing it was to walk in the way of duty; to do that which was right and meet to be done, and agreeable to the holy mind of God; that it caused me to break forth into a kind of loud weeping, which held me some time, so that I was forced to shut myself up, and fasten the doors. I could not but, as it were, cry out, "How happy are they which do that which is right in the sight of God! They are blessed indeed, they are the happy ones!" I had, at the same time, a very affecting sense, how meet and suitable it was that God should govern the world, and order all things according to his own pleasure; and I rejoiced in it, that God reigned, and that his will was done.

Jonathan Edwards, "Personal Narrative" (1739)

PRAYER

It is right and good that you are the Lord of creation! Praise be your name! Amen.

───── **August 20** ─────

Then one of them, when he saw that he was healed, turned back, praising God with a loud voice. He prostrated himself at Jesus' feet and thanked him. And he was a Samaritan. Then Jesus asked, "Were not ten made clean? But the other nine, where are they? Was none of them found to return and give praise to God except this foreigner?" (Luke 17:15–18)

To pass now to the matter of gratitude and ingratitude. There was never any man yet so wicked as not to approve of the one, and detest the other. . . . The very story of an ungrateful action puts us out of all patience, and gives us a loathing for the author of it. . . .

There is no question, but gratitude for benefits received is the ready way to procure more, and in requiting one friend we encourage many, but . . . if I were sure that the doing of good offices would be my ruin, yet I would pursue them.

Seneca, "Of Benefits"

REFLECTION

Have you ever been angry at someone for his or her total lack of gratitude? How did their actions remind you of yourself?

——— **August 21** ———

Give thanks in all circumstances; for this is the
will of God in Christ Jesus for you.
(1 Thessalonians 5:18)

If your life seems devoid of blessings right now, the fact remains that God's love for you is so great that Jesus Christ shared in human loneliness, poverty, homelessness, and crucifixion, and you can thank God for that love. At particularly dark times, find consolation in your solidarity with God's other children who are suffering. Difficult times in our lives can either isolate and embitter us or give us a greater understanding of our unity with the whole human family.

Nancy Roth, *The Breath of God*

ACTION

Roth suggests that we move our hands in the air over anything we are grateful for (a family member, a garden, an Oreo) and thank God for it as we draw a halo around it. Try this today.

——— **August 22** ———

For by grace you have been saved through faith, and this is
not your own doing; it is the gift of God—not the result of
works, so that no one may boast. (Ephesians 2:8–9)

It's a strange feeling to be so completely dependent on other people; but at least it teaches one to be grateful, and I hope I shall never forget that. In ordinary life we hardly realize that we receive a great deal more than we give, and that it is only with gratitude that life becomes rich. It's very easy to overestimate the importance of our own achievements in comparison with what we owe to others.

Dietrich Bonhoeffer, letter to his parents from Tegel prison,
September 13, 1943

REFLECTION

How do your achievements rest on the kindness and generosity of other people? What do you owe those people for any success you have had?

———— **August 23** ————

*How long shall this wicked congregation complain
against me? (Numbers 14:27)*

People suffering from a style of living marked by ungratefulness miss seeing it in their own personality. As a result, both they, and the persons around them, suffer. Even when they do say thank you, their gratitude is tainted. They say it because others expect it, politically it's the right thing to do, or they like the person they are thanking and want to be appreciated in return for being seen as a grateful person. This is pretty sad when you think about it. Yet, little, if any, of this is done consciously, so blaming them for it or expecting them to change should you point it out is a waste of time.

Robert J. Wicks, *Crossing the Desert*

PRAYER

Teach my heart to be grateful, and curb my tendency to complain or criticize. Amen.

August 24

I have learned to be content with whatever I have. I know what it is to have little, and I know what it is to have plenty. In any and all circumstances I have learned the secret of being well-fed and of going hungry, of having plenty and of being in need. (Philippians 4:11–12)

Evidently people consider me a happy man. And I suppose in a way I really am. But I spoil it for myself by my stubborn, interior refusal of happiness.

What a sad and silly thing! God has been consistently and incessantly good to me in everything, and I refuse to be content.

Thomas Merton, ocso, journal entry, April 29, 1961

ACTION

Decide today to practice being content with what you have. Every time an "I wish" thought comes to mind, drown it out with careful rehearsal of all your many blessings.

August 25

I will extol you, O Lord, for you have drawn me up, and did not let my foes rejoice over me. (Psalm 30:1)

If you think of gratitude as the disagreeable task of the inferior who "owes" the superior, reading the lavish praise of the Psalmist is uncomfortable. . . .

True gratitude isn't cringing or uncomfortable at all: It is the purest expression of joy. Ungrateful people—you may have met a few—are not happy people. If we humans were

making good use of our consciousness, we would wander around in a flabbergasted daze of gratitude all the time: *I could be hungry . . . but instead, I've got French fries! There could be nothing . . . but instead, there's something!*

There could be only birth, pain, and death. Instead there is also love.

_____

Kate Braestrup, Beginner's Grace

ACTION
Pray for an ungrateful person today.

——— August 26 ———

Rejoice always. (1 Thessalonians 5:16)

The mark of a Christian who strives for a vibrant relationship with God is joy, prayer, and gratitude. These are not one-time offerings but perpetual and ongoing expressions—for every situation, in all circumstances—rooted in the will of God and given as gifts by God.

Paul never suggests that believers deny the grief or pain that adversity brings but rather that they recognize, even in the midst of hardship, God's spirit infusing them with joy.

_____

Margaret Feinberg, Wonderstruck

REFLECTION
Sometimes Christians recommend simply ignoring all sadness, depression, or trauma in order to "conquer" it. As Feinberg indicates, that isn't what Paul is saying at all. Consider that it is within your power to live alongside such pain, fully acknowledging its reality but also making daily decisions to choose joy and gratitude instead.

For the LORD God is a sun and shield;
he bestows favor and honor.
No good thing does the LORD withhold
from those who walk uprightly.
O LORD of hosts,
happy is everyone who trusts in you.
(Psalm 84:11–12)

AUGUST

Gratitude

To be grateful is to recognize the Love of God in everything He has given us—and He has given us everything. Every breath we draw is a gift of His love, every moment of existence is a grace, for it brings with it immense graces from Him. Gratitude therefore takes nothing for granted, is never unresponsive, is constantly awakening to new wonder and to praise of the goodness of God. For the grateful person knows that God is good, not by hearsay but by experience. And that is what makes all the difference.

*

199

Thomas Merton, OCSO, in *Words of Gratitude*

PRAYER

Lord of life, every breath I take is your gift. Thank you for life, and for your goodness! Amen.

"Give, and it will be given to you. A good measure,
pressed down, shaken together, running over, will be put
into your lap; for the measure you give will be the
measure you get back." (Luke 6:38)

We use "for" to introduce the reason for gratitude, and when we do so, "for" implies that someone else has been involved in or is responsible for the action: "We were grateful for the fruit" entails somebody else having provided it. . . .

Gratitude includes accepting—not resenting—dependence on something provided by someone who is not ourselves. It means concentrating on that person and on her kind intentions, just as she has concentrated her attention on me.

Margaret Visser, *The Gift of Thanks*

ACTION

Start at least one conversation today in which you and another person discuss the people you are grateful for.

 **August 29** ————

And my God will fully satisfy every need of yours according to his riches in glory in Christ Jesus. (Philippians 4:19)

One of the advantages of having lived a long time is that you can often remember when you had it worse. I am grateful to have lived long enough to have known some of the blessings of adversity. My memory goes back to the Great Depression, when we had certain values burned into our souls. One of these values was gratitude for that which we had because we had so little. The Great Depression in the United States in the early thirties was a terrible schoolmaster. We had to learn provident living in order to survive. Rather than create in us a spirit of envy or anger for what we did not have, it developed in many a spirit of gratitude for the meager, simple things with which we were blessed, like hot, homemade bread and oatmeal cereal and many other things.

——

James E. Faust, "Gratitude as a Saving Principle"

REFLECTION

When have hard economic times taught you gratitude, and helped you count your blessings?

——————— **August 30** ———————

So God created the great sea monsters and every living creature that moves, of every kind, with which the waters swarm, and every winged bird of every kind. And God saw that it was good. (Genesis 1:21)

Sam and I sat side by side on the deck as we sped along on the endless blue. Then Sam leaned forward, craning his neck to see something over the side of the boat. . . . The next thing we knew, the boat was surrounded on both sides by dolphins, literally hundreds of dolphins leaping out of the waves everywhere you looked, in arcs like rainbows, vaulting in and out of the water like aquatic clowns. It was almost too much; I hung my head and laughed. Everyone on board was crying out in joy as more and more dolphins leapt on both sides of the boat; it was like the end of the Fourth of July when they set off every last firework they have, and a new explosion follows before the last has even disappeared.

——

Anne Lamott, *Traveling Mercies*

PRAYER

Thank you for dolphins and all other creatures that leap for joy. Amen.

——— **August 31** ———

*I thank my God every time I remember you, constantly
praying with joy in every one of my prayers for all of you,
because of your sharing in the gospel from the first day
until now. (Philippians 1:3–5)*

This afternoon I wrote many postcards. While writing I experienced a deep love for all the friends I was writing to. My heart was full of gratitude and affection, and I wished I could embrace each of my friends and let them know how much they mean to me and how much I miss them. It seems that sometimes distance creates closeness, absence creates presence, loneliness creates community! I felt my whole being, body, mind, and spirit, yearning to give and receive love without condition, without fear, without reservation.

Why should I ever think or say something that is not love? Why should I ever hold a grudge, feel hatred or jealousy, act suspiciously? Why not always give and forgive, encourage and empower, give thanks and offer praise? Why not?

Henri J. M. Nouwen, *Sabbatical Journey*

REFLECTION

As we close our month on gratitude, what have you learned from this spiritual practice?

SEPTEMBER

Hospitality

Hospitality

*

204

———— **September 1** ————

The alien who resides with you shall be to you as the citizen among you; you shall love the alien as yourself, for you were aliens in the land of Egypt: I am the LORD your God.
(Leviticus 19:34)

Let all guests who arrive be received like Christ,
for He is going to say,
"I came as a guest, and you received Me" (Matt. 25:35).
And to all let due honor be shown,
especially to the domestics of the faith and to pilgrims.
As soon as a guest is announced, therefore,
let the Superior or the brethren meet him
with all charitable service.
And first of all let them pray together,
and then exchange the kiss of peace.
For the kiss of peace should not be offered
until after the prayers have been said,
on account of the devil's deceptions.

The Rule of Saint Benedict

REFLECTION

Saint Benedict encourages us to show particular honor to guests, receiving them as if they were Christ himself. As we explore the spiritual practice of hospitality this month, be thinking about this question: What would it require for you to welcome every stranger as Christ? How would your life need to change?

———— September 2 ————

*The natives showed us unusual kindness. Since it had begun
to rain and was cold, they kindled a fire and welcomed all
of us around it. (Acts 28:2)*

I n the ancient world (the one Jesus was born into), people
saw the sharing of meals as having eternal consequences. If
you ate meals with the right kind of people, paradise waited
for you. If you ate with the wrong kind of people . . . well,
you get it. Jesus challenged this organizing principle of his
culture. Understanding how the culture viewed having the
"right" dinner companions sheds a whole new light on the
old story of feeding the five thousand. People marvel at a
little bit of food feeding a whole bunch of people and miss
a whole other point. Jesus wanted them to *EAT* together. If
they did this, it would change everything, they would be
joining the revolution.

Father Daniel Homan, osb, and Lonni Collins Pratt,
Radical Hospitality

ACTION

Open your home for a meal. This can be with friends you
know well to start out, or with acquaintances you know
only a little, if you're feeling adventurous.

———— September 3 ————

*Contribute to the needs of the saints;
extend hospitality to strangers. (Romans 12:13)*

S ome people need a beautiful floral tea cup, others a sturdy
coffee mug that they can wrap their hands around. Not

long ago, I served a guest whose father had recently passed away. I had a sense that I should set the breakfast table with china we seldom use. It was decorated in sprays of violets. At the end of the meal, this particular guest told me how much the china meant to her, as her father had given her violets each year on her birthday.

In the beginning God created. And he did it in an orderly manner. First came the heavens and the earth, next the light, dry land and seas, and so forth. He didn't plunk down some vegetation, add an animal or two, toss in some fish, and say, "Oops, forgot the water!" He carried out a perfect plan that provided for and allowed each creation to flourish. His garden was beautiful. Each creature was known by name. When we create a home, and offer it to others, this is the sort of template we should follow.

⎯⎯

Sister Sharon Hunter, *The Paraclete Book of Hospitality*

REFLECTION

When has someone taken the time to carefully plan a meal or other act of welcome for you? How did that attention to detail make you feel?

⎯⎯⎯⎯ **September 4** ⎯⎯⎯⎯

Do not neglect to show hospitality to strangers, for by doing that some have entertained angels without knowing it.
(Hebrews 13:2)

A hospitality house, you learn soon enough, is sustained by a grace that's beyond you—beyond your community meetings and your lofty commitments—to see the stranger as a gift. There is, for sure, always work to be done. Yet nothing

you do guarantees that any of this will be here tomorrow. . . .
This way of living leads a person to pray. . . .

"Benedict taught us to greet every guest as if the guest were Christ," a monk says to me with exaggerated earnestness. And then, with a twinkle in his eye, he adds, "But sometimes, when the knock comes at the door, we say, 'Oh Christ, it's *you* again.'" He chuckles, and I know he knows how much I need the prayers he's teaching me.

Jonathan Wilson-Hartgrove, *Strangers at My Door*

PRAYER

Open my heart, Lord, so that I may receive strangers with gratitude and be honored by their presence—even if they aren't the easiest people to be around. Amen.

——— September 5 ———

"For I was hungry and you gave me food." *(Matthew 25:35)*

All who present themselves are to be welcomed as Christ," writes Benedict.

"When did we see you?" asked the disciples.

Perhaps "every day" is the answer. At the door and in the neighborhood and at the corner. At the breakfast table and in the back seat and on the bus. In the break room and the grocery store. Naked and lonely and sick and imprisoned and thirsty and hungry covers a lot of ground, you know.

Benedict calls us to a constant awareness that those who enter our world are all to be treated as though they were the Christ. He calls us to a posture, a way of seeing and of welcoming and of serving that is rooted in the sense of adoration of the Christ that is present in us all.

He calls for particular honor and care to be given to the poor, the sick, the needy, the guest, and the pilgrims. And who among us, who among those we know, who among those we shall meet tomorrow is not some or all or each at some time or all of the time?

———

Robert Benson, *A Good Life*

ACTION

Take five minutes today when you are in a place where you can observe people you don't know—at a café, in your pew, in line at the post office. One by one, imagine that each person you see is actually, really, truly Jesus.

——— **September 6** ———

You shall not oppress a resident alien; you know the heart of an alien, for you were aliens in the land of Egypt. (Exodus 23:9)

Many early Christian texts deliberately confuse the roles of host and guest. Particularly in stories about hospitality offered, it is sometimes hard to tell who is giving and who is receiving. For example, Palladius tells the story of Elias, a solitary ascetic who lived near a road. When a large group of visitors stopped by looking for refreshment, Elias was eager to offer hospitality but only had three loaves of bread to feed them all. Miraculously two loaves were plenty to fill all twenty guests, and the loaf that was left fed Elias for twenty-five days. Elias the host became the recipient of abundance as a result of his visitors. This reversal of roles is a common theme in early Christian stories of hospitality.

———

Amy Oden, *And You Welcomed Me*

—————— **September 7** ——————

Let each of you look not to your own interests, but to the interests of others. (Philippians 2:4)

[S]outh Korean reformer] Kim [Dae Jung] . . . counsels that every occasion offers [people] an opportunity for prayer. While riding a bus, they should pray for the safety of their fellow passengers. When crossing a street, they should pray for those at the intersection. . . . Kim's effort here is to make the neighbor visible.

Invisibility is a major detriment to the practice of hospitality in urban areas. Because we encounter dozens or hundreds of people each day, everyone becomes a stranger to us. . . . Kim feels this has to be overcome. His recommendations about prayer are the first attempt at seeing what we really see all the time.

———

Arthur Sutherland, *I Was a Stranger*

PRAYER

Show me the invisible people who cross my path today. Teach me to see them as you do, Lord. Amen.

—————— **September 8** ——————

"My lord, if I find favor with you, do not pass by your servant. Let a little water be brought, and wash your feet,

SEPTEMBER

*and rest yourselves under the tree. Let me bring a little
bread, that you may refresh yourselves, and after that
you may pass on—since you have come to your servant."
(Genesis 18:3–5)*

Hospitality

*

210

The heart of hospitality is about creating space for someone
to feel seen and heard and loved. It's about declaring your
table a safe zone, a place of warmth and nourishment. . . .

When I first began cooking and hosting, I felt more pressure to work around each possible dislike and preference—
serve this on the side, serve that three ways so everyone can
have it their way. But, really, "have it your way" is a fast-
food ad campaign, not a compelling rationale for how we
should gather around one another's tables.

So this is the dance, it seems to me: to be the kind of host
who honors the needs of the people who gather around his or
her table, and to be the kind of guest who comes to the table
to learn, not to demand.

Shauna Niequist, *Bread and Wine*

ACTION

Practice the discipline of hospitality today by being an
undemanding guest. Be teachable, grateful, and easy to
please.

———— September 9 ————

*"Love your enemies and pray for those who persecute you."
(Matthew 5:44)*

Praying for others is an act of hospitality. It involves
opening the door of our hearts and minds and admitting

people into our consciousness. We invite them to take up residence for a time and allow them to engage our feelings and thoughts. Like entertaining guests for a weekend, praying for others requires time and energy. . . .

Praying for our friends and loved ones is one thing. Offering the same kind of hospitality to our enemies is a lot to ask. Praying for the people who irk us, the people who hurt us, or the people we dislike or even hate is difficult because we do not want to think about them, let alone permit them to enter the sacred privacy of our prayers. We want to avoid our enemies, to forget that they exist. Even saying their names gives them a prestige we do not want them to have. Hospitality is out of the question.

Sybil MacBeth, *Praying in Color*

ACTION

Even if you're not an artist—and I am *so* not—you're going to draw a picture today. Call to mind someone you would consider an enemy (or at the very least someone who not only knows which buttons to push but is also in possession of your secret launch code). Draw their picture. It doesn't have to be representational. Then pray for that person's health, relationships, and peace. You may want to put the picture in a place where you will see it regularly as a reminder to pray for your enemy several times today.

——— **September 10** ———

Because there is one bread, we who are many are one body, for we all partake of the one bread. (1 Corinthians 10:17)

Common assumptions regard worship as *motivation* for hospitality or as a place we might garner some useful *information* about hospitality. But such assumptions miss the mark; they make worship a means to an end, and they locate hospitality outside of worship. . . . The alternative vision I wish to set forth sees worship itself as our participation in God's own triune life, a life we can characterize as hospitality. To sing, to pray, to pass the peace, to listen to God's word, to eat at God's table is to share, through the gift and power of the Spirit, in God's own giving and receiving.

Elizabeth Newman, *Untamed Hospitality*

REFLECTION

When has worship been hospitality for you?

——— September 11 ———

"And who is my neighbor?" (Luke 10:29)

The parable of the Good Samaritan from Luke 10:25–37 has become a cultural cliché of sorts. But when we realize that it occurs in the most serious of contexts—that is, how do we acquire eternal life?—we begin to see that the illustration Jesus gives stretches far and wide in meaning. Mercy becomes the defining factor in what qualifies someone as a "neighbor." In the ultimate judgment, "the King will reply, 'truly I tell you, whatever you did for one of the least of these brothers and sisters of mine, you did for me'" (Matt 25:40).

Carolyn Weber, *Holy Is the Day*

PRAYER

Show me the way to eternal life through love and mercy. Amen.

———— September 12 ————

Jesus said to them, "They need not go away; you give them something to eat." (Matthew 14:16)

J esus consistently chose unconventional table fellowship as the sign of God's kingdom. And so faced with a crowd of five thousand, he drives home the message he's been preaching—about the spiritual unimportance of religious and social barriers—by inviting everyone to share a meal on the spot. The point is not food. It is hands-on learning. Do this, Jesus says, and you'll taste what life in the kingdom of God is like.

Hospitality

*

213

The kingdom of heaven is not privatized. It is not about commerce, about buying what you need for yourself. It is not passive; Jesus doesn't ask his disciples to wait for a miracle, but commands them, with a brusque authority . . . "*You* give the people something to eat." Because life in the kingdom means there's more than enough for everyone.

Sara Miles, *Jesus Freak*

ACTION

"*You* give them something to eat." Today, spontaneously invite someone to share a meal—maybe even the homeless person who asks you for change.

———— September 13 ————

Be hospitable, a lover of goodness, prudent, upright, devout, and self-controlled. (Titus 1:8)

Hospitality begins with an invitation. A host offers to share his home, to welcome another, to extend "self." A good hostess provides shelter, food, and companionship and treats the guest as one worthy of attention and care. The host needs an attitude of poverty. . . . When the host is filled with ideas, prejudices, and worries, there is no room for the guest to relax, unwind, and be herself. The good hostess is a person who is empty enough (thus "poor" enough) to receive a guest.

———

Doris Donnelly, *Spiritual Fitness*

REFLECTION

Having what Donnelly describes as an "attitude of poverty" marks the difference between true hospitality, which is about meeting the needs of a guest, from entertaining, which is about making a good impression. When have you practiced hospitality? When have you entertained?

———— **September 14** ————

'This is my commandment, that you love one another as I have loved you." (John 15:12)

If we're really honest with ourselves, there are probably times when we think, "What possible use can I be in this world? What need is there for somebody like me to fill?" That's one of the deeper mysteries. Then God's grace comes to us in the form of another person who tells us we have been of help, and what a blessing that is.

I remember one of my seminary professors saying people who were able to appreciate others—who looked for what was good and healthy and kind—were about as close as you could get to God—to the eternal good. And those people who were always looking for what was *bad* about themselves and others were really on the side of evil. "That's what the evil wants," he would say. "Evil wants us to feel so terrible about who we are and who we know, that we'll look with condemning eyes on anybody who happens to be with us at the moment." I encourage you to look for the good where you are and embrace it.

Mr. Rogers, quoted in Jeremy Langford, *Seeds of Faith*

ACTION

Be on the side of good today by looking for what is positive about yourself. What are your good qualities, and how have those qualities made others feel welcomed?

——— **September 15** ———

"But you are not to be called rabbi, for you have one teacher, and you are all brothers." (Matthew 23:8)

"All men are brothers." How often we hear this refrain, the rallying call that strikes a response in every human heart. These are the words of Christ, "Call no man master, for ye are all brothers." It is a revolutionary call which has even been put to music. The last movement of Beethoven's Ninth Symphony has that great refrain—"All men are brothers." Going to the people is the purest and best act in Christian tradition and revolutionary tradition and is the beginning of world brotherhood.

Never to be severed from the people, to set out always from the point of view of serving the people, not serving the interests of a small group or oneself. . . . It is almost another way of saying that we must and will find Christ in each and every man, when we look on them as brothers.

Dorothy Day, *The Long Loneliness*

Hospitality

PRAYER

All of your people are my brothers and sisters, Lord. Help me today to remember it. Amen.

*

——— **September 16** ———

And Jesus said to him, "Foxes have holes, and birds of the air have nests; but the Son of Man has nowhere to lay his head." (Matthew 8:20)

Throughout the Gospels, Jesus enters into the lives of people who are on the margins of society, struggling with hunger, shame, disease, and homelessness. He does this out of deep compassion for them, but also because he shares their experience of being a homeless stranger, with no place to lay his head (Matt. 8:20). His own experience of homelessness, hunger, thirst, and nakedness shapes his empathy for the distressed of this world and motivates him to heal and to save those who are in the greatest need. In the Gospel of Matthew, when Jesus says that anyone who feeds the hungry and welcomes strangers is really feeding and welcoming him, he is not exaggerating; he knows this deprivation firsthand (Matt. 25:34–35).

Henry G. Brinton, *The Welcoming Congregation*

ACTION

Volunteer at a homeless shelter, soup kitchen, or food bank this week. Remember to see Christ in everyone you serve.

——— **September 17** ———

You do well if you really fulfill the royal law according to the scripture, "You shall love your neighbor as yourself." But if you show partiality, you commit sin and are convicted by the law as transgressors. (James 2:8–9)

The truth is that we are too comfortable with our prejudices. They become so deeply ingrained that we're scarcely aware of them. We can go on happily for a lifetime, barely aware of the thoughts, needs, and talents of others who look, sound, and behave differently from us. By his own example, Jesus shows us how to overcome the barriers that separate us from other people, and the amazing ways our lives can be enriched when we dare to take the first step toward an "unattractive" person.

———

Jimmy Carter, *Sources of Strength*

REFLECTION

What prejudices are you aware of harboring? How do they separate you from others?

———— **September 18** ————

*Pray in the Spirit at all times in every prayer and
supplication. To that end keep alert and always persevere
in supplication for all the saints. (Ephesians 6:18)*

Hospitality

There have been days that I have prayed for people in the
news, a face from the newspaper, a person on Facebook,
or from the profile of a person on Twitter. In these days of
social media and massive social interaction through the
Internet, there's no end to the number of people that I can
touch in a positive way without ever stepping foot outside
my door. The beautiful thing is it still counts. . . . There are
really no restrictions and no end to the possibilities.

River Jordan, Praying for Strangers

ACTION
Actively pray for five people whose stories you encounter
in the media today. (And no, it doesn't count if you pray
for cats on Buzzfeed.com.)

———— **September 19** ————

*Jesus said to them, "I am the bread of life. Whoever comes
to me will never be hungry, and whoever believes in me will
never be thirsty." (John 6:35)*

Baking invites and creates community. Although most of
us could eat an entire loaf of bread straight from the oven
by ourselves, most often bakers are eager to share. The very
word "companion" comes from the Latin *cum pane*: "with
bread." A companion is someone with whom we share our
bread. The word "company" comes from the same root; we

bake a special loaf when company is coming. I'm sometimes distressed when someone says, "I used to bake bread all the time when my children were younger, but now that it's just me and my husband. . . ." I always say, "God bless you, but don't you have any neighbors?"

Father Dominic Garramone, *Bake and Be Blessed*

REFLECTION
How does baking invite and create community?

─────── **September 20** ───────

No one shall be able to stand against you all the days of your life. As I was with Moses, so I will be with you; I will not fail you or forsake you. (Joshua 1:5)

The Christian way of life does not take away our loneliness; it protects and cherishes it as a precious gift. Sometimes it seems as if we do everything possible to avoid the painful confrontation with our basic human loneliness, and allow ourselves to be trapped by false gods promising immediate satisfaction and quick relief. But perhaps the painful awareness of loneliness is an invitation to transcend our limitations and look beyond the boundaries of our existence. The awareness of loneliness might be a gift we must protect and guard, because our loneliness reveals to us an inner emptiness that can be destructive when misunderstood, but filled with promise for him who can tolerate its sweet pain.

Henri J. M. Nouwen, *The Wounded Healer*

REFLECTION
Thank you for your presence in my loneliness, and for the knowledge that loneliness can be a gift. Amen.

SEPTEMBER

Hospitality

*

220

———— **September 21** ————

"The kingdom of heaven may be compared to a king who gave a wedding banquet for his son. He sent his slaves to call those who had been invited to the wedding banquet, but they would not come." (Matthew 22:2–3)

Most of us are familiar with the parable of the wedding banquet told in Matthew 22:1–14. A king invites guests to a great feast. But when the time comes, most of the guests who sent in positive RSVPs find themselves too busy with business meetings or piano recitals or the big game on TV to show up. Jesus is making the point that God has prepared a feast for each of us—eternal life—yet many of us get too consumed with the busyness of existence to accept his grace-filled invitation.

Nancy Sleeth, *Almost Amish*

REFLECTION

God has prepared a great banquet for you. Are you too busy with other things to accept divine hospitality?

———— **September 22** ————

They devoted themselves to the apostles' teaching and fellowship, to the breaking of bread and the prayers.
(Acts 2:42)

As I cover the lasagnas and carry them to another house where our community potluck is to begin, I know there are easier, more efficient ways to get the calories I need at dinner time. . . . But we've gone to the trouble to make this particular dinner for roughly the same reason we make an effort to eat with these particular people—because it seems more in keeping with the sort of community we are made for, even if it costs more time and money, even if it forces us to deal with people we'd sometimes rather avoid. One of the things we learn to name by eating together is that we are creatures, inextricably connected in a membership called creation. To deny that connection in practice is to reject the gift of life and to march, however slowly and blindly, toward our collective death.

Jonathan Wilson-Hartgrove, *The Awakening of Hope*

ACTION

Have a potluck! Maybe you can invite the neighbors that you haven't yet met.

———— September 23 ————

For the whole law is summed up in a single commandment, "You shall love your neighbor as yourself." (Galatians 5:14)

Hospitable places are comfortable and lived in; they are settings in which people are flourishing. Although not necessarily beautifully maintained or decorated, they are evidently cared for. . . . Such places are safe and stable, offering people a setting where "they can rest for awhile to collect themselves." When sanctuary and a slower pace are combined, there is a sense of peace.

In such places life is celebrated, yet the environment also has room for brokenness and deep disappointments. Such places make faith and a hospitable way of life seem natural, not forced. Hospitable settings are often enhanced by the simple beauty of creation, where body, soul, and spirit are fed by attention to small details such as attractively prepared and good-tasting food, or flowers from a nearby garden. Attention to these details expresses an appreciation for life which has more to do with taking time than with having money.

Christine Pohl, *Making Room*

REFLECTION

Is your home a stable place that exudes a sense of peace? Is it a safe environment where broken people don't have to put up a false show?

──────── **September 24** ────────

Bear one another's burdens, and in this way you will fulfill the law of Christ. (Galatians 6:2)

Sometimes *communitas* happens where people come together not voluntarily but because they are pulled together by events out of their control. Think of the experience of being in something like a blizzard or an earthquake or a hurricane. During a blizzard that brought four-foot drifts of snow up to my door, I got to know neighbors I had never even spoken with before, and some of us hiked to the store to get supplies for others less able to make the walk. I have also lived in the path of more than one hurricane over the years. What I remember more than all the hours of cleanup and repair is the time we had a neighborhood cookout after about a week without water or electricity. Take away a few of our basic human comforts, and we are invited to shed some of the personal veneer as well.

Sarah York, *Pilgrim Heart*

REFLECTION

When has a disaster or unusual circumstance helped forge a bond between you and your neighbors?

——— **September 25** ———

Greet one another with a holy kiss. All the churches of Christ greet you. (Romans 16:16)

As one arrives at a gathering—in the parking lot, on the sidewalk—others are arriving too, and how one treats them is, it turns out, a highly significant communal practice. . . . Interestingly, it was precisely this so-called detail—of how we welcome one another when we gather—that was of great concern to the first apostles (1 Corinthians 11; James 2). For example, Paul's call to "greet one another with a holy kiss" (repeated four times in his epistles) was more significant than it appears. Class-conscious Roman society required that people only exchange the kiss with peers, but the early churches brought together Jew and Gentile, men and women, slave and free, rich and poor. That people transgressed (or transcended) normal social convention was essential to the early church in maintaining its higher allegiance to the way of Jesus instead of the way of Rome.

Brian D. McLaren, *Finding Our Way Again*

ACTION

Be bold. Give someone a hug or kiss today who would not normally expect one from you. However, I don't recommend trying this spiritual practice on a total stranger.

SEPTEMBER

Hospitality

*

224

———— **September 26** ————

*We have gifts that differ according to the grace given to us:
prophecy, in proportion to faith; ministry, in ministering;
the teacher, in teaching; the exhorter, in exhortation;
the giver, in generosity; the leader, in diligence; the
compassionate, in cheerfulness. (Romans 12:6–8)*

Embracing a faith community is more than "attending church." Church "services" are not about being "serviced by" the church. Some see church attendance as a form of entertainment—some place they go, some actions they observe, some people they watch, followed by some food at a restaurant, and then home they go. Embracing a faith community means becoming a community *participant*, and that means accepting something very important and noticeable: being the person to the community that we are meant to be. The apostle Paul calls this "spiritual gifts" in several of his letters, but whatever we want to call it we are to participate by performing what we have been gifted to do.

Scot McKnight, *Embracing Grace*

PRAYER

Lord, show me the ways I can use whatever gifts you have given me to build up your church and welcome others. Amen.

———— **September 27** ————

*But while he was still far off, his father saw him and was
filled with compassion; he ran and put his arms around him
and kissed him. (Luke 15:20)*

My neighbor and I fell to talking about . . . the young adult child of someone we know. This young man has had some struggles lately and has come home to regroup. He has made some mistakes, I understand, some of which he does not even want to talk about. Parents are not always sure what to do or say when their child, who is now a young adult, turns up at their door.

My neighbor said she thought the answer was easy. "You do the only thing you can do," she said. "Stand at the door with your arms open. Ask as few questions as is possible. Make no judgments. Say 'hello, we are so glad to see you.'"

I am reasonably certain she has never read Saint Benedict's Rule. But she knows what the saint knew. She knows what the Good Shepherd knows, and the father of the prodigal son, for that matter: "Always let mercy triumph over judgment."

Always be ready to leave the ninety and the nine. Always be ready to run down the road to greet the one who was lost.

Robert Benson, *A Good Neighbor*

REFLECTION

Who do you know who needs an open-arm reception without judgment?

——— September 28 ———

And let us consider how to provoke one another to love and good deeds, not neglecting to meet together, as is the habit of some, but encouraging one another.
(Hebrews 10:24–25)

In today's Facebook world, "friend" has become a verb. So you friend someone by clicking on a little request button online . . . and as a result you can end up with thousands of friends, most of whom you would not recognize if they actually came to your home and rang your doorbell.

I do like the idea of "friending," though. It *should* be a verb, because friendship requires action. It doesn't happen passively, particularly in today's busy world. Just as we have to make an intentional choice to sit down and spend time with Jesus in order to know Him, we also have to purposefully sit down with friends. In order to truly know others and be known by them, we have to invest time. It won't happen automatically or on the run.

Ellen Vaughn, *Come, Sit, Stay*

PRAYER
Lord, show me which friends need my encouragement today.

—————— **September 29** ——————

*Those who withhold kindness from a friend
forsake the fear of the Almighty. (Job 6:14)*

When I think of *friendship* as a verb, when I think of actions that shape friendship, what comes to mind first and foremost is the willingness to take initiative. Over and over.

Initiative means making some kind of response after a friend has surgery. Perhaps a card, a meal, a gift, a phone call or a visit. Initiative means creating opportunities to listen when a friend is going through a crisis—suggesting a conversation over coffee, making time for a phone call or sending an email with specific questions about the situation. Initiative means checking in with friends when you haven't heard from them for a while. Initiative means remembering to pray for a friend's needs.

Lynne Baab, *Friending*

ACTION

Send a note to an old friend today, just to check in. (A note written on paper is lovely, but an e-mail is fine too.) Take the initiative to stay in touch.

——— September 30 ———

Be hospitable to one another without complaining.
(1 Peter 4:9)

Everyone is so busy these days. Extending hospitality is often difficult. We're prevented from getting our work done. Or we have to be somewhere else very soon. We can spare only a few minutes of our time. To tell the truth, Christ often presents himself as an inconvenience in our lives. This is when monastics and oblates remind themselves that Benedict in chapter 53, "The Reception of Guests," tells us to greet everyone "with the courtesy of love."

. . . Benedict says we are to see Christ in our guests. We always hope they can see him in us.

Benet Tvedten, OSB,
How to Be a Monastic and Not Leave Your Day Job

REFLECTION

As we conclude our focus on hospitality, what have you learned from this practice?

OCTOBER

Compassionate
Eating
and
Creation
Care

OCTOBER

Compassionate
Eating
and
Creation
Care

*

230

——— **October 1** ———

*For the fate of humans and the fate of animals is the same;
as one dies, so dies the other. They all have the same
breath, and humans have no advantage over the animals;
for all is vanity. (Ecclesiastes 3:19)*

Spiritual readings of animals start with one important understanding: animals are our teachers. . . . In countless stories, myths, and dreams, animals are wise elders, imparting wisdom about the world and hinting at the great mysteries of life.

Some people minimize the value of entering into relationships with animals, regarding them as inferior beings put on Earth to serve humans as food, tools, entertainment, and transportation. But to be spiritually literate means to recognize that animals are much more than what humans might do with them. The word "animal" actually comes from the Latin *animalis*—having a soul—and is closely linked to the noun *animus* or breath.

Frederic and Mary Ann Brussat, *Spiritual Literacy*

REFLECTION

During October, we'll be thinking about creation care, mindful eating, and the worth of animals. Do you believe that animals have souls? If so, does that change how you treat them?

——— **October 2** ———

*Beloved, I pray that all may go well with you and that you
may be in good health, just as it is well with your soul.
(3 John 2)*

One day a young woman came into the library to ask me for prayer for the healing of terrible pain in the bones of her jaw. . . . Doc quietly got out from under my desk, sat in front of Naomi, raised her paw, and put it gently on Naomi's knee and kept it there. . . . I think we slipped out of time. I don't know how long Doc sat there before she finally dropped her paw and slid back under my desk.

There was no question in either Naomi's or my mind who had been chosen as the instrument of healing that afternoon. . . . What I felt was an amazed sense of gratitude for God's love, and a humble joy that in witnessing it I had been part of God's healing power.

OCTOBER

Compassionate
Eating
and
Creation
Care

*

231

———

Madeleine L'Engle, *Bright Evening Star*

REFLECTION

Has an animal ever been an instrument of healing in your life?

——— **October 3** ———

The earth is the LORD's and all that is in it,
the world, and those who live in it. (Psalm 24:1)

The world is also discovering we were made for interdependence not just with human beings; we are finding out that we depend on what used to be called inanimate nature. When Africans said, "Oh, don't treat that tree like that, it feels pain," others used to say, "Ah, they're prescientific, they're primitive." It is wonderful now how we are beginning to discover that it is true—that the tree does hurt, and if you hurt the tree, in an extraordinary way you hurt yourself.

———

Desmond Tutu, *God Has a Dream*

Compassionate
Eating
and
Creation
Care

*

232

PRAYER

Help me to perceive the interconnectedness of all life, for everything is your creation. Amen.

———— **October 4** ————

FEAST DAY OF SAINT FRANCIS OF ASSISI

Who teaches us more than the animals of the earth, and makes us wiser than the birds of the air? (Job 35:11)

When I try to visualize the final paradise in which animals and humans live together in peace and harmony, I often think of animal blessings that I have taken part in. This is particularly true on the Feast Day of St. Francis, when churches all over the world hold "Blessing of the Animals" services, in which creatures are invited into the sanctuary and offered special blessings as members of God's family. An ideal alternative setting for such a ceremony is a park or a church courtyard with lots of trees and flowers in it and perhaps a fountain or a pool of water.

Ironically, when people bring their pets from different parts of town, there can be disharmony and trouble. Dogs start barking at cats and people struggle to keep animals from fighting, growling, and hissing. But often in my experience, once the blessings begin, a spirit of harmony and peace prevails among pets and people.

Jack Wintz, OFM, *I Will See You in Heaven*

ACTION

Seek out a Blessing of the Animals service this week, and attend it with an animal in tow. You may have to borrow someone's pet for an hour.

October 5

Then shall the trees of the forest sing for joy
before the LORD. (1 Chronicles 16:33)

In a word, we talk about a man who cannot see the wood for the trees. St. Francis was a man who did not want to see the wood for the trees. He wanted to see each tree as a separate and almost a sacred thing, being a child of God and therefore a brother or sister of man. But he did not want to stand against a piece of stage scenery used merely as a background, and inscribed in a general fashion: "Scene; a wood." . . . This is the quality in which, as a poet, he is the very opposite of a pantheist. He did not call nature his mother; he called a particular donkey his brother or a particular sparrow his sister. If he had called a pelican his aunt or an elephant his uncle, as he might possibly have done, he would still have meant that they were particular creatures assigned by their Creator to particular places; not mere expressions of the evolutionary energy of things. That is where his mysticism is so close to the common sense of the child.

G. K. Chesterton, *St. Francis of Assisi*

PRAYER

All praise by yours, my Lord, through Sister Earth, our mother, who feeds us in her sovereignty and produces various fruits and colored flowers and herbs.

—Saint Francis, "The Canticle of the Creatures"

Compassionate
Eating
and
Creation
Care

*

233

——— **October 6** ———

Is the hyena greedy for my heritage at my command?
Are the birds of prey all around her? (Jeremiah 12:9)

Compassionate
Eating
and
Creation
Care

*

234

The animal kingdom holds for us such an infinite variety of delights: beauty, majesty, delicacy, comedy, gaiety, strength, speed, song, grace, grandeur. What a God, to think of such forms to create, such ways of life to set in motion!

But mosquitoes seem unnecessary; buzzards are, to the merely human eye, unattractive; the ferocity of the wolverine lacks the burning-brightness of the tiger. It's the hyena, though, that gives me pause. A more depraved looking animal cannot be imagined. The very sight of him is really nauseating.

But since he is an animal, he cannot be depraved. It is a fault of vision in me that sees that sneaky, ungainly body, those cold intrusive eyes, those hideous, loose jaws, as evil.

God didn't simply install the hyena as you would plumbing, to take care of a sanitation problem. He *made* him. Given what I say I believe of the nature of God, I am absolutely required to believe that he made the hyena with pleasure, looked upon him with love, and saw that he was good. God *enjoys* the hyena, just as if he were a meadowlark.

Fae Malania, *The Quantity of a Hazelnut*

REFLECTION

Is there a particular animal or insect that makes you hesitate to say that *all* creation is good? (Insert tarantula here.) Do you think God enjoys that creature even if you do not?

They are like trees
planted by streams of water,
which yield their fruit in its season,
and their leaves do not wither.
In all that they do, they prosper. (Psalm 1:3)

OCTOBER

Compassionate
Eating
and
Creation
Care

*

235

The tree that I sit by is not so ancient; however, she is one of my teachers. She grows beside a stream, and I cross a little bridge and walk down an embankment to get to her. The stream has washed away some of the soil around the tree, exposing the top of her wonderfully marbled roots. I sit on these roots with my questions, my longings, and my prayers, and I begin to feel grounded and rooted myself. I remember who I am, where I have come from, and where I'll return to. This tree contains the great cycle of the seasons in her being, and I witness the passage of time through her branches. My life is put into a much larger perspective, and I hear the invitation to align myself with the energy that animates this tree and all of this incredible creation.

As I sit under this tree, it makes perfect sense to me that the first place where Jesus was led after the Spirit came upon him in the Jordan was the wilderness.

Denise Roy, *My Monastery Is a Minivan*

ACTION

Spend a few minutes sitting under a tree today. If you're lucky enough to live in a place where the leaves are changing color right now, so much the better. Marvel at the trees as one of God's best creations.

Compassionate
Eating
and
Creation
Care

*

236

—— **October 8** ——

Yonder is the sea, great and wide,
creeping things innumerable are there,
living things both small and great.
There go the ships,
and Leviathan that you formed to sport in it.
(Psalm 104:25–26)

Several winters ago my wife and I and our then twenty-year-old daughter, Sharmy, went to that great tourist extravaganza near Orlando, Florida, called Sea World. . . .

What with the dazzle of sky and sun, the beautiful young people on the platform, the soft southern air, and the crowds all around us watching the performance matched only by what seemed the delight of the performing whales, it was as if the whole creation—men and women and beasts and sun and water and earth and sky and, for all I know, God himself—was caught up in one great, jubilant dance of un-imaginable beauty. And then, right in the midst of it, I was astonished to find that my eyes were filled with tears.

Frederick Buechner, *The Longing for Home*

PRAYER

Holy God, the wonder of your creation moves me deeply.
Thank you for the beauty and variety of the animals you
have made. Amen.

—— **October 9** ——

The wolf shall live with the lamb,
the leopard shall lie down with the kid. (Isaiah 11:6)

In a northern California community a large prison and the local Humane Society match prisoners with dogs who aren't adoptable for health or sociability reasons. Two prisoners are assigned to one dog, and live with it and provide 24/7 care, whether that be nursing care or just practice in being more sociable. The dogs become adoptable and easier to match with a permanent family or individual. The prison's warden, and even the prisoners themselves, affirm that the need to pay attention to the dogs' needs encourages the practice of compassion, and draws prisoners away from focusing exclusively on themselves—something that happens easily in prison environments. . . .

What is true for prisoners is true for the rest of us as well. Animals draw us out of ourselves, and away from our own agendas and our self-absorption.

OCTOBER

Compassionate
Eating
and
Creation
Care

*

237

Debra Farrington, *All God's Creatures*

REFLECTION

Are you aware of any animals in need—or of any people in need of animals?

———— **October 10** ————

"All things are lawful for me," but not all things are beneficial. (1 Corinthians 6:12)

Some choices that would make a difference in my own life and would make me more mindful that food is God's gift to us are ones like these: fasting from fast food. Eating less meat. Paying attention to my body's hunger and then eating no more than I need to satisfy it. Taking care never to let

OCTOBER

Compassionate
Eating
and
Creation
Care

*

238

food go to waste (a perennial problem in my refrigerator). Really trying to eat those five fruits and vegetables every day that our bodies need to thrive. Never eating without giving thanks. Even a few such choices, embraced with consciousness, might teach us . . . that in the midst of the ordinary activities of preparing and eating food we might touch something holy and find our lives changed. And our bodies might become for us not only a sign of our mortality and vulnerability but also the place where we meet God.

Stephanie Paulsell, *Honoring the Body*

ACTION

Of the many options that Paulsell lists above, choose one to focus on for the next three days. It may be reducing meat, eating less food overall, or being sure to thank God for each meal. Just select one thing and try to stick to it for three days.

———— October 11 ————

The righteous know the needs of their animals,
but the mercy of the wicked is cruel. (Proverbs 12:10)

Love all of God's creation, love the whole, and love each grain of sand. Love every leaf, every ray of God's light. Love animals, love plants, love every kind of thing. If you love every kind of thing, then everywhere God's mystery will reveal itself to you. Once this has been revealed to you, you will begin to understand it ever more deeply with each passing day. And finally you will be able to love the whole world with an all-encompassing universal love. Love animals. God gave them the beginnings of thought and a sense of untroubled joy. Do not disturb this, do not torment them, do not take away their joy, do not oppose God's intent. Man, set not thyself up above the animals.

——

Fyodor Dostoevsky, *The Brothers Karamazov*

REFLECTION

What could you do in your life to obey the injunction not to torment animals or take away their joy?

Compassionate
Eating
and
Creation
Care

*

239

——— **October 12** ———

Stop and consider the wondrous works of God.
(Job 37:14)

Most High, all-powerful, good Lord,
Yours are the praises, the glory, and the honor, and all blessing,
To You alone, Most High, do they belong,
and no human is worthy to mention Your name.
Praised be You, my Lord, with all Your creatures,
especially Sir Brother Sun,
Who is the day and through whom You give us light.
And he is beautiful and radiant with great splendor;
and bears a likeness of You, Most High One.
Praised be You, my Lord, through Sister Moon and the stars,
in heaven You formed them clear and precious and beautiful.

——

St. Francis of Assisi, "The Canticle of the Creatures"

ACTION

Pray the Canticle selection above out loud, preferably when you are outdoors in nature.

Compassionate
Eating
and
Creation
Care

*

240

———— **October 13** ————

Can anyone understand the spreading of the clouds,
the thunderings of his pavilion?
See, he scatters his lightning around him
and covers the roots of the sea. (Job 36:29–30)

Reading the Canticle as a poem of St. Francis's soul, rather than a poem describing nature, reveals that St. Francis did not simply view nature from a comfortable distance. Rather, he lived in intimate communion with the natural world in all *its* moods and seasons. Nature was the book where he read God's providence and presence, the metaphor of his own soul in *its* moods and seasons. It is not surprising, then, that when he sang the song that summarized his whole life, the images that rose into his consciousness were images of the natural world.

By the time he sang "The Canticle of the Creatures," St. Francis had allowed the Creator to heal all divisions within him; and he sang of the unity and harmony of all creation. His eyes were incarnational, wholistic; his heart was one with everything that existed.

———

Murray Bodo, OFM, *Saint Francis of Assisi: Poetry as Prayer*

PRAYER

I will sing the goodness of the natural world, and glorify you, O God. Amen.

———— **October 14** ————

All the birds of the air made their nests in its boughs.
(Ezekiel 31:6)

The connection between Francis of Assisi and animals is the single fact about him that most people know. We have tales of his encounters with animals, fish, invertebrates, and plants. In all of these ways, Franciscans emphasized that creation includes more than humankind. Just as they redefined what it means to be family, they further widened the fraternity to link humans and creatures in the same relationship to God.

OCTOBER

Compassionate
Eating
and
Creation
Care

*

241

On one warm afternoon, Francis wandered outside of Assisi, questioning his motives for ministry, asking God if perhaps everything he had done up until that point had been for the wrong reasons. He wondered if he should have simply gotten married and raised a family as his father wanted him to do. Francis was always the most critical of himself, but it was on just such an afternoon that Francis first met the birds and spoke to them as if to equals. That day marks the beginning of the era when we began to understand ourselves as intrinsically connected to all creation.

Jon M. Sweeney, *Francis and Clare*

ACTION

Talk to a bird. Out loud. Thank the bird for being beautiful, for singing to you each morning, for eating pesky insects . . . whatever makes you grateful for birds. Tell the bird that it is part of God's glorious creation! (Then go home and try not to eat chicken, turkey, or other poultry today, for that duck could be somebody's mother.)

——— October 15 ———

I am the vine, you are the branches. Those who abide in me and I in them bear much fruit, because apart from me you can do nothing. (John 15:5)

OCTOBER

Compassionate
Eating
and
Creation
Care

*

242

The gap seemed suddenly to close between matter and spirit, between soil and soul, in these vineyards caressed daily and predictably by the California sun. In the dry, hot air the grapes ripened. They needed the intensity of the climate and its unwavering steadiness to fulfill the grapiness they were destined to become. Dryness evoked their ripening. . . .

As I handled the purple clusters on the vine, I felt a ripening in me, one that could perhaps only happen in the intensity of this pilgrimage. Is this how God reveals himself? I paid closer attention to the natural order to see what nature exposed about spirit and divinity; we were all from the same stock, the same vine, grafted perhaps onto the main vine but branching out in our own unique ways.

Dennis Patrick Slattery, *Grace in the Desert*

REFLECTION

Have you experienced moments in nature when the division between yourself and other parts of God's creation seemed to collapse? When you felt connected to all things?

——— October 16 ———

And just as he was coming up out of the water, he saw the heavens torn apart and the Spirit descending like a dove on him. And a voice came from heaven, "You are my Son, the Beloved; with you I am well pleased." (Mark 1:10–11)

Pigeons want to be close to us. They are where we are—in some of the worst places we have made (our neglected projects and abandoned buildings) and some of the best (art museums, parks, Rome's piazzas). They won't leave us alone.

Yet there's hardly a bird that people are more likely to want to shoot and exterminate. People are very often not fond of pigeons. They call them rats with wings. They are considered pests who "infest" urban areas. Cities have tried countless ways of exterminating them, usually unsuccessfully. What if the Spirit of God descends like a pigeon, somehow—always underfoot, routinely ignored, often disdained?

Debbie Blue, *Consider the Birds*

REFLECTION

Blue points out that the pigeon and the dove are actually the same bird. While we've romanticized and spiritualized the dove, we have done our best to slaughter the pigeon. With that in mind, what would it mean for you if the Holy Spirit descended in the Gospels not in the form of a holy dove, but a reviled pigeon?

OCTOBER

Compassionate
Eating
and
Creation
Care

*

243

--- **October 17** ---

But ask the animals, and they will teach you;
the birds of the air, and they will tell you. (Job 12:7)

Everything [animals] are is in every move they make. When a dachshund takes a shine to you, it is not likely to be because he has thought it over ahead of time. Or in spite of certain reservations. Or in expectation of certain benefits. It seems to be just because it feels to him like a good idea at the time. Such as he is, he gives himself to you hook, line, and sinker, the bad breath no less than the frenzied tail and the front paws climbing in the air. Needless to say the whole picture can change in a flash if you try to make off with his

OCTOBER

Compassionate
Eating
and
Creation
Care

*

244

dinner, but for the moment his entire being is an act of love bordering on the beatific.

_____

Frederick Buechner, *Whistling in the Dark*

PRAYER

Thank you for the spontaneous and unconditional joy of animals. Amen.

———— October 18 ————

God said, "See, I have given you every plant yielding seed that is upon the face of all the earth, and every tree with seed in its fruit; you shall have them for food. And to every beast of the earth, and to every bird of the air, and to everything that creeps on the earth, everything that has the breath of life, I have given every green plant for food." And it was so. (Genesis 1:29–30)

In the book of Genesis, prior to the fall there existed a vegetarian world for both humans and animals. . . . Humans ate grain and fruit, and animals ate grass. This is what a world is like without sin, a world not yet marred by human rebellion, a world in which humans are at peace with God, with animals, and with the world of nature. Here there is no killing, no eating of flesh, no infliction of pain and suffering on any of God's creatures. Here were realized God's perfect intentions for humans and animals.

_____

Robert N. Wennberg, *God, Humans, and Animals*

REFLECTION

Do you agree with this author that human beings should be vegetarians since the Bible suggests we were vegetarians before the Fall?

October 19

As for me, I am establishing my covenant with you and your descendants after you, and with every living creature that is with you, the birds, the domestic animals, and every animal of the earth with you, as many as came out of the ark.
(Genesis 9:8–10)

OCTOBER

Compassionate
Eating
and
Creation
Care

*

245

Though I am by no means a vegetarian, I dislike the thought that some animal has been made miserable in order to feed me. If I am going to eat meat, I want it to be from an animal that has lived a pleasant, uncrowded life outdoors, on bountiful pasture, with good water nearby and trees for shade. And I am getting almost as fussy about food plants. I like to eat vegetables and fruits that I know have lived happily and healthily in good soil.

Wendell Berry, "The Pleasures of Eating"

ACTION

Strive to make sure that any animal you may eat today was humanely treated and not raised on a factory farm.

October 20

Their confidence is gossamer,
a spider's house their trust. (Job 8:14)

We can learn a lesson from the little spider. Watch a spider as she patiently rebuilds her web each time it is broken or removed. Seldom will she move its location but chooses to rebuild it with patience. She reweaves broken strands each time they are broken. She waits, in patience, for dinner to come into her white cosmos of tiny threads. . . .

OCTOBER

Compassionate
Eating
and
Creation
Care

*

246

Like the spider, we must return again and again to rebuild our webs by bringing together the threads of our lives and uniting them to the divine center within. Without such work, our lives become disconnected, unpeaceful and broken. Perhaps the next time we see a spider's web, we can see it as a spiritual classroom and not simply something to be swept away.

Edward Hays, *Pray All Ways*

REFLECTION

In what way is a spider's web a "spiritual classroom"?

——— **October 21** ———

Run, say to that young man: Jerusalem shall be inhabited like villages without walls, because of the multitude of people and animals in it. (Zechariah 2:4)

When a child tells us her dog has died and asks if her dog will go to heaven, we are usually quick to respond with a yes, and then we hope the conversation ends right there. But then the child might ask us if all dogs go to heaven, and that should stop and make us think very hard about what we think heaven is. If heaven is the place where God will redeem and restore all that God values, then is it really so childish to think about animals being there? If God is omnipotent and God's love knows no limits, is it really so innocent to think about God loving animals enough to make them a part of heaven?

Stephen Webb, *Good Eating*

REFLECTION

Are there beloved pets or animals that you hope will be in heaven with you?

By the streams the birds of the air have their habitation;
they sing among the branches. (Psalm 104:12)

O f all the creatures that I can see in this landscape, the geese best represent the communion of saints. They depend on one another. The lead goose does the most work, but when it is tired, it falls back and another takes its place. To be able to rely on others is a deep trust that does not come easily.

The geese fly in the wake of one another's wings. They literally get a lift from one another. I want to be with others this way. Geese tell me that it is, indeed, possible to fly with equals.

Compassionate
Eating
and
Creation
Care

*

247

Gunilla Norris, *Journeying in Place*

PRAYER

Lord, teach me the trust that comes naturally to geese and other creatures. Amen.

And God said, "Let the earth bring forth living creatures of
every kind: cattle and creeping things and wild animals of
the earth of every kind." And it was so. God made the wild
animals of the earth of every kind, and the cattle of every
kind, and everything that creeps upon the ground of every
kind. And God saw that it was good. (Genesis 1:24–25)

T he first chapter of Genesis says that on the fifth day of creation God made all the life of the sea and of the air, and on the sixth day He made all the life on the land. . . .

OCTOBER

Compassionate
Eating
and
Creation
Care

*

248

As a Christian who loves being in nature, I find these to be important words. On the sixth day God goes on to create humans—but even before He does, He has already pronounced the living world as pleasing *to Him.* It's His, and He's glad He made it.

Scott Savage, *A Plain Life*

PRAYER

Your creation is good, Lord. Holy is your name! Amen.

October 24

The hearing ear and the seeing eye—
the Lord has made them both. (Proverbs 20:12)

St. Augustine reminds us that something as simple as a seed sprouting reveals the awesome power of God, because God causes the seed to evolve from "secret and invisible folds" into more "visible forms of beauty"—a "work of such wonder and grandeur as to astound the mind that seriously considers it, and to evoke praise of the Creator."

The existence, wonder, and worthiness of God are broadcast daily for all to see if we will simply step outside and open our minds and hearts to the truth.

Gary Thomas, *Sacred Pathways*

ACTION

Identify at least one dormant plant in your neighborhood that will one day rebound with life—perhaps a bulb you've placed in the ground, waiting for spring, or a perennial that dies back every year only to burst forth again after winter. Pray for that plant's growth.

October 25

A glad heart makes a cheerful countenance,
but by sorrow of heart the spirit is broken. (Proverbs 15:13)

Chimpanzees engage life fully, every moment. They wear their emotions for all to see, or hear. . . . The quality of their friendships and family relationships to a large extent determines the quality of their lives. Watching the social vignettes of chimpanzees through the years has taught me to recognize my own pretenses. We are such similar apes. But they bring a primal pureness and immediacy to their expressions of intimacy, which I have come to cherish in my friendships with them. From knowing chimpanzees I have learned to live more honestly and vulnerably.

Compassionate
Eating
and
Creation
Care

*

249

Sheri Speede, *Kindred Beings*

REFLECTION
When has an animal taught you how to express emotion?

October 26

Can you draw out Leviathan with a fishhook,
or press down its tongue with a cord?
Can you put a rope in its nose,
or pierce its jaw with a hook?
Will it make many supplications to you?
Will it speak soft words to you? (Job 41:1–3)

In Africa, two men stand at a river which they are about to cross, when they notice crocodiles looking at them. "Are you afraid?" says one to the other. "Don't you know that God is merciful and good?" "Yes, I do," says the frightened man. "But what if God suddenly chooses right now to be good to the crocodiles?"

Elie Wiesel, *Sages and Dreamers*

Compassionate Eating and Creation Care

*

ACTION

Read Job 41 slowly. Marvel at the terrible, fierce strength of some of God's creatures.

——— **October 27** ———

"Be merciful, just as your Father is merciful." (Luke 6:36)

We can practice a compassionate vegetarianism, at least on a small scale at first if the task seems daunting. Selecting one day a week to eliminate animal products would be congruent with the many generations of Christians who abstained from these products on Fridays in solidarity with the crucified Jesus. Holding compassionate potlucks, and using these events to educate the congregation and larger community, creates a new possibility for agape meals and love feasts. Finding local, humane products to replace mass-produced, unhealthy and cruel products is another component of a merciful eating lifestyle. . . . All of these are steps in the direction of a truly compassionate Christian life.

Laura Hobgood-Oster, *The Friends We Keep*

ACTION

On Friday of this week, abstain from eating meat and animal products.

He makes his sun rise on the evil and on the good, and
sends rain on the righteous and on the unrighteous.
(Matthew 5:45)

Local eating could seem like a choice that only hippies or Yuppies might make, but it is actually a collective project for a shared future. How to do that is the question. How do we have our (local) cake and eat it too (not sacrifice the benefits of anywhere food)? This is the challenge. . . .

The task now is to gather up our hard-earned freedoms and apply them to shaping a future that works for all. As it says in the Bible in Matthew 5:45, "He makes his sun to rise on the evil and on the good, and sends rain on the just and on the unjust." Same with the earth's living systems—what affects them affects us all. The sun and rain of climate change fall on everyone.

Compassionate
Eating
and
Creation
Care

*

251

———

Vicki Robin, *Blessing the Hands That Feed Us*

REFLECTION

For the book quoted above, Robin undertook a "ten-mile diet," in which all the food she ate was grown or raised within a ten-mile radius of her home. How would eating locally benefit your family? How might it help the planet?

———— **October 29** ————

But he would withdraw to deserted places and pray.
(Luke 5:16)

Marveling at creation is easy to do when you're sitting on the porch of a cabin in the mountains of Montana,

OCTOBER

Compassionate
Eating
and
Creation
Care

*

252

listening to the rush of a spring-swollen river and the occasional cry of two hawks that have been chasing a smaller bird around the hills all afternoon. . . . All of western Montana is like God boasting, "Look what I can do! Look what I can do!"

But you don't have to be in a place as preposterously pretty as Big Sky to reap the benefits of stepping outside. This is particularly true for those of us who have been holed up trying to wrestle something out—spiritually, emotionally, existentially. Take the example of Jesus. When he was trying to come to terms with himself . . . he went into the wild, whether it was the desert, the Sea of Galilee, or the Garden of Gethsemane.

———

Cathleen Falsani, *Sin Boldly*

ACTION
Go outside and see what God has done!

——— **October 30** ———

Praise the LORD from the earth,
you sea monsters and all deeps. (Psalm 148:7)

Francis believed that all creatures were created for the explicit purpose of worshipping God. Hence, the annihilation of any species would diminish the adoration that is God's due. He derived such conviction from Psalm 148. . . .

I, personally, am sensitized to the Franciscan perspective on animals each year when my wife and I go whale watching off the shores of Provincetown, Massachusetts. The naturalist on the boat with us talks about the decimation of whales and how they are on the verge of extinction. It is then that I remember that the psalmist declared that whales were created to sing hymns of praise to God. Whales sing! . . . Silencing their voices of worship by annihilating them is sinful. It might even be considered blasphemous.

Tony Campolo, *Letters to a Young Evangelical*

PRAYER

Teach me to love and protect all your creatures, Lord. Amen.

OCTOBER

Compassionate
Eating
and
Creation
Care

*

253

October 31

The LORD is good to all, and his compassion is over all that he has made. (Psalm 145:9)

And since He has suffered so many things for us and has done and will do so much good to us, let every creature which is in heaven and on earth and in the sea and in the abysses render praise to God and glory and honor and benediction; for He is our strength and power who alone is good, alone most high, alone almighty and admirable, glorious and alone holy, praiseworthy and blessed without end forever and ever. Amen.

St. Francis of Assisi, "Letter to Faithful Christians"

REFLECTION

As we end our month of focusing on creation and the compassionate treatment of animals, what will you take away?

NOVEMBER

Fixed-Hour Prayer

——— **November 1** ———

Therefore, since we are surrounded by so great a cloud of witnesses, let us also lay aside every weight and the sin that clings so closely, and let us run with perseverance the race that is set before us. (Hebrews 12:1)

On All Saints' Day, it is not just the saints of the church that we should remember in our prayers, but all the foolish ones and wise ones, the shy ones and overbearing ones, the broken ones and whole ones, the despots and tosspots and crackpots of our lives who, one way or another, have been our particular fathers and mothers and saints, and whom we loved without knowing we loved them and by whom we were helped to whatever little we may have, or ever hope to have, of some kind of seedy sainthood of our own.

Frederick Buechner, *The Sacred Journey*

REFLECTION

It's appropriate that we begin our November practice of praying the Divine Office, or the Liturgy of the Hours, with the annual celebration of All Saints' Day. This month, can you try to remember that you and those you love are counted among the saints, despite your failings?

——— **November 2** ———

Devote yourselves to prayer, keeping alert in it with thanksgiving. (Colossians 4:2)

There is a great temptation to succumb to the notion that one can go from saying no Office at all to saying all of the four daily Offices, complete with all of the Collects and all of the Lessons, in one gigantic leap. Unless one joins a community where that is part of the practice, and where, therefore, everything about the daily life is arranged for that purpose, such a leap is seldom possible. Indeed, even thinking that one might make such a leap is to create an enormous potential for failure and frustration.

The experience of many who, as individuals drawn to pray the daily prayer on their own, have traveled this way before is that the best approach is to begin slowly, and to add to your practice as you become familiar with the ways of the liturgy. Begin with one Office, the one that speaks to you most clearly, and work with it for a time until it has become part of your habit. . . . There is no hurry, this is not a contest. We are called to pray, not to achieve.

Robert Benson, *Venite*

ACTION

Go to the website divineoffice.org. If you don't already own a breviary or a print copy of Phyllis Tickle's *The Divine Hours*, you will be using this website all month to access the daily prayers. For today, choose one time from the tabs near the top (morning prayer, noontime prayer, etc.) and prayerfully read that one service aloud. It should take between five and fifteen minutes. We are starting slowly, with just one office of your choice. If you can, try to continue doing one office a day.

——— November 3 ———

O come, let us worship and bow down,
let us kneel before the Lord, our Maker! (Psalm 95:6)

At the beginning of our prayer life we are self-centered. Prayer means little more to us than "asking." We ask for personal favors, for blessings upon ourselves and those belonging to us. In our prayer vocabulary personal pronouns occupy a disproportionate place. It is *my* needs, *my* relations, *my* friends. . . .

But in the normal course of our spiritual growth, there comes a time when the center of prayer shifts from self to God. Petition, in its narrower sense, recedes. True, it is not excluded, for nothing that touches us can be indifferent to our Father in heaven. . . . But petition will no longer be the pivot upon which prayer turns. The true motivation will now be to get nearer God, to know him better, to experience his friendship, to enter more fully into his thoughts and purposes.

Brigid E. Herman, *Creative Prayer*

PRAYER

God, help my prayers have more of you and less of me. I want to know you better. Amen.

———— **November 4** ————

"Keep awake and pray that you may not come into the time of trial; the spirit indeed is willing, but the flesh is weak."
(Mark 14:38)

The recitation of formulaic prayers . . . entails certain risks. Prayer may deteriorate into mumbling, automatic repetition, and I sometimes catch myself repeating the words of the prayer without consciously reflecting on them. Yet even so, the words themselves act as stepping stones.

Time and again a word will jump out at me and engage my attention. I tend to be busy with any number of things and, of course, I am also distracted. In this situation praying can certainly become an automatic process—just one more item on the list of things to be done. For me, however, it is more than background music; it has an important function. . . . Formulaic prayer often serves as a kind of background orchestration for me. I try to be with the Lord in my heart, and sometimes the prayer resonates more fully than at other times. Sometimes it is a rote exercise and sometimes I experience it as a refreshment of the spirit. It all depends on my mood, my other obligations, how tired or rested I feel. Prayer, though, is something I need, just as I need food and drink.

A. J. Cardinal Simonis, *Our Father*

REFLECTION

Is there anything in your religious background or experience that would cause you to feel suspicious of formal, written prayers?

———— November 5 ————

Call to me and I will answer you, and will tell you great and hidden things that you have not known. (Jeremiah 33:3)

When you go to church several times a day, every day, there is no way you can "do it right." You are not always going to sit up straight, let alone think holy thoughts. You're not going to wear your best clothes but whatever isn't in the dirty clothes basket. You come to the Bible's great "book of praises" through all the moods and conditions of life, and while you may feel like hell, you sing anyway. To your surprise, you find that the psalms do not deny your true feelings but allow you to reflect on them, right in front of God and everyone.

_____

Kathleen Norris, *The Cloister Walk*

REFLECTION

According to Norris, one of the gifts of fixed-hour prayer is that we come before God right in the middle of every kind of human experience. When the time comes to pray, we may be sad, anxious, or barely holding it together. Do you feel comfortable praying even in those times?

——— November 6 ———

"Pray then in this way:
Our Father in heaven,
hallowed be your name.
Your kingdom come.
Your will be done,
on earth as it is in heaven."
(Matthew 6:9–10)

In the first half of the [Lord's] prayer, we begin with acceptance. Then we allow ourselves a desire. Then we correct it by coming back to acceptance. In the second half, the order is changed; we finish by expressing desire. Only desire has now become negative; it is expressed as a fear; therefore it corresponds to the highest degree of humility and that is a fitting way to end.

The Our Father contains all possible petitions; we cannot conceive of any prayer not already contained in it. It is to prayer what Christ is to humanity. It is impossible to say it once through, giving the fullest possible attention to each word, without a change, infinitesimal perhaps but real, taking place in the soul.

Simone Weil, "The Our Father"

ACTION

As you pray the Office today, pay particular attention to each phrase of the Lord's Prayer near the end of your prayers. Think about the arc Weil identifies as we move among acceptance, desire, fear, and humility.

——— November 7 ———

*Seven times a day I praise you
for your righteous ordinances. (Psalm 119:164)*

Lauds begins the day, causing our first utterance to be those that are offered to the praise of God. At Midday we briefly break from our work in order to remember that God, not our work, gives meaning to our day and that whatever good we do will have prayer at its source. In the evening we celebrate Vespers, looking back upon the day with thanksgiving, while acknowledging that not all we have done has been to the glory of God. Finally, at Compline, we commend ourselves and the whole church to God's care for the night ahead, and we pray for God's blessing.

The Paraclete Psalter

ACTION

Add a second Office to the one you are already observing. Try to space them out through the day if possible—Lauds and Vespers, or Midday and Compline. Keep doing two Offices each day if you can. If you can't, don't beat yourself up about it. Fixed-hour prayer is hard—and, as I said before, this book is printed on flagellation-free paper.

——— **November 8** ———

*For a day in your courts is better
than a thousand elsewhere.
I would rather be a doorkeeper in the house of my God
than live in the tents of wickedness. (Psalm 84:10)*

Sit in your cell as in paradise. Put the whole world behind you and forget it. Watch your thoughts like a good fisherman watching for fish. The path you must follow is the Psalms—never leave it.

If you have just come to the monastery, and in spite of your good will you cannot accomplish what you want, take every opportunity you can to sing the Psalms in your heart and to understand them with your mind.

And if your mind wanders as you read, do not give up; hurry back and apply your mind to the words once more.

St. Romuald, *Brief Rule*

REFLECTION

Does your mind wander when you recite the Office? How can you bring your thoughts back to the Psalms?

November 9

Steadfast love and faithfulness will meet;
righteousness and peace will kiss each other. (Psalm 85:10)

When most of us look at the Missionaries of Charity [Mother Teresa's order], we see their physical labor—cooking, scrubbing, feeding, cleaning, tending the poor, picking people up off the streets or visiting shut-ins. But few know that Mother Teresa and the Missionaries see their first work as prayer and the work with the poor as a natural outcome of that prayer. They intentionally stop to pray six times a day in addition to praying as they go to and from their destinations and work. Mother wrote that these are times during the day "when we can regain our strength and fill up our emptiness with Jesus."

Mary Poplin, *Finding Calcutta*

PRAYER

Lord, may my daily times with you refresh my strength and enable me to care for your people. Amen.

November 10

May the God of steadfastness and encouragement grant
you to live in harmony with one another, in accordance
with Christ Jesus, so that together you may with one voice
glorify the God and Father of our Lord Jesus Christ.
(Romans 15:5–6)

Recently my family joined a church community whose regular morning service includes reciting the Lord's Prayer together. As I chant the well-worn words "Our Father, Who art in heaven, hallowed by thy name . . ." something unlocks inside me. When I close my eyes and repeat the words of centuries, I experience a connection with community that has eluded me for many years. . . .

Praying the Lord's Prayer, the psalms, and other traditional prayers alone at set hours during the day allows me to feel the invisible community of others all over the world, praying around the clock words that are two thousand years old. I feel the pull of this community, a supernatural strength of numbers, an energy force greater than my words and myself. I can lean on the prayers that have gone before me, the prayers said alongside me, the prayers that will continue long after my lips have ceased to utter another sentence. I'm a link in an unbroken chain that is greater than myself; building on the work of centuries and unfinished in my lifetime.

Cindy Crosby, *By Willoway Brook*

ACTION

As you pray your two Offices today, imagine yourself leaning on the prayers of those who have come before you and will come after you. You are a link in a chain unbroken by time.

 **November 11** ────

All these were constantly devoting themselves to prayer.
(Acts 1:14)

Christians today, wherever they practice the discipline of fixed-hour prayer, frequently find themselves filled with a conscious awareness that they are handing their worship, at its final "Amen," on to other Christians in the next time zone.

Like relay runners passing a lighted torch, those who do the work of fixed-hour prayer do create thereby a continuous cascade of praise before the throne of God. To participate in such a regimen with such an awareness is to pray, as did the Desert Fathers, from within the spiritual community of shared texts as well as within the company of innumerable other Christians, unseen but present, who have preceded one across time or who, in time, will follow one.

Phyllis Tickle, *The Divine Hours*

REFLECTION

When you recite the Office, do you feel surrounded by the invisible community Tickle describes—the Christians and Jews through time who have prayed these same Psalms before you?

——— **November 12** ———

Rejoice in hope, be patient in suffering, persevere in prayer.
(Romans 12:12)

To pray the Daily Office is to be connected to people all around the world praying the same prayers. It is to connect yourself across time to those who have prayed these prayers before and those who will pray them after. Just as the Christian tradition has always lauded solitude, so too prayer in the Christian tradition has always been deeply communal. . . .

To say that praying the hours, praying the psalms, will forge bonds between you and other praying people is not just a trope, a will-of-the-wisp. Another word for those bonds is "solidarity."

Lauren F. Winner, "Prayer Is a Place"

PRAYER

May I be mindful during prayer that I am not alone, dear Lord, but surrounded by your saints. Amen.

Fixed-Hour
Prayer

*

266

——— **November 13** ———

Be pleased, O LORD, to deliver me;
O Lord, make haste to help me. (Psalm 40:13)

As Love, God has equipped us with everything we need in our journey toward goodness, truth, and beauty. God, absolutely compassionate to all and eternally faithful in his love, is always with us. There is nothing we or anyone can do to separate us from that divine Love. Therefore, we read and pray the Scriptures, particularly the difficult passages of the Psalms, with awareness of God's loving presence. Enfolded as we are in the love of the Creator, we still cry and beg for deliverance and demand protection like the psalmist—because we are human. Even though we know that Christ conquered death, we still cry out in frustration like the psalmist. Because our fears, worldly desires, and need to control still "lurk in secret like a lion in its covert," waiting to tear us apart, we join with the psalmist, saying, *Be pleased, O God, to deliver me. O Lord, make haste to help me!*

———

Roy DeLeon, OblSB, *Praying with the Body*

REFLECTION

What psalms give you comfort? What psalms utterly freak you out? (Psalms 137 and 109 get my vote.) What does it mean to you that there are psalms of praise *and* psalms with such hostility in the Bible?

Because your steadfast love is better than life,
my lips will praise you.
So I will bless you as long as I live;
I will lift up my hands and call on your name.
(Psalm 63:3–4)

Some monastic communities say or sing the entire Psalter every day. Some Christians read five psalms a day, getting through it in a month; that's a good way to begin. (I once heard Billy Graham say that he read five psalms every day because they taught him how to get along with God, and a chapter of Proverbs every day because it taught him how to get along with other people. Psalms and Proverbs right through, every month: a great discipline.)

Things happen when you use the whole cycle that are less likely to happen when you only use part or skip back and forth by following your own principle of selection rather than that of the compilers and, we may suppose, the Holy Spirit. This, I think, is part of what it might mean to live as a community, or as an individual, under the authority of scripture.

N. T. Wright, *The Case for the Psalms*

ACTION
Pray Psalm 63 aloud. Away from friends and family, if you feel silly.

—— November 15 ——

"When you are praying, do not heap up empty phrases
as the Gentiles do; for they think that they will be heard
because of their many words." (Matthew 6:7)

Fixed-Hour
Prayer

*

268

I realize that for many, fixed-hour prayer is an unknown practice. It certainly was for me until I discovered it during Lent on, of all places, Capitol Hill. And for those who are familiar with it, you may have dismissed this discipline long ago as something entirely mechanical and impersonal. I think that was the case for my own church tradition. I think we didn't do this growing up because my tradition thought prayer would be reduced to something that was vainly and meaninglessly repetitious. This does not need to be the case, however; I would argue that if any prayer becomes vain repetition—fixed or spontaneous—it's because our own heart isn't engaged, rather than what we say or how we say it.

Jeremy Bouma, *Prayers for My City*

PRAYER
Keep my heart fixed on you as I pray, O Lord. Amen.

——— November 16 ———

About noon the next day, as they were on their journey and approaching the city, Peter went up on the roof to pray.
(Acts 10:9)

It is supremely to be hoped that the Liturgy of the Hours may pervade and penetrate the whole of Christian prayer, giving it life, direction and expression, and effectively nourishing the spiritual life of the people of God.

We have, therefore, every confidence that an appreciation of that "unceasing" prayer which our Lord Jesus Christ entrusted to his Church will take on new life, since the Liturgy of the Hours, distributed as it is over suitable intervals of time, continually strengthens and supports that prayer. The very celebration of the Liturgy of the Hours, especially when a community is assembled for this purpose, expresses the genuine nature of the praying Church and is seen as a wonderful sign of that Church.

"The General Instruction of Roman Catholic *Liturgy of the Hours*"

ACTION

Add a third Office to the two you are already observing. Keep doing three Offices each day if you can. If you can't, congratulate yourself on how prideful you aren't becoming. See, there's always a silver lining to flunking sainthood.

——— November 17 ———

*The LORD is near to all who call on him,
to all who call on him in truth. (Psalm 145:18)*

Apart from the Office [the daily prayer of the church], which is a daily joy, I do not have the courage to search through books of beautiful prayers. They are so numerous that it would make my head ache. Unable either to say them all or to choose between them, I do as a child would who cannot read—I just say what I want to say to God, quite simply, and he never fails to understand.

For me, prayer is an uplifting of the heart, a glance toward heaven, a cry of gratitude and love in times of sorrow as well as joy. It is something noble, something supernatural, which expands the soul and unites it to God.

St. Thérèse of Lisieux, *By Love Alone*

REFLECTION

Which do you prefer, fixed-hour prayer or spontaneous prayer? Or do you, like Thérèse, feel at home in both? (She is an actual, bona fide, canonized *saint*, remember. Most of us are not in the same league.)

——— **November 18** ———

You desire truth in the inward being;
therefore teach me wisdom in my secret heart. (Psalm 51:6)

"**E**ach of us should have two pockets," the rabbis teach. "In one should be the message, 'I am dust and ashes,' and in the other we should have written, 'For me the universe was made.'" These ideas are clearly Benedict's as well. Two things he does not want us to omit from our prayer lives, Psalm 67's plea for continued blessing and Psalm 51's need for continual forgiveness, a sense of God's goodness and our brokenness, a sense of God's greatness and our dependence, a sense of God's grandeur and our fragility. Prayer, for Benedict, is obviously not a routine activity. It is a journey into life, its struggles and its glories. It is sometimes difficult to remember, when days are dull and the schedule is full, that God has known the depth of my emptiness but healed this broken self regardless, which, of course, is exactly why Benedict structures prayer around Psalm 67 and Psalm 51. Day after day after day.

————

Joan Chittister, OSB, *The Rule of Benedict*

ACTION
Pray Psalms 67 and 51 aloud.

November 19

Then the LORD put out his hand and touched my mouth; and the Lord said to me, "Now I have put my words in your mouth." (Jeremiah 1:9)

Habit and obligation have both become bad words. That prayer becomes a habit must mean that it is impersonal, unfeeling, something of a ruse. . . . Sometimes, often, prayer feels that way to me, impersonal and unfeeling and not something I've chosen to do. I wish it felt inspired and on fire and like a real, love-conversation all the time, or even just more of the time. But what I am learning the more I sit with liturgy is that what I feel happening bears little relation to what is actually happening. It is a great gift when God gives me a stirring, a feeling, a something-at-all in prayer. But work is being done whether I feel it or not. Sediment is being laid. Words of praise to God are becoming the most basic words in my head. They are becoming the fallback words, drowning out advertising jingles and professors' lectures and sometimes even my own interior monologues.

Lauren F. Winner, *Girl Meets God*

REFLECTION
What are the "fallback words" in your head?

November 20

I love you, O LORD, my strength. (Psalm 18:1)

It may be helpful to consider each "hour" as a sacred dialogue with God which, like any dialogue, is made up of times to speak and times to listen. In the first segment, after gathering our thoughts and quieting our minds, we begin to speak. Through introductory sentences, an opening prayer, and a psalm, we address God. The second segment is a time to listen. It consists of a reading (though not at Midday—remember, this is just a quick stop in the day) and a space for reflection. This period of silence might be a good time to ponder certain questions: What word or phrase seems to "light up" from this reading? What does God seem to be saying *to me* through this word? What would I say to God in response? This leads to the final segment, when once again we speak, through closing prayers, through the Lord's Prayer, and through asking God's blessing upon ourselves and our loved ones.

The Community of Jesus, *The Little Book of Hours*

PRAYER
Speak, Lord, for I am listening. Amen.

———— November 21 ————

So teach us to count our days
that we may gain a wise heart. (Psalm 90:12)

I had been living under the regimen of praying my day every third hour on the hour for some four or five years before I began to perceive the economy of time that is built into such a routine. I am relatively sure that the reason for this is more psychological than holy or religious; but the truth of the thing is that those who spend an hour or so of each day's allotted twenty-four in praying the offices appear to have more time than do folk who do not keep the hours. Or certainly we perceive ourselves as having more time. . . .

But I also strongly suspect that determining to keep the offices as a way of increasing one's secular time is doomed from the outset to fail. Fixed-hour prayer will have its adherents on its own terms or not at all; but the terms are faith's most cordial ones.

———

Phyllis Tickle, *Prayer Is a Place*

REFLECTION

Now that you have been doing fixed-hour prayer for three weeks, how do you perceive time? Do you feel you have more or less time than when you began?

——— **November 22** ———

*O LORD, in the morning you hear my voice;
in the morning I plead my case to you, and watch.
(Psalm 5:3)*

Benedict defined the liturgy of the hours as a monastery's most important work: it is, as the prioress explained it, "a sanctification of each day by common prayer at established times." Many people think it's foolish to spend so much time this way, but the experience of Benedictines over 1,500 years has taught them that doing anything else is unthinkable. It may be fashionable to assert that all is holy, but not many are willing to haul ass to church four or five times a day to sing about it. It's not for the faint of heart.

———

Kathleen Norris, *Dakota*

PRAYER

Give me strength to persevere in prayer, O Lord. Amen.

———— **November 23** ————

*Evening and morning and at noon
I utter my complaint and moan,
and he will hear my voice. (Psalm 55:17)*

A few years ago . . . Kris and I began to say morning prayer and evening prayers together and have maintained the sacred rhythm ever since. We don't try to get something special from this each time, and we are not looking to learn something new on every occasion, but instead we are doing what millions of Christians have done for two millennia: We are simply reciting the prayers of the Church, centered as they are around the Psalter and the Lord's Prayer, to remind ourselves of something old as we express our worship to God.

. . . I find that the sacred rhythm centers my life, orders my day, enlarges my heart, reminds me of old truths, and provides me with words to express both what I feel and think as well as what is appropriate at this time of year in the Church calendar.

————

Scot McKnight, *Praying with the Church*

REFLECTION

Has the practice of the Divine Office ordered your day, enlarged your heart, and reminded you of old truths? If so, yay! Go eat a doughnut. If not, eat the doughnut anyway. You've been trying your best for crying out loud.

Come, bless the LORD, all you servants of the Lord,
who stand by night in the house of the LORD! (Psalm 134:1)

The Office of the Night Watch, as its name suggests, comes into human reckoning during those hours when sleep is upon almost all of us. For those who are restless or sleepless, however, the office is often a personal balm and an easing, as well as an act of worship. For others, its beauty alone is sufficient to justify setting a clock for its keeping. For those who travel across time zones and shift diurnal patterns abruptly, the Office of the Night Watch is often a portable sanctuary, a way of entering into the company of believers wherever one is and however skewed a schedule.

Fixed-Hour
Prayer

*

275

Phyllis Tickle, *The Night Offices*

ACTION

The next time you are struggling with insomnia, enter into restful prayer by saying the Office of the Night Watch, which can be observed on the hour or half hour from 1:30 to 4:30 AM.

Likewise the Spirit helps us in our weakness; for we do
not know how to pray as we ought, but that very Spirit
intercedes with sighs too deep for words. (Romans 8:26)

For months on end I could not pray. If I tried to pray I only fell inward into despair and empty silence. During this time I picked up the Anglican Book of Common Prayer and began to read each morning the order for Morning Prayer.

It was like being winched slowly out of a pit. The prayer of confession, the psalms and other prayers, expressed my own longing for forgiveness and for God's peace in a way I could never do on my own.

John Brook, *The School of Prayer*

REFLECTION

Have the words of the Divine Office ever expressed your longings in a way that you could not?

———— November 26 ————

Give ear, O my people, to my teaching;
incline your ears to the words of my mouth. (Psalm 78:1)

More than any other part of scripture, we can say that the psalms are not beloved because they are holy, but that they are holy because they are beloved. We do not turn to the psalms out of a sense of obligation. We read psalms because they help us confront the pains and challenges that are part of human life. Psalms help us put into words what we experience and feel; more than that, many will tell you, psalms help us overcome our problems and bear the burdens that life places on all of us.

Daniel F. Polish, *Bringing the Psalms to Life*

PRAYER

Thank you for the Psalms, Lord, and the way they express the full spectrum of joy and sorrow. Amen.

———— November 27 ————

Restore to me the joy of your salvation,
and sustain in me a willing spirit. (Psalm 51:12)

Written prayers serve an especially useful purpose, I have found, during periods of spiritual dryness, when spontaneous prayer seems an impossible chore. I borrow the words, if not the faith, of others when my own words fail. At such a time I have two options. I can stop praying completely, which only serves to distance me further from God. Or I can keep going, asking God to see me through this difficult period, meanwhile leaning on the prayers of others.

Fixed-Hour
Prayer

*

277

Philip Yancey, *Prayer*

REFLECTION

After this month, do you think you will turn to fixed-hour prayer during the inevitable spiritual dry spells or times of doubt?

———— November 28 ————

The tombs also were opened, and many bodies of the saints
who had fallen asleep were raised. After his resurrection
they came out of the tombs and entered the holy city and
appeared to many. (Matthew 27:52–53)

What are we to make of that phrase in the Apostles' Creed, "the communion of saints"? It is not something that comes up all that much in the normal process of "doing church." Perhaps it seems a bit superstitious to imagine ghostly figures flying around the sanctuary on Sunday morning, whispering hymns and prayers alongside us as we sit in our pews. . . .

We live within a web of holy obligation. We are connected to people of the world today, and to those who created the world with their own labor. We are also connected to other invisible people: the unknown number of generations yet to be born.

Margaret Bendroth, *The Spiritual Practice of Remembering*

PRAYER

Lord, teach me to be mindful of how much I owe to all those who came before, and to those who are yet to walk this earth. Amen.

———— November 29 ————

Make a joyful noise to the LORD, all the earth;
break forth into joyous song and sing praises. (Psalm 98:4)

Our praying of the psalter, which is the heart of the Daily Office, takes us ever deeper into the mystery of the incarnation; the psalms give voice to the whole range of human experience which Christ has embraced and redeemed as the Savior of the world. Although nothing essential is lacking when the office is said, we continue the tradition of our Society by singing whenever there are sufficient voices. As we sing and chant deep levels of our being are involved; our hearts are lifted up in greater exultation. And music enhances our worship with riches inherited from many ages.

The Rule of the Society of St. John the Evangelist

ACTION

Even if you don't feel you are much of a singer, try singing the Psalms in the Divine Offices today. You can make up your own tunes or try to make the words fit into a hymn you know.

*By day the L<small>ORD</small> commands his steadfast love,
and at night his song is with me,
a prayer to the God of my life. (Psalm 42:8)*

The first part of the Nativity triptych, Advent, is my favorite season of the year. The darkness and cold of impending winter set the stage for the four weeks of preparation before Christmas. If people have a home season, mine is winter. As the days shorten and the sunsets grow more colorful and more ominous, my mood becomes pensive and dark. Advent invites me to hunker down and nestle in. It encourages me to go indoors and inward. I love the waiting and the anticipation.

Advent, Christmas, and Epiphany are the opening acts and the pep rally for the rest of the liturgical year. They remind me to wake up, to watch, and to prepare for the events ahead.

Fixed-Hour
Prayer

*

279

Sybil MacBeth, *The Season of the Nativity*

REFLECTION

Today we conclude our experiment with fixed-hour prayer and move on to the practice of generosity, which is appropriate for the season of Advent. During Advent, does your mood become pensive?

DECEMBER

Generosity

DECEMBER

Generosity

*

282

———— **December 1** ————

"Whoever has two coats must share with anyone who has none; and whoever has food must do likewise." (Luke 3:11)

Faith is a gift from God. Without it there would be no life. And our work, to be fruitful and to be all for God, and beautiful, has to be built on faith. Faith in Christ who has said, "I was hungry, I was naked, I was sick, and I was homeless and you did that to me." On these words of his all our work is based. . . . Because we cannot see Christ we cannot express our love to him; but our neighbors we can always see, and we can do to them what if we saw him we would like to do for Christ.

———

Blessed Mother Teresa, in *Something Beautiful for God*

REFLECTION
December is often a time of generosity, as we prepare for Christmas with gift-giving and hospitality. Do you feel you are naturally a generous person, or is generosity a practice you need to work on?

———— **December 2** ————

As for those who in the present age are rich, command them not to be haughty, or to set their hopes on the uncertainty of riches, but rather on God who richly provides us with everything for our enjoyment. They are to do good, to be rich in good works, generous, and ready to share, thus storing up for themselves the treasure of a good foundation for the future, so that they may take hold of the life that really is life. (1 Timothy 6:17–19)

Charity enables us to spiritualize the material, and to actualize our virtuous intentions. G-d could have easily distributed wealth evenly to all people. But, as the sages say, "If everyone were wealthy or poor, who would be generous?" Just as G-d continues to give—every fraction of time, every day on earth—charity allows *us* to give, thus becoming G-dlike ourselves. Remember: The money you give away is not your own; G-d has lent it to you to allow you the gift of giving. Those who have been blessed with more money, then, are those who have been blessed by G-d with the opportunity and privilege to be more giving, to be more G-dlike.

———

Rabbi Menachem Schneerson, in *Toward a Meaningful Life*

PRAYER

God, thank you for the blessings I have, and that I am sometimes in a position to be generous. Open my heart. Amen.

——— **December 3** ———

Sell your possessions, and give alms. Make purses for yourselves that do not wear out, an unfailing treasure in heaven, where no thief comes near and no moth destroys.
(Luke 12:33)

Through a life open to community, we learn the needs of others, we are given an opportunity to give to others, and we experience generosity from others. The act of generosity means that we choose to liberally share with others without any personal gain. If you build a life that is separate from people who experience great need, you will always struggle to be a generous person. In large part, the people closest to us determine what we desire. So surround yourself with people who are in need, and you will desire to meet needs. Surround yourself with people living in excess, and your desires will become even more excessive. Generous people live in community with people who benefit from their generosity, which makes for a fuller life for the giver.

Jeff Shinabarger, *More or Less*

ACTION

Be aware today of the people around you. Are you always surrounding yourself with those who have more, which might tempt you to covet what they have? Or are you around people who have less, whose situation can prompt you toward the virtue of generosity? Try to immerse yourself in the lives of people with less.

———— December 4 ————

Let them turn away from evil and do good;
let them seek peace and pursue it. (1 Peter 3:11)

Lord, make me an instrument of your peace
Where there is hatred,
Let me sow love;
Where there is injury, pardon;
Where there is error, truth;
Where there is doubt, faith;
Where there is despair, hope;
Where there is darkness, light;
And where there is sadness, Joy.

O Divine Master, grant that I may not so much seek to be
consoled
As to console;
To be understood, as to understand;
To be loved, as to love.
For it is in giving that we receive,
It is in pardoning that we are pardoned,
And it is in dying that we are born to eternal life.

—

Attributed to St. Francis of Assisi

REFLECTION

How does this prayer's emphasis on placing other people's
needs before our own spur us toward generosity?

—————— **December 5** ——————

*Now you are the body of Christ and individually members
of it. (1 Corinthians 12:27)*

Christ has no body now on earth but yours; no hands but
yours; no feet but yours. Yours are the eyes through
which the compassion of Christ must look out on the world.
Yours are the feet with which he has to go about doing good.
Yours are the hands with which He is to bless the people.

—

Attributed to St. Teresa of Avila

ACTION

Say this prayer of St. Teresa aloud very slowly. As the
prayer mentions various parts of your body, touch them
and consecrate them to do the work Jesus would do if
he were here on earth. (You may want to be alone when
you do this spiritual practice, since it can look a little like
you are singing "Head, Shoulders, Knees, and Toes.")

DECEMBER

——— **December 6** ———

*"Truly I tell you, just as you did it to one of the least of
these who are members of my family, you did it to me."
(Matthew 25:40)*

Generosity

*

286

Today at our church Alms Ministry, we saw nineteen
people. They come to St. Paul's for any kind of help we
can offer. . . .

One week two brothers come together. We ask them to
sit down with us so we can hear their story. One, the deaf
one, can drive. The other, too weak to speak for himself, is
scheduled for a heart operation in Seattle later in the week.
They have an ancient Chevy but no money for gas. We give
them a voucher for thirty dollars made out to the local gas
station.

The relief on their faces, even tears! The driver sobs,
looking at us and hugging his brother, "Thank you. He's
all I've got." Fuel for a car, even an old, beat-up vehicle, is
like the living soul in an aged body. It speaks of freedom, of
forward momentum, of release, of hope, of possibility.

Luci Shaw, *Adventure of Ascent*

ACTION

This week, contribute something to others, whether it's
a generous offering in the Salvation Army kettle outside
the grocery store or a morning spent wrapping presents
for a charity.

——— **December 7** ———

*How does God's love abide in anyone who has the world's
goods and sees a brother or sister in need and yet
refuses help? (1 John 3:17)*

God insists that if we do not imitate God's concern for the poor, we are not really God's people—no matter how frequent our worship or how orthodox our creeds. Because Israel failed to correct oppression and defend poor widows, Isaiah insisted that Israel was really the pagan people of Gomorrah (Isa. 1:10–17). God despised their fasting because they tried to worship God and oppress their workers at the same time (Isa. 58:3–7). Jeremiah 22:13–19 teaches that knowing God is *inseparable* from caring for the poor. . . . Jesus was even harsher. At the last judgment, some who expect to enter heaven will learn that their failure to feed the hungry condemns them to hell (Matt. 25:31–46). If we do not care for the needy brother or sister, God's love does not abide in us (1 John 3:17).

Ronald J. Sider, *Just Generosity*

REFLECTION
How do you feel, hearing that the Bible teaches that "knowing God is *inseparable* from caring for the poor"?

———— December 8 ————

They would sell their possessions and goods and distribute the proceeds to all, as any had need. (Acts 2:45)

Do good. Do all the good thou canst. Let thy plenty supply thy neighbour's wants; and thou wilt never want something to do. Canst thou find none that need the necessaries of life, that are pinched with cold or hunger; none that have not raiment to put on, or a place where to lay their head; none that are wasted with pining sickness; none that are languishing in prison? If you duly considered our Lord's words, "The poor have you always with you," you would no more ask, "What shall I do?"

John Wesley, "On Worldly Folly"

PRAYER

Generosity

Help me see new opportunities to do good today, Lord. Amen.

*

—— **December 9** ——

"Consider the lilies, how they grow: they neither toil nor spin; yet I tell you, even Solomon in all his glory was not clothed like one of these." (Luke 12:27)

The poor of the gospel learn to live without certainty about the morrow, in joyful confidence that all will be given.

The spirit of poverty does not consist in looking poverty-stricken, but in setting everything in the simple beauty of creation.

The spirit of poverty is to live in the gladness of each day. If for God there is generosity in providing the good things of the earth, for human beings there is grace in giving what they have received.

The Rule of Taizé

REFLECTION

A big part of learning to be generous is recognizing that a God of abundance will care for our own needs. We don't have to hoard our resources. Do you trust that God will meet your future needs if you give away some of what you now have?

—— December 10 ——

Do not worry about anything, but in everything by prayer and supplication with thanksgiving let your requests be made known to God. (Philippians 4:6)

You can't outgive the Lord, an old missionary told me, and I found this to be true. No matter what I gave away to those in need, I never lacked because of it. . . . The Bible is full of wonderful promises to those who are generous—I guess God knows we need all the encouragement we can get in this regard.

But on my own pilgrimage, every step of the way, God has been more than generous with me—heaped down, running over generous. In the process I've learned a little about being generous with others. Throughout my life I've learned that incredible blessings come to those who give, but learning to be generous to the unworthy, the ungrateful and the unrepentant is too Christ-like for our justice-calibrated sensibilities. It is here, however, where our prayer life can help us finish a little of Christ's work on earth.

Faith Annette Sand, *Prayers of Faith*

ACTION

Identify your many blessings. In what ways has God's generosity "heaped down" on you? Say thank you to God today!

—— December 11 ——

A generous person will be enriched, and one who gives water will get water. (Proverbs 11:25)

Generosity

*

290

A [spiritual] leading can be something as simple as the time Nancy and I stood in the checkout line at the local grocery store, our cart well loaded. Our three sons lived at home at the time and they went through food quickly. In front of us was a member of our meeting, who also had three sons. Her cart held a few essentials. A single mother, she was between jobs and doing her best to get by. I felt a prompting inside me. *By almost any standards, you are rich,* the voice said. *What should you do?* Then I remembered Jesus' words, "For I was hungry and you gave me food, I was thirsty and you gave me something to drink." I looked at Nancy, she nodded, and I tapped our friend on the shoulder. "Nancy and I would like to buy your groceries, if you'll allow us," I said so only she could hear. A look of relief filled her eyes and she nodded yes. . . .

It wasn't that I suddenly became a saint there in the grocery store. The story is not about me being a good guy, but rather how, at least in that instance, I listened to the prompting of love—and responded. In doing so, I was helped more than my friend was—my soul was enlarged as my compassion for neighbors less well off than me became more than just some intellectual understanding. It became an exercise of faith.

J. Brent Bill, *The Sacred Compass*

PRAYER

Show me today the people who need my help, Lord, both for their sake and my own. Amen.

December 12

Each of you must give as you have made up your mind, not reluctantly or under compulsion, for God loves a cheerful giver. (2 Corinthians 9:7)

The habit of giving, of giving generously, is not an extra option for keen Christians. It is absolutely obligatory on all—because our whole calling is to reflect God the creator, and the main thing we know about this true God is that his very nature is self-giving, generous love. The reason why "God loves a cheerful giver" (2 Corinthians 9:7) is that that's what God himself is like. Someone like that is a person after God's own heart. Making a regular, formal, and public practice of giving money is designed to generate the habit of the heart which forms a key part of what Paul meant by *agape* love.

N. T. Wright, *After You Believe*

REFLECTION

Are you a cheerful giver? Or are you counting the cost of your generosity?

December 13

So Moses gave command, and word was proclaimed throughout the camp: "No man or woman is to make anything else as an offering for the sanctuary." So the people were restrained from bringing; for what they had already brought was more than enough to do all the work. (Exodus 36:6–7)

As predictable as decorating the tree, a moment arrives each Advent when I realize that I have once again lost sight of what makes the season holy and set apart. My focus has slipped from Christ and shifted to my bank account, all the gifts I still have to buy or make, and all the parties I still have to host or attend. . . . But in the middle of all the hustle and bustle, just as I am tempted to pitch over the edge in holiday desperation and frantic people-pleasing, along comes St. Lucy, calm, serene, and full of purpose. With her traditional Scandinavian wreath of candles crowning her head, she brings light to the darkness of early winter. I read her words in Ælfric's Life of St. Lucy: "You can take nothing with you from this life, and whatever you give away at death for the Lord's sake you give because you cannot take it with you. Give now to the true Savior, while you are healthy, whatever you intended to give away at your death," and I am reminded that it is not just material gifts that I need to give away, but also those things that are most precious to me: my time, my laughter, my friendship, my love, my attention, my prayers.

Jerusalem Jackson Greer, *A Homemade Year*

ACTION

Today is the feast day of St. Lucia, a third-century saint who is associated with celebrations of light in the darkness of winter. (She also plucked her own eyes out, but let's just not go there.) Light a candle in her honor today and remember that the material things we have in this life are things we cannot take with us after we die. How much better to give them away now in the name of Jesus?

———— December 14 ————

*Father of orphans and protector of widows
is God in his holy habitation. (Psalm 68:5)*

A few minutes later, the doorbell rang. . . . It was my neighbor, an elderly woman I had exchanged no more than a dozen words with in the ten years I'd lived in Thomason. She had pot holders on her hands, which held a pan of brownies still hot from the oven, and tears were rolling down her cheeks. "I just heard," she said.

That pan of brownies was, it later turned out, the leading edge of a tsunami of food that came to my children and me, a wave that did not recede for many months after Drew's death. I didn't know that my family and I would be fed three meals a day for weeks and weeks. I did not anticipate that neighborhood men would come to drywall the playroom, build bookshelves, mow the lawn, get the oil changed in my car. . . . All I knew was that my neighbor was standing on the front stoop with her brownies and her tears: she *was* the Good News.

———

Kate Braestrup, *Here If You Need Me*

REFLECTION

After Braestrup suddenly lost her husband, the community rallied around her and her children. Are there single parents in your world who need your generosity and support?

——— **December 15** ———

In all this I have given you an example that by such work we must support the weak, remembering the words of the Lord Jesus, for he himself said, "It is more blessed to give than to receive." (Acts 20:35)

DECEMBER

Generosity

*

294

After my father's suicide in October, Mama was left with thousands of dollars of debt, twelve dollars in daddy's wallet, and the support of her two youngest children. She was still immersed in the lonely darkness of grief and shock. She could not meet house payments, she needed employment, and she was aware that the holidays were around the corner. . . .

Weeks later, several friends dissolved suicide's prevalent stigma with holiday greetings, when they surprised Mama with a Christmas fir tree. They decorated it with the hand-blown ornaments passed down from my grandparents, and our traditional colorful bubble lights. Next to the crèche, they placed beautifully wrapped presents of board games, fire trucks with sirens and moveable ladders, super deluxe yoyos, and Mama's favorite rose-scented dusting powder. Then they delicately placed a tray of sugarcoated pecans and homemade pralines on the breakfast room table. Wiping away a tear, Mama quietly murmured how grateful she was that God takes care of us.

Bridget Haase, OSU, *Generous Faith*

PRAYER

This holiday season, Lord, show me who needs my help and protection. Amen.

——— December 16 ———

"So whenever you give alms, do not sound a trumpet before you, as the hypocrites do in the synagogues and in the streets, so that they may be praised by others."
(Matthew 6:2)

Saint Thérèse of Lisieux wrote, "When one loves, one does not calculate." I'm a big calculator, always looking for a return. . . .

No! Spend out. Don't think about the return. "It is by spending oneself," the actress Sarah Berhhardt remarked, "that one becomes rich." What's more, one intriguing study showed that Sarah Bernhardt's pronouncement is *literally* true: people who give money to charity end up wealthier than those who don't give to charity. . . .

It's certainly true in my household that spending out creates a wealth of love and tenderness, while calculation and scorekeeping build resentment.

Gretchen Rubin, *The Happiness Project*

REFLECTION

Rubin chastises herself for always looking for a "return on investment" when she is charitable or generous. Ironically, she follows this by observing that generous people receive blessings in return in the form of abounding love and even in more money. When have you been "a big calculator, always looking for a return"?

———— December 17 ————

"But when you give alms, do not let your left hand know what your right hand is doing." (Matthew 6:3)

Lord, teach me to be generous,
Teach me to serve you as you deserve,
To give and not to count the cost,
To fight and not to heed the wounds,
To toil and not to seek for rest,

To labor and not to ask for reward,
Save that of knowing that I do your will. Amen.

St. Ignatius of Loyola, "Prayer for Generosity"

ACTION

Generosity

Do an anonymous act of service today, whether it's putting untraceable cash in a collection plate or dropping off a casserole for a sick neighbor. Did we mention the "anonymous" part?

*

296

———— December 18 ————

But Jesus looked at them and said, "For mortals it is impossible, but for God all things are possible."
(Matthew 19:26)

I remember talking with a friend who has worked for many years at the Catholic Worker, a ministry to the poor in New York City. Daily she tries to respond to waves of human misery that are as ceaseless as surf in that community. Out of my deep not-knowing I asked her how she could keep doing a work that never showed any results, a work in which the problems keep getting worse instead of better. I will never forget her enigmatic answer: "The thing you don't understand, Parker, is that just because something is impossible doesn't mean you shouldn't do it!"

Parker J. Palmer, *The Active Life*

PRAYER

With you all things are possible, O God! Teach me to remember that, and to have courage. Amen.

———— December 19 ————

"Not everyone who says to me, 'Lord, Lord,' will enter the kingdom of heaven, but only the one who does the will of my Father in heaven." (Matthew 7:21)

I think everybody wants to go to heaven," my father used to say, "but if I announce that there is a train leaving for heaven in twenty minutes, the line will not be very long." And if you think *that* line is short, try the one marked "Lay down your life" or "Sell all you have and give it to the poor" or "Give to everyone who begs of you" or "Do good to those who hate you."

Robert Benson, *The Body Broken*

REFLECTION
Which of the statements above is most frightening?

———— December 20 ————

We know that we have passed from death to life because we love one another. (1 John 3:14)

Oh, may I join the choir invisible
Of those immortal dead who live again
In minds made better by their presence; live
In pulses stirred to generosity,
In deeds of daring rectitude, in scorn
For miserable aims that end with self,
In thoughts sublime that pierce the night like stars,
And with their mild persistence urge men's search
To vaster issues.

George Eliot, "O May I Join the Choir Invisible"

DECEMBER

Generosity

REFLECTION

In this poem, Eliot suggests that our most generous, selfless impulses are often inspired by loved ones who are deceased and now part of "the choir invisible." Whom do you remember when you read this poem? How can you honor that deceased person through acts of generosity?

—— **December 21** ——

When you reap the harvest of your land, you shall not reap to the very edges of your field, or gather the gleanings of your harvest. (Leviticus 19:9)

Our friend's dog believes that all the toys in the house are hers. She collects them, keeps all of them beside her food bowl, and watches them, as if they'll disappear if she's not careful.

Abundance is a blessing we are given by God, not [one] created by us. God is forever asking us not to hold on to life with clenched fists. The ancient Hebrews lived by a concept of generosity, taught not to harvest the edges of the fields to supply those who had nothing. Sharing brought more abundance. As care was taken to help others, there was enough for everyone.

Devon O'Day, in *Paws to Reflect*

ACTION

Make a donation to a favorite charity today. If you can swing it, make the amount a little larger than what you have given in the past. Don't tell anyone.

"The Spirit of the Lord is upon me,
because he has anointed me
to bring good news to the poor." (Luke 4:18)

When I was in high school, my church youth group fasted and raised money for World Vision; during the fast, we helped out in the kitchen of a Coney Island gospel mission. Somehow, I always thought that feeding people who were hungry—whether a world away in places of famine or a few neighborhoods away in our own city—was a cause worthy and good only insofar as it might give us an "in" to share the gospel verbally. I didn't think that the gospel was expressed in the making and serving of huge vats of spaghetti and meatballs, or in going without food to raise money for those who went chronically without; now I think that the good news—the gospel—was tangibly, edibly expressed in the shaky hunger of our fasts and the savory goodness of the food we helped prepare for hungry people.

I'm not suggesting that feeding the hungry *replace* a verbal declaration of the good news of Christ. But the gospel, as spoken by Jesus himself, is itself *good news to the poor* and must always be presented as such. Jesus feeds the multitudes physical bread *before* telling them that he is the Bread of Life.

———

Rachel Marie Stone, *Eat with Joy*

REFLECTION

Has your view of what "good news to the poor" means changed over time?

DECEMBER

Generosity

*

300

The greedy person stirs up strife,
but whoever trusts in the LORD will be enriched.
(Proverbs 28:25)

How many are the evils that come of this cursed sin of avarice! How many homicides and thefts! How much pillage with unlawful gain, how much cruelty of heart and injustice! Avarice kills the soul and makes it the slave of riches. . . .

Misers love no one except for their own profit. Their avarice proceeds from and feeds their pride. The one follows the other, because misers always carry with them the thought of their own reputation. . . . It is a fire that always gives rise to the smoke of vainglory and vanity of heart, and of boasting in that which does not belong to it.

———

St. Catherine of Siena, *Little Talks with God*

PRAYER

I confess my greed and selfishness to you, Lord. Help me overcome my avarice. Amen.

So they went with haste and found Mary and Joseph, and
the child lying in the manger. (Luke 2:16)

A plain photograph of the birth of Jesus would be altogether unremarkable—except that it showed a woman bearing her baby in a public place. . . .

If, for us, reality is material only—if we gaze at the birth with a modern eye that recognizes nothing spiritual, sees nothing divine, demands the hard facts only, data, documentation—then we're left with a photograph of small significance: a derelict husband, an immodest mother, an outdoor shelter for pack-animals, a baby left in a feed-trough. Simple, rude, dusty, and bare.

But if we gaze at Christmas thus, then our own lives must be bereft of meaning: nothing spiritual, nothing divine, no awe, never a gasp of adoration.

Walter Wangerin Jr., *Measuring the Days*

REFLECTION

What does it mean to see the manger scene with spiritual eyes?

———— December 25 ————

And she gave birth to her firstborn son and wrapped him in bands of cloth, and laid him in a manger, because there was no place for them in the inn. (Luke 2:7)

That first Christmas was miserable for everyone involved. The Christ child, we read, was in the manger "because there was no room for him in the inn." But that, of course, is nonsense. There was all the room in the inn for him, only no one—or so thought the innkeeper—would make room for a woman about to give birth. . . .

Nevertheless, "Joy to the world," because our inhumanity to one another and God notwithstanding, "the Lord has come." . . . As all the joy of Christmas comes from on high, it is quite proper for "Joy to the World" to start on a high D and come down the scale until it reaches us, a full octave lower.

William Sloane Coffin Jr., "The First Fruit of Love"

PRAYER

Lord, thank you for the gift of the Christ child. Joy to the world! Amen.

Generosity

*

302

———— **December 26** ————

Bring the full tithe into the storehouse, so that there may be food in my house, and thus put me to the test, says the LORD of hosts; see if I will not open the windows of heaven for you and pour down for you an overflowing blessing.
(Malachi 3:10)

A few years ago some people from new monastic communities got together with other Christians around the country and started something called the Relational Tithe. Darin Peterson really caught a vision for the difference generosity can make when it's tied to relationships. . . . Using the Internet, Darin developed a system to organize regional clusters of people who pool money and agree together on how to share it with the people we know. In a matter of days, we're able to meet economic needs of friends and neighbors who are struggling. . . . Often the requests aren't huge, but we have consistently met every genuine need that members have brought to the group over the past few years. It's an incredible thing to know you're part of a network that will help you take care of anyone you know who is in need.

Jonathan Wilson-Hartgrove, *New Monasticism*

ACTION

Practice a relational tithe by giving money to someone you know who needs it, either directly or through a third party. Disguise it as a Christmas gift if you need to.

Therefore encourage one another and build up each other, as indeed you are doing. (1 Thessalonians 5:11)

I recall a minister who had been experiencing long bouts of depression because of the seeming lack of success in his parish. One day he went to visit a woman who was very ill. As he started to leave the room, the woman spoke to him: "You have been such an important person in my life. I want you to know that I have great love for you." These kind words sailed straight into the minister's heart. He told me that he just couldn't believe it but by the time he reached his office he could sense that something very different was stirring within him. During the next several weeks the depression lifted and he felt a tremendous rejuvenation in his life.

Generosity

*

303

Joyce Rupp, *Little Pieces of Light*

ACTION

Speak generous words to someone today, telling that person how much he or she has meant to you and why.

You will be enriched in every way for your great generosity, which will produce thanksgiving to God through us; for the rendering of this ministry not only supplies the needs of the saints but also overflows with many thanksgivings to God. (2 Corinthians 9:11–12)

Give from the heart!" people say. But Jesus seemed to speak of something else: Give where you want your heart to be, and let your heart catch up. Don't just give to things you care about. Give to things you *want* to care about. Don't decide the amount of your giving by how much you care, but by how much you *want* to care. Ask yourself, If I were the sort of person I would really like to be, *then* what would I do? How would I spend my money (and my time, and everything else)? Then, do what you would do if you were that sort of person. Put your treasure where you want your heart to be, and Jesus promises, your heart will go there.

———

Mark Allan Powell, *Giving to God*

REFLECTION

If you were already the sort of person you would really like to be, what would you be doing with your money?

December 29

Will anyone rob God? Yet you are robbing me! But you say, "How are we robbing you?" In your tithes and offerings! (Malachi 3:8)

Often the rhetoric we use to describe our life in Christ bears only a thin resemblance to where we really are. We boast of what we are giving because it hides what we are withholding. We allow ourselves to believe that we are capable of love just because we are capable of devout sentiment. . . .

The gospel presses us to painful honesty. If nothing else, we ought to be sincere. Get out and pant with the money-making street, become hedonists, and "eat, drink, and be merry for tomorrow we may die," *or* repent and return to the spirit of the gospel. We are called to live as prophets and lovers in the Spirit of Jesus Christ. We can't live a lie.

Brennan Manning, *The Importance of Being Foolish*

ACTION

Have a "day of reckoning" today, where you add up your tithes and charitable offerings from this year. Gulp. What percentage of your income do those gifts represent? Do you feel you should give more, less, or about the same next year?

———— **December 30** ————

"You cannot serve God and wealth." (Matthew 6:24)

The rich young ruler's love of money and his greed made him an idolater (Eph. 5:5). He missed coming to know the true God and Jesus Christ whom God had sent. He wanted eternal life, but he refused to make the necessary adjustment of his life to the true God.

Many people may face some of the same struggle today. Prosperity and the love of the things of the world may tempt you to refuse to adjust your life to God. The love for money and things can become a substitute for a love relationship with God. Jesus said, "You cannot serve both God and mammon" (Matt. 6:24).

Henry Blackaby, *Experiencing God*

REFLECTION

Are you trying to serve both God and wealth?

—— **December 31** ——

. . . so that, with the eyes of your heart enlightened, you may know what is the hope to which he has called you, what are the riches of his glorious inheritance among the saints. (Ephesians 1:18)

Generosity

Humanly speaking, in fact, who can say for sure about anything? And yet there are some things I would be willing to bet maybe even my entire life on.

That life is grace, for instance—the givenness of it, the fathomlessness of it, the endless possibilities of its becoming transparent to something extraordinary beyond itself. That . . . whether you call on him or don't call on him, God will be present with you. That if we really had our eyes open, we would see that all moments are key moments. That he who does not love remains in death. That Jesus is the Word made flesh who dwells among us full of grace and truth. On good days I might add a few more to the list. On bad days it's possible there might be a few less.

Frederick Buechner, *Now and Then*

REFLECTION

You have fought the good fight. You have finished the year! Today, think about all you have received this year in your journey through twelve spiritual disciplines— both the practices you enjoyed and the ones that didn't "take." Which will you be continuing? Which would you be happy to never, ever attempt again?

Acknowledgments

I'd like to thank Susan Bantz, Leighton Connor, Nancy Hopkins-Greene, Aaron Klinefelter, Sybil MacBeth, Jamie Noyd, Phyllis Tickle, and other friends for suggesting quotations and loaning me books. Jamie and the other campus pastors at the Edge House deserve my thanks for their weekly hospitality each Wednesday as I was researching this book, as does the staff at the Episcopal Church of the Redeemer in Cincinnati for allowing me to use their excellent library. As always, I'm grateful to the Community of Jesus and the wonderful people at Paraclete Press, including but not limited to Jon Sweeney, Sister Mercy, Sister Antonia, Pam Jordan, Jennifer Lynch, Carol Showalter, Lillian Miao, and Brother Christopher.

The original language and spellings were retained in all of these quotations, even when the traditional language was not gender-inclusive.

Notes

JANUARY

1 Joyce Rupp, *Fresh Bread and Other Gifts of Spiritual Nourishment* (Notre Dame, IN: Ave Maria Press, 1985), 19–20. Also, the Frederick Buechner quotation is from *Beyond Words*, and is quoted in full on January 7.

2 Paul Wilkes, *Beyond the Walls: Monastic Wisdom for Everyday Life* (New York: Image, 1999), 58–59. "Conversatio" for Wilkes means a sort of incremental conversion, in contrast to our cultural ideal of a "one-time, apocalyptic moment that forever changes a person" (45). Real conversion is a slow, "continuing process, one punctuated with more failures than successes" (46).

3 Barbara Essex, pastoral perspective on Matthew 5:38-48, *Feasting on the Word Year A, Volume 1* (Louisville, KY: Westminster John Knox Press, 2010), 384.

4 Eugene H. Peterson, *Practice Resurrection: A Conversation on Growing Up in Christ* (Grand Rapids, MI: Eerdmans, 2010), 133.

5 C. S. Lewis, *Mere Christianity* (San Francisco: HarperSanFrancisco, 2001), 203–4.

6 Richard Rohr, *Falling Upward: A Spirituality for the Two Halves of Life* (San Francisco: Jossey-Bass, 2011), 66–67.

7 Frederick Buechner, *Beyond Words: A Word a Day to Keep the Demons at Bay* (San Francisco: HarperSanFrancisco, 2004), 59.

8 Brené Brown, *The Gifts of Imperfection: Let Go of Who You Think You're Supposed to Be and Embrace Who You Are* (Center City, MN: Hazelden, 2010), 61.

9 Frederica Mathewes-Green, *At the Corner of East and Now: A Modern Life in Ancient Christian Orthodoxy* (New York: Tarcher/Putnam, 1999), 40–41.

10 Richard J. Foster, *Prayer: Finding the Heart's True Home* (San Francisco: HarperSanFrancisco, 1992), 8.

11 Patty Kirk, *Confessions of an Amateur Believer* (Nashville: Thomas Nelson, 2006), ix–x.

12 John Henry Newman, "Lead, Kindly Light" (1833), http://www.hymnary.org/text/lead_kindly_light_amid_the_encircling_gl. [accessed June 2014]

13 Heather King, *Redeemed: A Spiritual Misfit Stumbles Toward God, Marginal Sanity, and the Peace That Passes All Understanding* (New York: Viking, 2008), 234.

14 Adolfo Quezada, *Loving Yourself for God's Sake* (Totowa, NJ: Resurrection Press, 1997), 51–52.

15 John McQuiston II, *Finding Time for the Timeless: Spirituality in the Workweek* (Woodstock, VT: SkyLight Paths, 2004), 139–40.

16 Mark Nepo, *The Book of Awakening: Having the Life You Want by Being Present to the Life You Have* (York Beach, ME: Conari Press, 2000), 205.

17 Greg Garrett, *The Other Jesus: Rejecting a Religion of Fear for the God of Love* (Louisville, KY: Westminster John Knox Press, 2011), 56.

18 Lynne Baab, *Joy Together: Spiritual Practices for Your Congregation* (Louisville, KY: Westminster John Knox Press, 2012), 177.

19 John Wesley, *The New Birth,* edited by Thomas C. Oden (New York: Harper & Row, 1984), 38.

20 Kelly James Clark, *When Faith Is Not Enough* (Grand Rapids, MI: Eerdmans, 1997), 98.

21 Heather King, *Shirt of Flame: A Year with Saint Thérèse of Lisieux* (Brewster, MA: Paraclete Press, 2011), 96–97.

22 Margot Starbuck, *Small Things with Great Love: Adventures in Loving Your Neighbor* (Downers Grove, IL: InterVarsity Press, 2011), Kindle location 2115.

23 Louisa May Alcott, *Little Women* (New York: Bantam Classics, 1983), 10–11.

24 Rachel Held Evans, *The Year of Biblical Womanhood: How a Liberated Woman Found Herself Sitting on Her Roof, Covering Her Head, and Calling Her Husband Master* (Nashville: Thomas Nelson, 2012).

25 Eugene H. Peterson, *Subversive Spirituality* (Grand Rapids, MI: Eerdmans, 1997), 30.

26 Ronald Rolheiser, *The Restless Heart: Finding Our Spiritual Home in Times of Loneliness* (New York: Doubleday, 2004), 169.

27 Evelyn Underhill, *Radiance: A Spiritual Memoir of Evelyn Underhill,* compiled and edited by Bernard Bangley (Brewster, MA: Paraclete Press, 2004), 178.

28 Dante Alighieri, *Convivio,* book 4, chapter 12, http://dante.ilt.columbia.edu/books/convivi/convivio04.html.

29 Richard J. Foster and Gayle D. Beebe, *Longing for God: Seven Paths of Christian Devotion* (Downers Grove, IL: InterVarsity Press, 2009), 51–52.

30 The Monks of New Skete, *In the Spirit of Happiness* (Boston: Little, Brown 1999), 44.

31 Nadia Bolz-Weber, *Pastrix: The Cranky, Beautiful Faith of a Sinner and Saint* (Nashville: Jericho Books, 2013), 186–87.

FEBRUARY

1 Lynne Baab, *Fasting: Spiritual Freedom Beyond Our Appetites* (Downers Grove, IL: InterVarsity Press, 2006), 32.

2 Augustine of Hippo, "The Sermon on the Mount," 12.40, http://www.lectionarycentral.com/ashwed/AugustineGospel1.html.

3 John P. Burgess, *Encounters with Orthodoxy: How Protestant Churches Can Reform Themselves Again* (Louisville, KY: Westminster John Knox Press, 2013), 62.

4 Sara Miles, *City of God: Faith in the Streets* (New York: Jericho Books, 2014), 20–21.

5 Scot McKnight, *Fasting* (Nashville: Thomas Nelson, 2009), 49–50.

6 Lauren F. Winner, *Mudhouse Sabbath* (Brewster, MA: Paraclete Press, 2003), 66–67.

7 Frederica Mathewes-Green, *The Illumined Heart: The Ancient Christian Path of Transformation* (Brewster, MA: Paraclete Press, 2001), 57–58.

8 Edith Schaeffer, quoted in Richard Foster and Julia Roller, eds., *A Year with God: Living out the Spiritual Disciplines* (Grand Rapids, MI: Zondervan, 2009), 232.

9 Timothy [Kallistos] Ware, *The Orthodox Church,* new ed. (New York: Penguin, 1993), 116.

10 Dan B. Allender, *To Be Told: Know Your Story, Shape Your Future* (Colorado Springs, CO: WaterBrook Press, 2009), 186.

11 Scott Hahn, *Signs of Life: 40 Catholic Customs and Their Biblical Roots* (New York: Doubleday, 2009), 177–78.

12 Reba Riley, *Post-Traumatic Church Syndrome* (St. Louis, MO: Chalice Press, 2015), n.p.

13 John Henry Newman: "Parochial and Plain Sermons," book 6, Sermon 1, http://www.fordham.edu/halsall/mod/newman-fasting.asp.

14 Tony Jones, *The Teaching of the Twelve: Believing and Practicing the Primitive Christianity of the Ancient Didache Community* (Brewster, MA: Paraclete Press, 2010), 71.

15 Dallas Willard, *The Great Omission,* http://www.dwillard.org/articles/artview.asp?artID=40.

16 Valerie E. Hess, *Spiritual Disciplines Devotional* (Downers Grove, IL: InterVarsity Press, 2007), 62–63.

17 Antony the Great, quoted in *Eternal Wisdom from the Desert: Writings from the Desert Fathers,* edited and mildly modernized by Henry L. Carrigan (Brewster, MA: Paraclete Press, 2001), 79.

18 George Fox, *Journal,* http://www.strecorsoc.org/gfox/ch01.html.

19 Donald Altman, *Art of the Inner Meal: Eating as a Spiritual Path* (San Francisco: HarperSanFrancisco, 1999), 164–65.

20 Ambrose, quoted in *The Doubleday Christian Quotation Collection,* compiled by Hannah Ward and Jennifer Wild (New York: Doubleday, 1998), 12.

21 Paula Huston, *The Holy Way: Practices for a Simple Life* (Chicago: Loyola Press, 2003), 74–75.

22 Chris Seay, *A Place at the Table: 40 Days of Solidarity with the Poor* (Grand Rapids, MI: Baker Books, 2012), 35–36.

23 Richard J. Foster, *Celebration of Discipline: The Path to Spiritual Growth,* Twentieth Anniversary Edition (San Francisco: HarperSanFrancisco, 1998), 54.

24 Alan P. Johnson, *Fasting: The Second Step to Eternal Life* (Salt Lake City: Deseret Book Company, 1964), 9.

25 Evelyn Underhill, "Food," in *Lent with Evelyn Underhill*, ed. G. P. Mellick Belshaw (Harrisburg, PA: Morehouse Publishing, 1990), 80.

26 The Desert Mother Amma Syncletica, quoted in Laura Swan, *The Forgotten Desert Mothers: Sayings, Lives, and Stories of Early Christian Women* (Mahwah, NJ: Paulist Press, 2001), 50.

27 Patricia D. Brown, *Paths to Prayer: Finding Your Own Way to the Presence of God* (San Francisco: Jossey-Bass, 2003), 107.

28 Enzo Bianchi, *Echoes of the Word: A New Kind of Monk on the Meaning of Life* (Brewster, MA: Paraclete Press, 2013), 130–31.

MARCH

1 Brother Lawrence, *Practicing the Presence of God,* introduction and notes by Tony Jones (Brewster, MA: Paraclete Press, 2007), 50, 55.

2 Cecily Hallack, "The Divine Office of the Kitchen," quoted in *The Paraclete Book of Hospitality* (Brewster, MA: Paraclete Press, 2012), 56.

3   Archbishop Desmond Tutu, preface to *Words for Silence: A Year of Contemplative Meditations* by Gregory Fruehwirth, ojn (Brewster, MA: Paraclete Press, 2008), 7–8.

4   Thérèse of Lisieux, *Story of a Soul: The Autobiography of Saint Thérèse of Lisieux* (Washington, DC: ICS Publications, 1996), 179.

5   Martin Luther, in *Luther's Works: The American Edition, Volume 3: Lectures on Genesis 15-20*, edited by Jaroslav Pelikan (St. Louis, MO: Concordia Publishing House, 1995), 321.

6   William Sloane Coffin Jr., *Letters to a Young Doubter* (Louisville, KY: Westminster John Knox Press, 2005), 58–59.

7   Alexandra Stoddard, *Feeling at Home: Defining Who You Are and How You Want to Live* (New York: William Morrow, 1999), xv; quoted in LaVonne Neff, *The Gift of Faith: Thoughtful Reflection by Faithful Anglicans* (New York: Morehouse Publishing, 2004), 104.

8   Kathleen Norris, *The Quotidian Mysteries: Laundry, Liturgy, and "Women's Work"* (Mahwah, NJ: Paulist Press), 35.

9   Rick Warren, *The Purpose Driven Life: What on Earth Am I Here For?* (Grand Rapids, MI: Zondervan, 2002), 260–61.

10 Margaret Kim Peterson, *Keeping House: The Litany of Everyday Life* (San Francisco: Jossey-Bass, 2007), 39–40.

11 Gene Edward Veith Jr., *God at Work: Your Christian Vocation in All of Life* (New York: Crossway, 2002) 13–14.

12 Ross West, *Go to Work and Take Your Faith Too!* (Macon, GA: Peake Road, 1997), 83–84.

13 A. A. Milne, *Winnie-the-Pooh* (New York: Dutton, 1954), 160.

14 Lillian Daniel, *When "Spiritual But Not Religious" Is Not Enough: Seeing God in Surprising Places, Even the Church* (Nashville: Jericho Books, 2013), 27–28.

15 Shauna Niequist, *Bittersweet* (Grand Rapids, MI: Zondervan, 2010), 38–39.

16 Thomas Merton, "Work and the Shakers," transcript of an oral talk given at the Abbey of Gethsemani on July 23, 1964, in Thomas Merton, *Seeking Paradise: The Spirit of the Shakers* (Maryknoll, NY: Orbis Books, 2003), 92.

17 Molly Wolf, *Hiding in Plain Sight: Sabbath Blessings* (Collegeville, MN: The Liturgical Press, 1998), 124.

18 Amy Julia Becker, *A Good and Perfect Gift: Faith, Expectations, and a Little Girl Named Penny* (Minneapolis: Bethany House, 2011), 88.

19 Madeleine L'Engle with Carole F. Chase, *Glimpses of Grace: Daily Thoughts and Reflections* (San Francisco: HarperSanFrancisco, 1996), 46.

20 Thomas Moore, *Care of the Soul: A Guide for Cultivating Depth and Sacredness in Everyday Life* (New York: HarperPerennial, 1994), 287–88.

21 Gunilla Norris, *Being Home: A Book of Meditations* (New York: Bell Tower, 1991), xi–xii.

22 Isaac Cronin, *The Mindful Cook: Finding Awareness, Simplicity, and Freedom in the Kitchen* (New York: Villard Books, 1999), 59.

23 Scott Russell Sanders, *Staying Put: Making a Home in a Restless World* (Boston: Beacon Press, 1993), 34.

24 Elizabeth J. Andrew, *Home, Hardwood, and Holiness* (Cambridge, MA: Perseus Book Group, 2005), 9.

25 Craig Barnes, *Searching for Home: Spirituality for Restless Souls* (Grand Rapids, MI: Brazos Press, 2003), 28–29.

26 Nancy Roth, *Spiritual Exercises: Joining Body and Spirit in Prayer* (New York: Seabury Books, 2005), 76–77.

27 Thomas Moore, *A Life at Work: The Joy of Discovering What You Were Born to Do* (New York: Broadway Books, 2008), 168–69.

28 Brenda Peterson, *Nature and Other Mothers: Reflections on the Feminine in Everyday Life* (New York: HarperCollins, 1992), 119.

29 Brennan Manning, *Ruthless Trust: The Ragamuffin's Path to God* (San Francisco: HarperSanFrancisco, 2000), 153.

30 John D. Beckett, *Mastering Monday: A Guide to Integrating Faith and Work* (Downers Grove, IL: InterVarsity Press, 2006), 78.

31 Gunilla Norris, *Becoming Bread: Meditations on Loving and Transformation* (New York: Bell Tower, 1993), 3–4.

APRIL

1 Eugene H. Peterson, *Eat This Book: A Conversation in the Art of Spiritual Reading* (Grand Rapids, MI: Eerdmans, 2006), 81–82.

2 Marjorie Thompson, *Soul Feast: An Invitation to the Christian Spiritual Life* (Louisville, KY: Westminster John Knox Press, 2005), 25.

3 Bert Ghezzi, *Everyday Encounters with God: What Our Experiences Teach Us about the Divine* (Ijamsville, MD: The Word Among Us Press, 2008), 131.

4 David G. Benner, *Opening to God: Lectio Divina and Life as Prayer* (Downers Grove, IL: InterVarsity Press, 2010), 59.

5 The prayer "Before Prayer" is by David Adam, in *Landscapes of Light: An Illustrated Anthology of Prayers* (Brewster, MA: Paraclete Press, 2002), n.p.

6 Anne Lamott, *Plan B: Further Thoughts on Faith* (New York: Riverhead, 2005), 73.

7 Debra Farrington, *Living Faith Day by Day* (San Francisco: Jossey-Bass, 2003), 127–28.

8 M. Basil Pennington, ocso, *Praying the Holy Scriptures*, Ancient Spiritual Disciplines series (Brewster, MA: Paraclete Press, 2012), 12–13.

9 Mariano Magrassi, *Praying the Bible: An Introduction to Lectio Divina* (Collegeville, MN: The Liturgical Press, 1998), 83–84.

10 Henri J. M. Nouwen, quoted in *Seeds of Hope: A Henri Nouwen Reader*, edited by Robert Durback (New York: Bantam Books, 1989), 69–70.

11 Mary Margaret Funk, in *The Gethsemani Encounter: A Dialogue on the Spiritual Life by Buddhist and Christian Monastics,* ed. Donald Mitchell and James Wiseman (New York: Bloomsbury USA, 1999), 65.

12 Sharon Garlough Brown, *Sensible Shoes* (Downers Grove, IL: InterVarsity Press, 2013), 102.

13 Augustine of Hippo, *Confessions* 3.5.9 http://www.ourladyswarriors.org/saints/augcon3.htm#chap5.

14 Debbie Blue, *From Stone to Living Word: Letting the Bible Live Again* (Grand Rapids, MI: Brazos Press, 2008), 42–43.

15 Kathleen Norris, *Amazing Grace: A Vocabulary of Faith* (New York: Riverhead, 1998), 196.

16 Tullian Tchividjian, *One Way Love: Inexhaustible Grace for an Exhausted World* (Colorado Springs, CO: David C. Cook, 2013), 31.

17 Madeleine L'Engle, *The Rock That Is Higher: Story as Truth* (Colorado Springs, CO: Shaw Books, 2002), 126–27.

18 Raymond Studzinski, "Lectio Divina: Reading and Praying," in *The Tradition of Catholic Prayer*, ed. the monks of Saint Meinrad (Collegeville, MN: Liturgical Press, 2007), 203–4.

19 Jane E. Vennard, *Be Still: Designing and Leading Contemplative Retreats* (Herndon, VA: The Alban Institute, 2000), 76.

20 Gary Jansen, *Exercising Your Soul: Fifteen Minutes a Day to a Spiritual Life* (Nashville: FaithWords, 2010), 66.

21 Michael Casey, *Sacred Reading: The Ancient Art of Lectio Divina* (Liguori, MO: Liguori/Triumph, 1995), 90–91.

22 Thomas Keating, *The Heart of the World: An Introduction to Contemplative Christianity* (New York: The Crossroad Publishing Company, 1981), 53.

23 Megan McKenna, *Not Counting Women and Children: Neglected Stories from the Bible* (Maryknoll, NY: Orbis Books, 1994), 222.

24 Lonni Collins Pratt and Father Daniel Holman, *Benedict's Way: An Ancient Monk's Insights for a Balanced Life* (Chicago: Loyola Press, 2000), 181.

25 Dietrich Bonhoeffer, *Meditating on the Word*. ed. and trans. by David McI. Gracie (Cambridge, MA: Cowley Publications, 1986), 32–33.

26 Roger Ferlo, *Sensing God: Reading Scripture with All Our Senses* (Cambridge, MA: Cowley Publications, 2002), 17–18.

27 Teresa A. Blythe, *50 Ways to Pray: Practices from Many Traditions and Times* (Nashville: Abingdon Press, 2006), 52.

28 David McKenna, *How to Read a Christian Book: A Guide to Selecting and Reading Christian Books as a Christian Discipline* (Grand Rapids, MI: Baker Books, 2001), 18–19.

29 Mary Margaret Funk, *Tools Matter for Practicing the Spiritual Life: The Jesus Prayer, Ceaseless Prayer, Fasting* (New York: Continuum, 2001), 14.

30 Alice Fryling, *The Art of Spiritual Listening: Responding to God's Voice Amid the Noise of Life* (Colorado Springs, CO: Shaw, 2003), 41.

MAY

1 Richard J. Foster, *Freedom of Simplicity: Finding Harmony in a Complex World,* rev. and updated ed. (San Francisco: HarperOne, 2005), 217.

2 A. W. Tozer, *The Pursuit of God,* chapter 2, 31, http://www.gutenberg.org/ebooks/25141.

3 Murray Bodo, *Celtic Daily Prayer* (San Francisco: HarperSanFrancisco, 2002), 70–71.

4   John Chrysostom, "Concerning the Power of Demons," in Bobby Gross, *Living the Christian Year: Time to Inhabit the Story of God* (Downers Grove, IL: InterVarsity Press, 2009), 249.

5   David Janzen, *The Intentional Christian Community Handbook: For Idealists, Hypocrites, and Wannabe Disciples of Jesus* (Brewster, MA: Paraclete Press, 2013), 219–20.

6   C. Christopher Smith and John Pattison, *Slow Church: Cultivating Community in the Patient Way of Jesus* (Downers Grove, IL: InterVarsity Press, 2014), 180–82.

7   Martin Luther, "Do Not Be Anxious," quoted in Martin E. Marty, *Speaking of Trust: Conversing with Martin Luther about the Sermon on the Mount* (Minneapolis: Augsburg Books, 2003), 37.

8   Andrew Foster Connors, *Feasting on the Word Year A, Volume 1: Advent through Transfiguration* (Louisville, KY: Westminster John Knox Press, 2012), 338.

9   Thomas à Kempis, *The Imitation of Christ*, William C. Creasy, rev. ed., (Notre Dame, IN: Ave Maria, 1989, 2004), 34.

10 Philip Gulley, *Living the Quaker Way: Timeless Wisdom for a Better Life Today* (San Francisco: HarperOne, 2013), 29–30.

11 Arthur Simon, *How Much Is Enough? Hungering for God in an Affluent Culture* (Grand Rapids, MI: Baker Books, 2003), 53.

12 Hildegard of Bingen, *The Book of Divine Works,* in Carmen Acevedo Butcher, *St. Hildegard of Bingen, Doctor of the Church: A Spiritual Reader* (Brewster, MA: Paraclete Press, 2007, 2013), 153.

13 Annie Dillard, *Pilgrim at Tinker Creek,* quoted in Catherine Albanese, *American Spiritualities: A Reader* (Bloomington: Indiana University Press, 2001), 441.

14 Dolores R. Leckey, *7 Essentials for the Spiritual Journey* (New York: Crossroad Publishing Company, 1999), 96.

15 Carl Honoré, *In Praise of Slowness: How a Worldwide Movement Is Challenging the Cult of Speed* (San Francisco: HarperSanFrancisco, 2004), 30–31.

16 Sheena Iyengar, *The Art of Choosing* (New York: Twelve, 2010), 204–5.

17 Adele Ahlberg Calhoun, *The Spiritual Disciplines Handbook: Practices That Transform Us* (Downers Grove, IL: InterVarsity Press, 2005), 75–76.

18 Bruce and Stan, *God Is in the Small Stuff: And It All Matters* (Ulrichsville, OH: Barbour Press, 1998), 102–3.

19 Teresa of Avila, *The Way of Perfection*, quoted in Bernard Bangley, ed., *A Little Daily Wisdom: Through the Year with Saint Teresa of Avila* (Brewster, MA: Paraclete Press, 2011), November 30 entry.

20 Brother Peter Reinhart, *Brother Juniper's Bread Book: Slow Rise as Method and Metaphor* (Cambridge, MA: Perseus Books, 1991), 1–2.

21 Thomas Traherne, *Centuries of Meditations,* quoted in Henry Morgan, *A Time to Reflect: 365 Classic Meditations to Help You Through the Year* (Nashville: Abingdon Press, 1998), 150–51.

22 Gregory L. Jantz, *Gotta Have It! Freedom from Wanting Everything Right Here, Right Now* (Colorado Springs, CO: David C. Cook, 2010), 190–91.

Notes

*

314

23 Jon M. Sweeney, *Cloister Talks: Learning from My Friends the Monks* (Grand Rapids, MI: Brazos Press, 2009), 100.

24 Henry David Thoreau, *Walden*, http://www.walden.org/Library/Quotations/Simplicity.

25 Marsha Sinetar, *Sometimes, Enough Is Enough: Finding Spiritual Comfort in a Material World* (New York: Cliff Street Books, 2000), 98.

26 Jeff Golliher, *A Deeper Faith: A Journey into Simplicity* (New York: Tarcher/Penguin, 2008), 216.

27 Marietta McCarty, *The Philosopher's Table: How to Start Your Philosophy Dinner Club* (New York: Tarcher, 2013), 98.

28 Michelle Singletary, *The 21 Day Financial Fast: Your Path to Financial Peace and Freedom* (Grand Rapids, MI: Zondervan, 2013), 150–51.

29 Marcus Aurelius, *The Meditations of Marcus Aurelius: Spiritual Teachings and Reflections*, book 4, section 3 (London: Watkins Publishing, 2006), 45–46.

30 David Timms, *Living the Lord's Prayer* (Bloomington, MN: Bethany House Publishers, 2008), 142–43.

31 Lauren F. Winner, *Still: Notes on a Mid-Faith Crisis* (San Francisco: HarperOne, 2012), 108.

JUNE

1 *The Cloud of Unknowing*, ed. and modernized by Bernard Bangley (Brewster, MA: Paraclete Press, 2006), 7–8.

2 Cynthia Bourgeault, *Centering Prayer and Inner Awakening* (Cambridge, MA: Cowley Publications, 2004), 39–40.

3 Richard J. Foster, *Sanctuary of the Soul: Journey into Meditative Prayer* (Downers Grove, IL: InterVarsity Press, 2011), 104.

4 Julia Roller, *Mom Seeks God* (Nashville: Abingdon Press, 2014), 21.

5 Garrison Keillor, *Lake Wobegon Days,* (New York: Viking, 1985), 102–3.

6 C. S. Lewis, *Letters to Malcolm: Chiefly on Prayer* (New York: Harcourt Brace Jovanovich, 1964), 81–82.

7 Doris Grumbach, *The Presence of Absence: On Prayers and Epiphany* (Boston: Beacon Press, 1998), 91.

8 M. Basil Pennington, ocso, *Centering Prayer: Renewing an Ancient Christian Art Form* (New York: Doubleday, 1982, 2001), 112–13.

9 David G. Benner, *Spirituality and the Awakening Self: The Sacred Journey of Transformation* (Downers Grove, IL: InterVarsity Press, 2012), 227.

10 Thomas Keating, "The Practice of Attention/Intention," in Gustave Reininger, ed., *Centering Prayer in Daily Life and Ministry* (New York: Continuum, 1998), 15.

11 Thomas Merton, *What Is Contemplation?* (Springfield, IL: Templegate, 1950), 7–8.

12 Thomas Keating, "Cultivating the Centering Prayer," in M. Basil Pennington and Thomas Keating with Thomas E. Clarke, *Finding Grace at the Center: The Beginning of Centering Prayer* (Woodstock, VT: SkyLight Paths, 2002), 58–59.

13 Richard Rohr, *Immortal Diamond: The Search for Our True Self* (San Francisco: Jossey-Bass, 2013), 90–91.

14 John Michael Talbot, *The Jesus Prayer: A Cry for Mercy, A Path of Renewal* (Downers Grove, IL: InterVarsity Press, 2013), 17–18.

15 Norris Chumley, *Mysteries of the Jesus Prayer: Experiencing the Presence of God and a Pilgrimage to the Heart of an Ancient Spirituality* (San Francisco: HarperOne, 2011), 171.

16 *The Way of a Pilgrim,* trans. Olga Savin (Boston: Shambhala, 1996), fourth narrative, 115.

17 Frederica Mathewes-Green, *The Jesus Prayer: The Ancient Desert Prayer That Tunes the Heart to God* (Brewster, MA: Paraclete Press, 2009), 81.

18 Blessed Isaac is quoted by John Cassian (360–435) in Philip and Carol Zaleski, *Prayer: A History* (New York: Houghton Mifflin, 2005), 141.

19 Father Ruwais, quoted in Norris J. Chumley, *Mysteries of the Jesus Prayer: Experiencing the Presence of God and a Pilgrimage to the Heart of an Ancient Spirituality* (San Francisco: HarperOne, 2011), 59.

20 Tony Jones, *The Sacred Way: Spiritual Practices for Everyday Life* (Grand Rapids, MI: Zondervan, 2010), 64.

21 St. John Chrysostom, *Letter to Monks*, http://glory2godforallthings.com/2007/12/31/st-john-chrysostom-on-the-jesus-prayer/.

22 Mark Buchanan, *Spiritual Rhythm: Being with Jesus Every Season of Your Soul* (Grand Rapids, MI: Zondervan, 2010), 303.

23 Frederica Mathewes-Green, *Facing East: A Pilgrim's Journey into the Mysteries of Orthodoxy* (San Francisco: HarperOne, 1997) 142–43.

24 Wendy Murray Zoba, *On Broken Legs: A Shattered Life, A Search for God, A Miracle That Met Me in a Cave in Assisi* (Colorado Springs, CO: NavPress, 2004), 30–31.

25 Frederica Mathewes-Green, *Praying the Jesus Prayer* (Brewster, MA: Paraclete Press, 2011), 50–53.

26 Scott Cairns, *Short Trip to the Edge: Where Earth Meets Heaven: A Pilgrimage* (San Francisco: HarperOne, 2007), 35–36.

27 Ed Dobson, *The Year of Living Like Jesus: My Journey of Discovering What Jesus Would Really Do* (Grand Rapids, MI: Zondervan, 2009), 83–84.

28 Madeleine L'Engle, *The Irrational Season: The Crosswicks Journal—Book 3* (New York: HarperCollins, 1977), 211.

29 St. Gregory of Sinai, "Instructions to Hesychasts," in *Writings from the Philokalia: On Prayer of the Heart*, trans. by E. Kadloubovsky and G. E. H. Palmer (New York: Farrar, Straus, and Giroux, 1995), 74.

30 Kallistos Ware, "The Beginnings of the Jesus Prayer," in Benedicta Ward and Ralph Waller, eds., *Joy of Heaven: Springs of Christian Spirituality* (London: SPCK, 2003), 17.

JULY

1 Abraham Joshua Heschel, *The Sabbath: Its Meaning for Modern Man* (New York: Farrar, Straus and Giroux, 1951), 13.

2 Elizabeth Ehrlich, *Miriam's Kitchen: A Memoir* (New York: Viking, 1997), 358.

3 Andy Crouch, *Playing God: Redeeming the Gift of* Power (Downers Grove, IL: InterVarsity Press, 2013), 116.

4 Walter Brueggemann, *Sabbath as Resistance: Saying No to the Culture of Now* (Louisville, KY: Westminster John Knox Press, 2014), 29–30.

5 Dorothy Bass, *Receiving the Day: Christian Practices for Opening the Gift of Time* (San Francisco: Jossey-Bass, 2000), 64–65. Today's prayer is from the nineteenth-century theologian Søren Kierkegaard and is quoted in George Appleton, ed., *The Oxford Book of Prayer* (New York: Oxford University Press, 1985), 79.

6 John Greenleaf Whittier, "The Brewing of Soma," http://www.poemhunter.com /poem/the-brewing-of-soma. Quote from Søren Kierkegaard taken from Angela Ashwin, ed., *The Book of a Thousand Prayers* (Grand Rapids, MI: Zondervan, 2002), 98.

7 Wayne Muller, *Sabbath: Finding Rest, Renewal, and Delight in Our Busy Lives* (New York: Bantam, 1999) 51.

8 Henri J. M. Nouwen, *The Living Reminder: Service and Prayer in Memory of Jesus Christ* (New York: Seabury Press, 1977), 50.

9 A Jewish blessing for the Sabbath, in Appleton, ed., *The Oxford Book of Prayer*, 278.

10 James Bryan Smith, *The Good and Beautiful God: Falling in Love with the God Jesus Knows* (Downers Grove, IL: InterVarsity Press, 2009), 33.

11 Marva Dawn, *Keeping the Sabbath Wholly: Ceasing, Resting, Embracing, Feasting* (Grand Rapids, MI: Eerdmans, 1989), 29–30.

12 Matthew Sleeth, *24/6: A Prescription for a Healthier, Happier Life* (Carol Stream, IL: Tyndale House, 2012), 65–66.

13 Isaac Bashevis Singer, "Short Friday," in Steven J. Rubin, *Celebrating the Jewish Holidays: Poems, Stories, Essays* (Hanover, NH: University Press of New England, 2003), 60.

14 Eugene H. Peterson, *Working the Angles: The Shape of Pastoral Integrity* (Grand Rapids, MI: Eerdmans, 1987), 72–73. The poem is "As Kingfishers Catch Fire" by Gerard Manley Hopkins, in *Poems and Prose of Gerard Manley Hopkins*, ed. W. H. Gardner (Baltimore: Penguin Books, 1953), 51.

15 John Main, *Being on the Way*, quoted in *Silence and Stillness in Every Season*, ed. Paul Harris (New York: Continuum, 1997), 297.

16 MaryAnn McKibben Dana, *Sabbath in the Suburbs: A Family's Experiment with Holy Time* (St. Louis, MO: Chalice Press, 2012), 33.

17 William Powers, *Hamlet's BlackBerry: A Practical Philosophy for Building a Good Life in the Digital Age* (New York: HarperCollins, 2010), 2.

18 Patty Kirk, *The Easy Burden of Pleasing God* (Downers Grove, IL: InterVarsity Press, 2013), 88–89.

19 Barbara Brown Taylor, *Leaving Church: A Memoir of Faith* (San Francisco: HarperOne, 2006), 140.

20 Walter J. Jarrelson, *The Ten Commandments for Today* (Louisville, KY: Westminster John Knox Press, 2006), 45.

21 Keri Wyatt Kent, *Rest: Living in Sabbath Simplicity* (Grand Rapids, MI: Zondervan, 2009), 147–48.

22 Maya Angelou, *Wouldn't Take Nothing for My Journey Now* (New York: Random House, 1993), 139.

23 Barbara Rush, *The Jewish Year: Celebrating the Holidays* (New York: Stewart, Tabori & Chang, 2001), 16.

24 Dan B. Allender, *Sabbath* (Nashville: Thomas Nelson, 2009), 192–93.

25 Greg Cootsona, *Say Yes to No: Using the Power of NO to Create the Best in Life, Work, and Love* (New York: Doubleday, 2008), 81.

26 Tricia McCary Rhodes, *Sacred Chaos: Spiritual Disciplines for the Life You Have* (Downers Grove, IL: InterVarsity Press, 2008), 85–86.

27 Kim Thomas, *Even God Rested: Why It's Okay for Women to Slow Down* (Eugene, OR: Harvest House Publishers, 2003), 200.

28 Robert Ellsberg, *The Saints' Guide to Happiness: Everyday Wisdom from the Lives of the Saints* (New York: North Point Press, 2003), 60–61.

29 Augustine of Hippo, *Sermon* 8.6, quoted in Cindy Crosby, *Ancient Christian Devotional: A Year of Weekly Readings* (Downers Grove, IL, 2007), 223–24.

30 Judith Shulevitz, *The Sabbath World: Glimpses of a Different Order of Time* (New York: Random House, 2010), 217.

31 Rabbi Nina Beth Cardin, *The Tapestry of Jewish Time: A Spiritual Guide to Holidays and Life-Cycle Events* (Springfield, NJ: Behrman House, 2000), 44.

AUGUST

1   Mark Scandrette, *Free: Spending Your Time and Money on What Matters Most* (Downers Grove, IL: InterVarsity Press, 2013), 90.

2   Vinita Hampton Wright, *Simple Acts of Moving Forward: A Little Book about Getting Unstuck* (Colorado Springs, CO: Shaw, 2003), 61–62.

3   Dietrich Bonhoeffer, *Life Together: A Discussion of Christian Fellowship* (San Francisco: Harper & Row, 1954), 29.

4   Lewis Smedes, *Days of Grace through the Year* (Downers Grove, IL: InterVarsity Press, 2007), 167.

5   Gordon B. Hinckley, *Standing for Something: Ten Neglected Virtues That Will Heal Our Hearts and Homes* (New York: Times Books, 2000), 90.

6   Maya Angelou, *Mom & Me & Mom* (New York: Random House, 2013), 135–37.

7   Ranald Macaulay and Jerram Barrs, *Being Human: The Nature of Spiritual Experience* (Downers Grove, IL: InterVarsity Press, 1978), 73.

8   Edna St. Vincent Millay, "Afternoon on a Hill" (1917), http://www.public-domain-poetry.com/edna-st-vincent-millay/afternoon-on-a-hill-26269.

9   Os Guinness, *The Call: Finding and Fulfilling the Central Purpose of Your Life* (Nashville: Thomas Nelson, 2003), 193, 195.

10 Brian D. McLaren, *Naked Spirituality: A Life with God in 12 Simple Words* (San Francisco: HarperOne, 2011), 77.

11 Nevada Barr, *Seeking Enlightenment Hat by Hat: A Skeptic's Path to Religion* (New York: G. P. Putnam's Sons, 2003), 25–26.

12 Henri J. M. Nouwen, *The Return of the Prodigal Son: A Story of Homecoming* (New York: Image/Doubleday, 1994), 85–86.

13 Gerard Manley Hopkins, "Pied Beauty" (1877), http://www.poetryfoundation.org/poem/173664.

14 Anne Lamott, *Help Thanks Wow: The Three Essential Prayers* (New York: Riverhead, 2013), 56–57.

15 Thich Nhat Hanh, *Living Buddha, Living Christ* (New York: Riverhead, 1995), 26–27.

16 Brennan Manning, *Reflections for Ragamuffins: Daily Devotions* (San Francisco: HarperSanFrancisco, 1998), 178.

17 Helen Keller, *Light in My Darkness* (West Chester, PA: Chrysalis Books, 2000), 112.

18 Amy Grant, *Mosaic: Pieces of My Life So Far* (New York: Doubleday/Flying Dolphin Press, 2007), 144.

19 Jonathan Edwards, "Personal Narrative" (1739). http://mith.umd.edu/eada/html/display.php?docs=edwards_personalnarrative.xml&action=show.

20 Lucius Annaeus Seneca, "Of Benefits," *Seneca's Morals: By Way of Abstract* (Ann Arbor: University of Michigan Library, 2009), 48–49.

21 Nancy Roth, *The Breath of God* (New York: Church Publishing, 2006), 87.

22 Dietrich Bonhoeffer, letter to his parents from Tegel prison, September 13, 1943, in *Letters and Papers from Prison: New Greatly Enlarged Edition*, ed. Eberhard Bethge (New York: The Macmillan Company, 1971), 109.

23 Robert J. Wicks, *Crossing the Desert: Learning to Let Go, See Clearly, and Live Simply* (Notre Dame, IN: Sorin Books, 2007), 73.

24 Thomas Merton, journal entry, April 29, 1961, in *Turning Toward the World: The Journals of Thomas Merton, vol. 4, 1960–1963* (San Francisco: HarperSanFrancisco, 1996), 112.

25 Kate Braestrup, *Beginner's Grace: Bringing Prayer to Life* (New York: Simon & Schuster, 2010), 21–22.

26 Margaret Feinberg, *Wonderstruck: Awaken to the Nearness of God* (Brentwood, TN: Worthy Publishing, 2012), 147.

27 Thomas Merton, quoted in *Words of Gratitude*, ed. Robert A. Emmons and Joanna Hill (Philadelphia: Templeton Foundation Press, 2001), 14.

28 Margaret Visser, *The Gift of Thanks: The Roots and Rituals of Gratitude* (New York: Houghton Mifflin Harcourt, 2009), 366–67.

29 James E. Faust, "Gratitude as a Saving Principle," *Ensign* (May 1990): 85.

30 Anne Lamott, *Traveling Mercies: Some Thoughts on Faith* (New York: Anchor Books, 1999), 242.

31 Henri J. M. Nouwen, *Sabbatical Journey: The Diary of His Final Year* (New York: The Crossroad Publishing Company, 1998), 73.

SEPTEMBER

1 The Rule of Saint Benedict, chapter 53, http://www.osb.org/rb/text/rbeaad1.html.

2 Father Daniel Homan, osb, and Lonni Collins Pratt, *Radical Hospitality: Benedict's Way of Love* (Brewster, MA: Paraclete Press, 2002), 115–16.

3 Sister Sharon Hunter, quoted in *The Paraclete Book of Hospitality,* by the editors of Paraclete Press (Brewster, MA: Paraclete Press, 2012), 25–26.

4 Jonathan Wilson-Hartgrove, *Strangers at My Door: An Experiment in Radical Hospitality* (New York: Convergent, 2013), 65–66.

5   Robert Benson, *A Good Life: Benedict's Guide to Everyday Joy* (Brewster, MA: Paraclete Press, 2004), 51–52.

6   Amy Oden, *And You Welcomed Me: A Sourcebook on Hospitality in Early Christianity* (Nashville: Abingdon Press, 2001), 36.

7   Arthur Sutherland, *I Was a Stranger: A Christian Theology of Hospitality* (Nashville: Abingdon Press, 2006), 60.

8   Shauna Niequist, *Bread and Wine: A Love Letter to Life around the Table with Recipes* (Grand Rapids, MI: Zondervan, 2013), 114–15.

9   Sybil MacBeth, *Praying in Color: Drawing a New Path to God* (Brewster, MA: Paraclete Press, 2006), 90–91.

10 Elizabeth Newman, *Untamed Hospitality: Welcoming God and Other Strangers* (Grand Rapids, MI: Brazos Press, 2007), Kindle location 661.

11 Carolyn Weber, *Holy Is the Day: Living in the Gift of the Present* (Downers Grove, IL: InterVarsity Press, 2013), 81.

12 Sara Miles, *Jesus Freak: Feeding, Healing, Raising the Dead* (San Francisco: Jossey-Bass, 2010), 25–26.

13 Doris Donnelly, *Spiritual Fitness: Everyday Exercises for Body and Soul* (San Francisco: HarperSanFrancisco, 1993), 49–50.

14 Jeremy Langford, *Seeds of Faith: Practices to Grow a Healthy Spiritual Life* (Brewster, MA: Paraclete Press, 2007), 48–49.

15 Dorothy Day, *The Long Loneliness* (New York: Harper & Row, 1952), 216.

16 Henry G. Brinton, *The Welcoming Congregation: Roots and Fruits of Christian Hospitality* (Louisville, KY: Westminster John Knox Press, 2012), 117–18.

17 Jimmy Carter, *Sources of Strength: Meditations on Scripture for a Living Faith* (New York: Times Books, 1997), 75.

18 River Jordan, *Praying for Strangers: An Adventure of the Human Spirit* (New York: Berkley Books, 2011), 296.

19 Father Dominic Garramone, *Bake and Be Blessed: Bread Baking as a Metaphor for Spiritual Growth* (St. Louis, MO: KETC, 2002), 18–19.

20 Henri J. M. Nouwen, *The Wounded Healer* (New York: Image/Doubleday, 1979), 84.

21 Nancy Sleeth, *Almost Amish: One Woman's Quest for a Slower, Simpler, More Sustainable Life* (Carol Stream, IL: Tyndale House, 2012), 12.

22 Jonathan Wilson-Hartgrove, *The Awakening of Hope: Why We Practice a Common Faith* (Grand Rapids, MI: Zondervan, 2012), 41–42.

23 Christine Pohl, *Making Room: Recovering Hospitality as a Christian Tradition* (Grand Rapids, MI: Eerdmans, 1999), 152.

24 Sarah York, *Pilgrim Heart: The Inner Journey Home* (San Francisco: Jossey-Bass, 2001), 133–34.

25 Brian D. McLaren, *Finding Our Way Again: The Return of the Ancient Practices* (Nashville: Thomas Nelson, 2008), 103.

26 Scot McKnight, *Embracing Grace: A Gospel for All of Us* (Brewster, MA: Paraclete Press, 2005), 159–60.

27 Robert Benson, *A Good Neighbor: Benedict's Guide to Community* (Brewster, MA: Paraclete Press, 2009), 40–41.

28 Ellen Vaughn, *Come, Sit, Stay: Finding Rest for Your Soul* (Brentwood, TN: Worthy Press, 2012), 159.

29 Lynne Baab, *Friending: Real Relationships in a Virtual World* (Downers Grove, IL: InterVarsity Press, 2011), 96.

30 Brother Benet Tvedten, *How to Be a Monastic and Not Leave Your Day Job: An Invitation to Oblate Life* (Brewster, MA: Paraclete Press, 2006), 52–53.

OCTOBER

1 Frederic Brussat and Mary Ann Brussat, *Spiritual Literacy: Reading the Sacred in Everyday Life* (New York: Scribner, 1996), 169.

2 Madeleine L'Engle, *Bright Evening Star: Mystery of the Incarnation* (Colorado Springs, CO: Shaw Books, 1997), 110–11.

3 Desmond Tutu, *God Has a Dream: A Vision of Hope for Our Time* (New York: Doubleday, 2004), 28.

4 Friar Jack Wintz, *I Will See You in Heaven* (Brewster, MA: Paraclete Press, 2011), 25–27.

5 G. K. Chesterton, *St. Francis of Assisi* (London: Hodder and Stoughton, 1958), 103–104. The text of the "Canticle of the Creatures" can be found online at http://www.custodia.org/default.asp?id=1454.

6 Fae Malania, *The Quantity of a Hazelnut* (Brewster, MA: Paraclete Press, 2005), 33–34.

7 Denise Roy, *My Monastery Is a Minivan: Where the Daily Is Divine and the Routine Becomes Prayer* (Chicago: Loyola Press, 2001), 119–20.

8 Frederick Buechner, *The Longing for Home: Recollections and Reflections* (San Francisco: HarperSanFrancisco, 1996), 126–27.

9 Debra Farrington, *All God's Creatures: The Blessings of Animal Companions* (Brewster, MA: Paraclete Press, 2006), 23–24.

10 Stephanie Paulsell, *Honoring the Body: Meditations on a Christian Practice* (San Francisco: Jossey-Bass, 2002), 95–96.

11 Fyodor Dostoevsky, *The Karamazov Brothers: A New Translation by Ignat Avsey* (New York: Oxford University Press, 1994), book 6, chapter 3, 399–400.

12 Saint Francis of Assisi, "The Canticle of the Creatures," Custodia Tearrae Sanctae, http://www.custodia.org/default.asp?id=1454.

13 Murray Bodo, OFM, *Saint Francis of Assisi: Poetry as Prayer* (Boston: Pauline Books & Media, 2003), 70–71.

14 Jon M. Sweeney, *Francis and Clare: A True Story* (Brewster, MA: Paraclete Press, 2014), 102.

15 Dennis Patrick Slattery, *Grace in the Desert: Awakening to the Gifts of Monastic Life* (San Francisco: Jossey-Bass, 2004), 27–28.

16 Debbie Blue, *Consider the Birds: A Provocative Guide to Birds of the Bible* (Nashville: Abingdon Press, 2013), 10.

17 Frederick Buechner, *Whistling in the Dark: An ABC Theologized* (New York: Harper & Row, 1988), 7.

18 Robert N. Wennberg, *God, Humans, and Animals: An Invitation to Enlarge Our Moral Universe* (Grand Rapids, MI: Eerdmans, 2003), 292.

19 Wendell Berry, "The Pleasures of Eating," in Michael Schut, ed., *Food and Faith: Justice, Joy, and Daily Bread* (Harrisburg, PA: Morehouse Publishing, 2006), 146.

20 Edward Hays, *Pray All Ways* (Leavenworth, KS: Forest of Peace Publishing, 1981), 119.

21 Stephen Webb, *Good Eating* (Grand Rapids, MI: Brazos Press, 2001), 161.

22 Gunilla Norris, *Journeying in Place: Reflections from a Country Garden* (New York: Bell Tower, 1994), 31.

23 Scott Savage, *A Plain Life: Walking My Belief* (New York: Ballantine Books, 2000), 160–61.

24 Gary Thomas, *Sacred Pathways: Discover Your Soul's Path to God* (Nashville: Thomas Nelson, 1996), 46.

25 Sheri Speede, *Kindred Beings: What Seventy-Three Chimpanzees Taught Me About Life, Love, and Connection* (New York: HarperCollins, 2013), 249.

26 Elie Wiesel, *Sages and Dreamers: Biblical, Talmudic, and Hasidic Portraits and Legends* (New York: Simon & Schuster, 1993), 108.

27 Laura Hobgood-Oster, *The Friends We Keep: Unleashing Christianity's Compassion for Animals* (Waco, TX: Baylor University Press, 2010), 110.

28 Vicki Robin, *Blessing the Hands That Feed Us: What Eating Closer to Home Can Teach Us about Food, Community, and Our Place on Earth* (New York: Viking, 2014), 8–9.

29 Cathleen Falsani, *Sin Boldly: A Field Guide for Grace* (Grand Rapids, MI: Zondervan, 2008), 182.

30 Tony Campolo, *Letters to a Young Evangelical* (New York: Basic Books, 2006), 207-8.

31 Saint Francis of Assisi, "Letter to Faithful Christians," http://www.sacred-texts.com/chr/wosf/wosf12.htm.

NOVEMBER

1   Frederick Buechner, *The Sacred Journey: A Memoir of Early Days* (San Francisco: HarperCollins, 1982), 74.

2   Robert Benson, *Venite: A Book of Daily Prayer* (New York: Tarcher/Putnam, 2000), 5.

3   Brigid E. Herman, *Creative Prayer* (Brewster, MA: Paraclete Press, 1998), 62–63.

4   A. J. Cardinal Simonis, *Our Father: Reflections on the Lord's Prayer* (Grand Rapids, MI: Eerdmans, 1999), 11–12.

5   Kathleen Norris, *The Cloister Walk* (New York: Riverhead Books, 1996), 92.

6   Simone Weil, *Waiting on God* (New York: Routledge Revivals, 2009), 89.

7   *The Paraclete Psalter* (Brewster, MA: Paraclete Press, 2010), viii.

8   Saint Romuald's Brief Rule is posted at the website for the new Camoldoli Hermitage in Big Sur, California, http://www.contemplation.com/community/history.html.

9   Mary Poplin, *Finding Calcutta: What Mother Teresa Taught Me about Meaningful Work and Service* (Downers Grove, IL: InterVarsity Press, 2008), 73–74.

10 Cindy Crosby, *By Willoway Brook: Exploring the Landscape of Prayer* (Brewster, MA: Paraclete Press, 2003), 81–83.

11 Phyllis Tickle, *The Divine Hours: Prayers for Autumn and Wintertime* (New York: Doubleday, 2000), ix.

12 Lauren F. Winner, "Prayer Is a Place," in Tony Jones, ed., *Phyllis Tickle, Evangelist of the Future: Reflections on the Impact She's Had on Publishing, Religion, and the Church in America* (Brewster, MA: Paraclete Press, 2014), 137.

13 Roy DeLeon, OblSB, *Praying with the Body: Bringing the Psalms to Life* (Brewster, MA: Paraclete Press, 2009), xvi.

14 N. T. Wright, *The Case for the Psalms: Why They Are Essential* (San Francisco: HarperOne, 2013), 166–67.

15 Jeremy Bouma, *Prayers for My City: A Fixed-Hour Prayer Guide for Grand Rapids* (Grand Rapids, MI: Theoklesia, 2012), Kindle location 127.

16 "The General Instruction of Roman Catholic *Liturgy of the Hours*," quoted in Lorraine Kisley, *Watch and Pray: Christian Teachings on the Practice of Prayer* (New York: Harmony/Bell Tower, 2002), 194–95.

17 Thérèse of Lisieux, *By Love Alone: Daily Readings with St. Thérèse of Lisieux*, ed. Michael Hollings (London: Darton, Longman, and Todd, 1986).

18 Joan Chittister, *The Rule of Benedict: Insights for the Ages* (New York: Crossroad Publishing Company, 1992), 80–81.

19 Lauren F. Winner, *Girl Meets God: On the Path to a Spiritual Life* (Chapel Hill, NC: Algonquin Books, 2002), 143–44.

20 The Community of Jesus, *The Little Book of Hours: Praying with the Community of Jesus* (Brewster, MA: Paraclete Press, 2007), x–xi.

21 Phyllis Tickle, *Prayer Is a Place: America's Religious Landscape Observed* (New York: Doubleday, 2005), 257.

22 Kathleen Norris, *Dakota: A Spiritual Geography* (New York: Houghton Mifflin, 1993), 185.

23 Scot McKnight, *Praying with the Church: Following Jesus Daily, Hourly, Today* (Brewster, MA: Paraclete Press, 2006), 144–45.

24 Phyllis Tickle, *The Night Offices: Prayers for the Hours from Sunset to Sunrise* (New York: Oxford University Press, 2006), ix.

25 John Brook, *The School of Prayer: An Introduction to the Divine Office for All Christians* (Collegeville, MN: Liturgical Press, 1992), 4.

26 Daniel F. Polish, *Bringing the Psalms to Life: How to Understand and Use the Book of Psalms* (Woodstock, VT: Jewish Lights, 2000), xii–xiii.

27 Philip Yancey, *Prayer: Does It Make Any Difference?* (Grand Rapids, MI: Zondervan, 2006), 179–80.

28 Margaret Bendroth, *The Spiritual Practice of Remembering* (Grand Rapids, MI: Eerdmans, 2013), 113–14, 118–19.

29 *The Rule of the Society of St. John the Evangelist* (Cambridge, MA: Cowley Publications, 1997), 36.

30 Sybil MacBeth, *The Season of the Nativity: Confessions and Practices of an Advent, Christmas, and Epiphany Extremist* (Brewster, MA: Paraclete Press, 2014), 11, 41.

1   Mother Teresa, quoted in *Something Beautiful for God: The Classic Account of Mother Teresa's Journey into Compassion*. ed. Malcolm Muggeridge (San Francisco: Harper & Row, 1971), 112–13.

2   Rabbi Menachem Schneerson, quoted in Simon Jacobson, *Toward a Meaningful Life: The Wisdom of the Rabbi Menachem Mendel Schneerson* (New York: Perennial Currents, 2004), 103.

3   Jeff Shinabarger, *More or Less: Choosing a Lifestyle of Excessive Generosity* (Colorado Springs, CO: David C. Cook, 2013), 248–49.

4   Attributed to Saint Francis of Assisi, but likely written in the twentieth century; see http://www.franciscan-archive.org/patriarcha/peace.html.

5   Quoted in Roger Housden, *For Lovers of God Everywhere: Poems of the Christian Mystics* (London: Hay House UK, 2010), 247.

6   Luci Shaw, *Adventure of Ascent: Field Notes from a Lifelong Journey* (Downers Grove, IL: InterVarsity Press, 2014), 51.

7   Ronald J. Sider, *Just Generosity: A New Vision for Overcoming Poverty in America* (Grand Rapids, MI: Baker Books, 1999), 58.

8   John Wesley, "On Worldly Folly," *The Sermons of John Wesley* 119, http://wesley.nnu.edu/john-wesley/the-sermons-of-john-wesley-1872-edition/sermon-119-on-worldly-folly/. Incidentally, the quote that was originally going to be used for this date ("Do all the good you can, by all the means you can, in all the ways you can, in all the places you can, at all the times you can, to all the people you can, as long as you ever can"), which is traditionally attributed to Wesley, was cut because Wesleyan scholars insist he did not say it. See Mary Jacobs, "Wesley, Misquoted: Methodism's Founder Gets a Little Too Much Credit," *The United Methodist Reporter* (Fall 2011), http://www.awfumc.org/pages/detail/534.

9   *The Rule of Taizé in French and English* (Brewster, MA: Paraclete Press, 2013), 83.

10   Faith Annette Sand, *Prayers of Faith: On Learning to Trust God* (Pasadena, CA: Hope Publishing House, 1996), 179–180.

11   J. Brent Bill, *The Sacred Compass: The Way of Spiritual Discernment* (Brewster, MA: Paraclete Press, 2008), 48–49.

12   N. T. Wright, *After You Believe: Why Christian Character Matters* (San Francisco: HarperOne, 2010), 282–83.

13   Jerusalem Jackson Greer, *A Homemade Year: The Blessings of Cooking, Crafting, and Coming Together* (Brewster, MA: Paraclete Press, 2013), 22–23.

14   Kate Braestrup, *Here If You Need Me: A True Story* (Boston: Little, Brown, 2007), 53–54.

15   Sister Bridget Haase, osu, *Generous Faith: Stories to Inspire Abundant Living* (Brewster, MA: Paraclete Press, 2009), 51–52.

16   Gretchen Rubin, *The Happiness Project: Or, Why I Spent a Year Trying to Sing in the Morning, Clean My Closets, Fight Right, Read Aristotle, and Generally Have More Fun* (New York: HarperCollins, 2009), 184–85.

17   St. Ignatius of Loyola, "Prayer for Generosity," http://www.bc.edu/bc_org/prs/stign/prayers.html.

Notes

*

324

18 Parker J. Palmer, *The Active Life: A Spirituality of Work, Creativity, and Caring* (San Francisco: Jossey-Bass, 1999), 76.

19 Robert Benson, *The Body Broken: Answering God's Call to Love One Another* (New York: Doubleday, 2003), 78.

20 George Eliot, "O May I Join the Choir Invisible" (1867), in *O May I Join the Choir Invisible! and Other Favorite Poems* (Boston: D. Lothrop and Company, 1884), http://www.gutenberg.org/files/20742/20742-h/20742-h.htm.

21 Devon O'Day, in Devon O'Day and Kim McLean, *Paws to Reflect: 365 Devotions for the Animal Lover's Soul* (Nashville: Abingdon Press, 2012), 296.

22 Rachel Marie Stone, *Eat with Joy: Redeeming God's Gift of Food* (Downers Grove, IL: InterVarsity Press, 2013), 44.

23 Catherine of Siena, *Little Talks with God*, ed. and mildly modernized by Henry L. Carrigan, Jr. (Brewster, MA: Paraclete Press, 2001), 61–62.

24 Walter Wangerin, Jr., *Measuring the Days: Daily Reflections* (San Francisco: HarperSanFrancisco, 1993), 352–53.

25 William Sloane Coffin Jr., "The First Fruit of Love," in *The Collected Sermons of William Sloane Coffin: The Riverside Years, Volume 1* (Louisville, KY: Westminster John Knox Press, 2008), 487.

26 Jonathan Wilson-Hartgrove, *New Monasticism: What It Has to Say to Today's Church* (Grand Rapids, MI: Brazos Press, 2008), 101–2.

27 Joyce Rupp, *Little Pieces of Light: Darkness and Personal Growth* (Mahwah, NJ: Paulist Press, 1994), 61.

28 Mark Allan Powell, *Giving to God: The Bible's Good News about Living a Generous Life* (Grand Rapids, MI: Eerdmans, 2006), 55–56.

29 Brennan Manning, *The Importance of Being Foolish: How to Think Like Jesus* (New York: HarperCollins, 2005), 46.

30 Henry Blackaby, *Experiencing God: How to Live the Full Adventure of Knowing and Doing the Will of God* (Nashville: Broadman & Holman, 1994), 236.

31 Frederick Buechner, *Now and Then: A Memoir of Vocation* (San Francisco: HarperSanFrancisco, 1991), 108–9.

Index of Authors Quoted